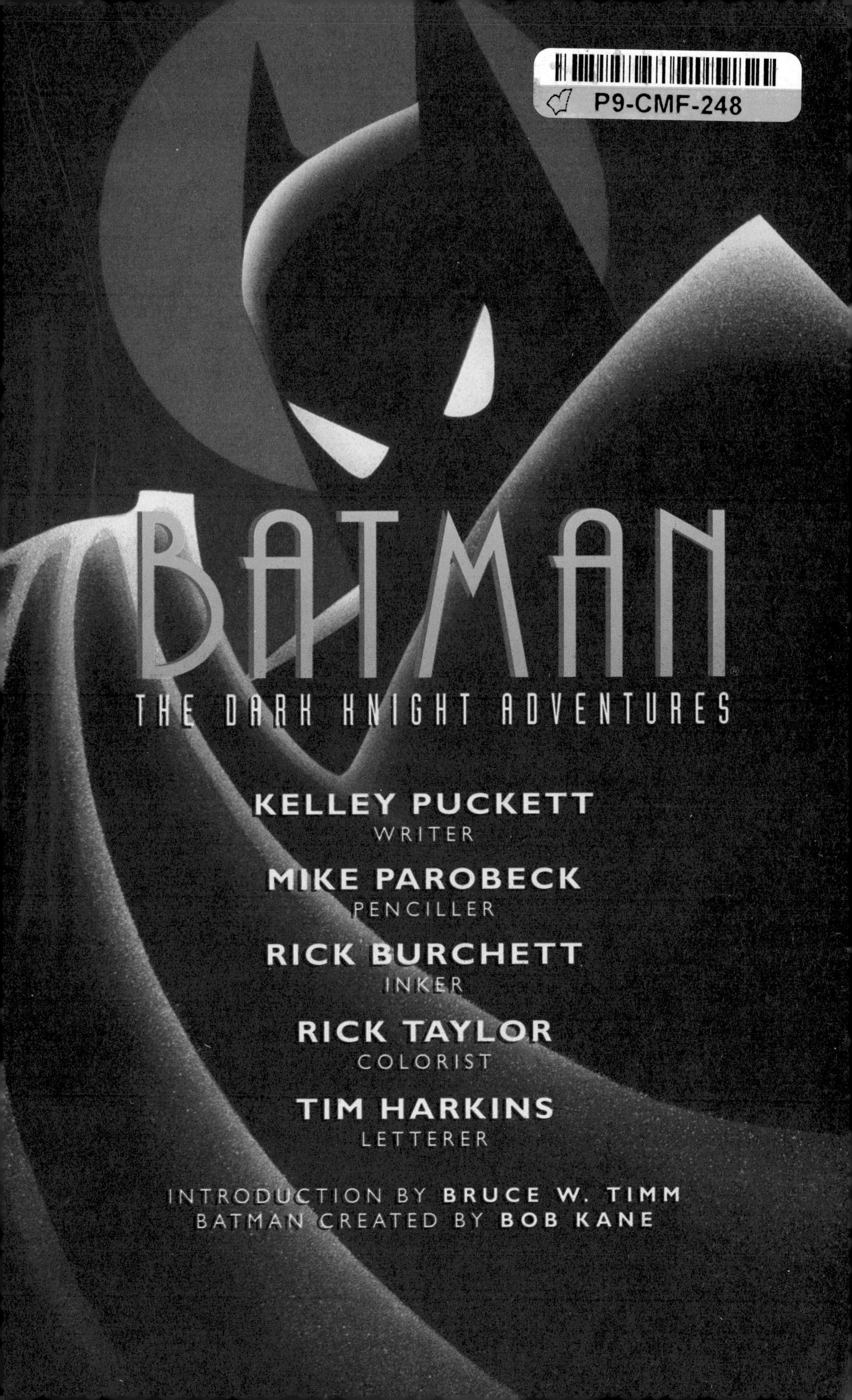

BATMAN®

THE DARK KNIGHT ADVENTURES

KELLEY PUCKETT
WRITER

MIKE PAROBECK
PENCILLER

RICK BURCHETT
INKER

RICK TAYLOR
COLORIST

TIM HARKINS
LETTERER

INTRODUCTION BY **BRUCE W. TIMM**
BATMAN CREATED BY **BOB KANE**

BATMAN: THE DARK KNIGHT ADVENTURES

Published by DC Comics. Cover and compilation copyright © 1994 DC Comics. All Rights Reserved.

Originally published in single magazine form as THE BATMAN ADVENTURES 7-12.
Copyright © 1993 DC Comics. All Rights Reserved. All characters, their distinctive likenesses and related indicia featured in this publication are trademarks of DC Comics. The stories, characters, and incidents featured in this publication are entirely fictional.

DC Comics, 1700 Broadway, New York, NY 10019
A division of Warner Bros. — A Time Warner Entertainment Company
Printed in Canada. Second Printing.
ISBN # 1-56389-124-7

Cover painting by Mike Parobeck & Rick Burchett
Publication design by Brian Pearce

INTRODUCTION

BY BRUCE W. TIMM

Back in 1990, when we here at Warner Bros. began developing *Batman: The Series,* one of our main objectives was to create a sophisticated super-hero show that would appeal to older genre fans as well as to young children. The epithet "too *Super Friends!*" was a common reaction to particularly lame story ideas.

Months before the series debuted, we arranged a number of "sneak preview" screenings of our first completed episode at comic book conventions around the country. The response from the fans was wildly enthusiastic. The good folks at DC Comics were so pleased, they decided to publish a monthly comic based on our version of the character. "Cool!" I thought.

Then I read in the *Comics Buyer's Guide* that the resultant comic, THE BATMAN ADVENTURES, was going to be skewed toward a younger audience. Visions of *Super Friends* and —worse! — *Spidey Super-Stories* danced in my head.

Man, was I ticked off!

"How dare they!" I ranted. "If it were *really* based on our show, it would be a serious, *adult* comic! Don't they get it? Do they think that just because it's a cartoon that only little kids will watch it? Blah blah blah, etc. etc."

I read the first issue of THE BATMAN ADVENTURES with a huge chip on my shoulder. And, against all odds...

I was thoroughly charmed.

Turning THE BATMAN ADVENTURES into a "kid's comic" was actually a very shrewd marketing decision. After all, there were already FOUR monthly "adult" Batman titles. A fifth would certainly be superfluous. By adapting the TV show's clean, "cartoony" art style and eliminating some of the darker, more violent elements of the modern Batman Mythos, the folks at DC have created a Batman comic that any parent can let their kids read without fear that it will warp their little minds.

And yet, it holds abundant pleasures for the savvy, adult comics fans as well.

Kelley Puckett's stories feature intriguing plots, witty dialogue, and an excellent sense of narrative drive, spiced with the occasional dash of irony. His Clayface story, "Larceny, My Sweet," with its bittersweet, doomed love affair scenario, reads like an unfilmed episode of our show. If you're looking for the ultrasimplistic plots, goofy villains and condescending "morals" of those horrid mid-1970s "kiddie superhero" comics, look elsewhere.

I first noticed Mike Parobeck's artwork on DC's recent
JUSTICE SOCIETY revival, where I thought his bouncy, "clean-line"
drawing style showed a lot of promise. When he took over BATMAN
ADVENTURES, his work immediately seemed to take a major leap
forward in quality. Suddenly, his storytelling became bolder, more
dynamic. His figures, already "cartoony" in a weird "John Byrne-
meets-Jaime Hernandez" manner, became even more stylized,
and yet, paradoxically, more "solid," due to his increased use of heavy
shadows and spot blacks. As good as he is now, I get the scary feeling
he's just getting warmed up.

   Inker Rick Burchett has been doing superlative work on the
book since the first issue, maintaining a consistent "look" over the
work of three very different pencillers, and yet playing up the
strengths of each. Not an easy feat, I'm sure! And Rick Taylor's unique
color stylings have given the book
a distinctive, moody-but-vibrant
look all its own.

Month after month, these
guys produce work of
amazingly high quality.
   I admit that I'm biased, but
I have to say that THE BATMAN
ADVENTURES is the Batman
comic I most look forward to
reading each month. Perhaps the
highest praise I can give them is
that the stories collected in this
book are, above all else, just plain
fun. That's something that sadly
can't be said of a lot of current
comics.
   I got a big kick out of these
stories. I know you will too.

BRUCE W. TIMM
Producer/Director
Batman: The Animated Series

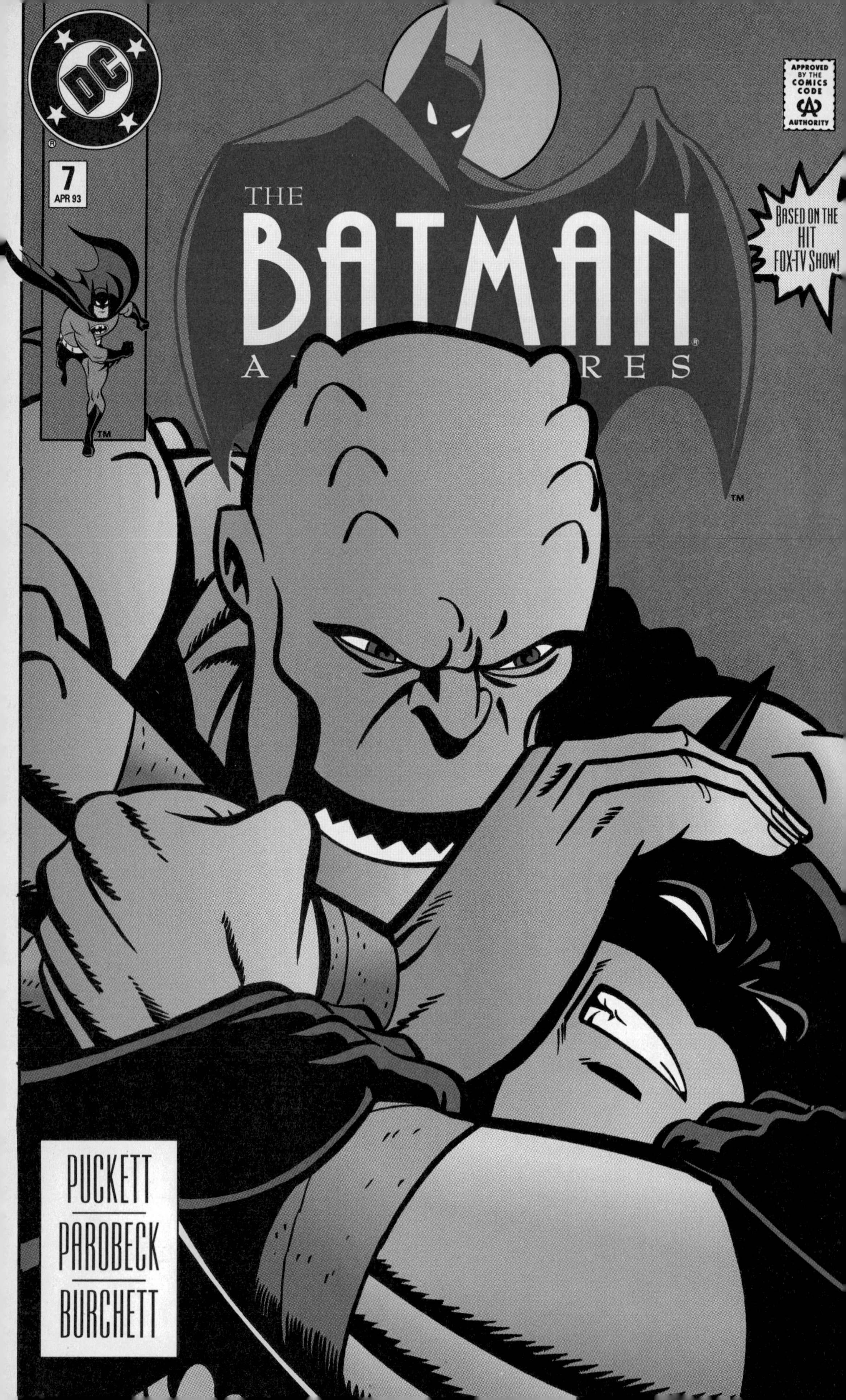
DC
7
APR 93
APPROVED BY THE COMICS CODE AUTHORITY
THE BATMAN
RES
BASED ON THE HIT FOX-TV SHOW!
PUCKETT
PAROBECK
BURCHETT

RAGING LIZARD!

ACT ONE: REQUIEM FOR A MUTANT!

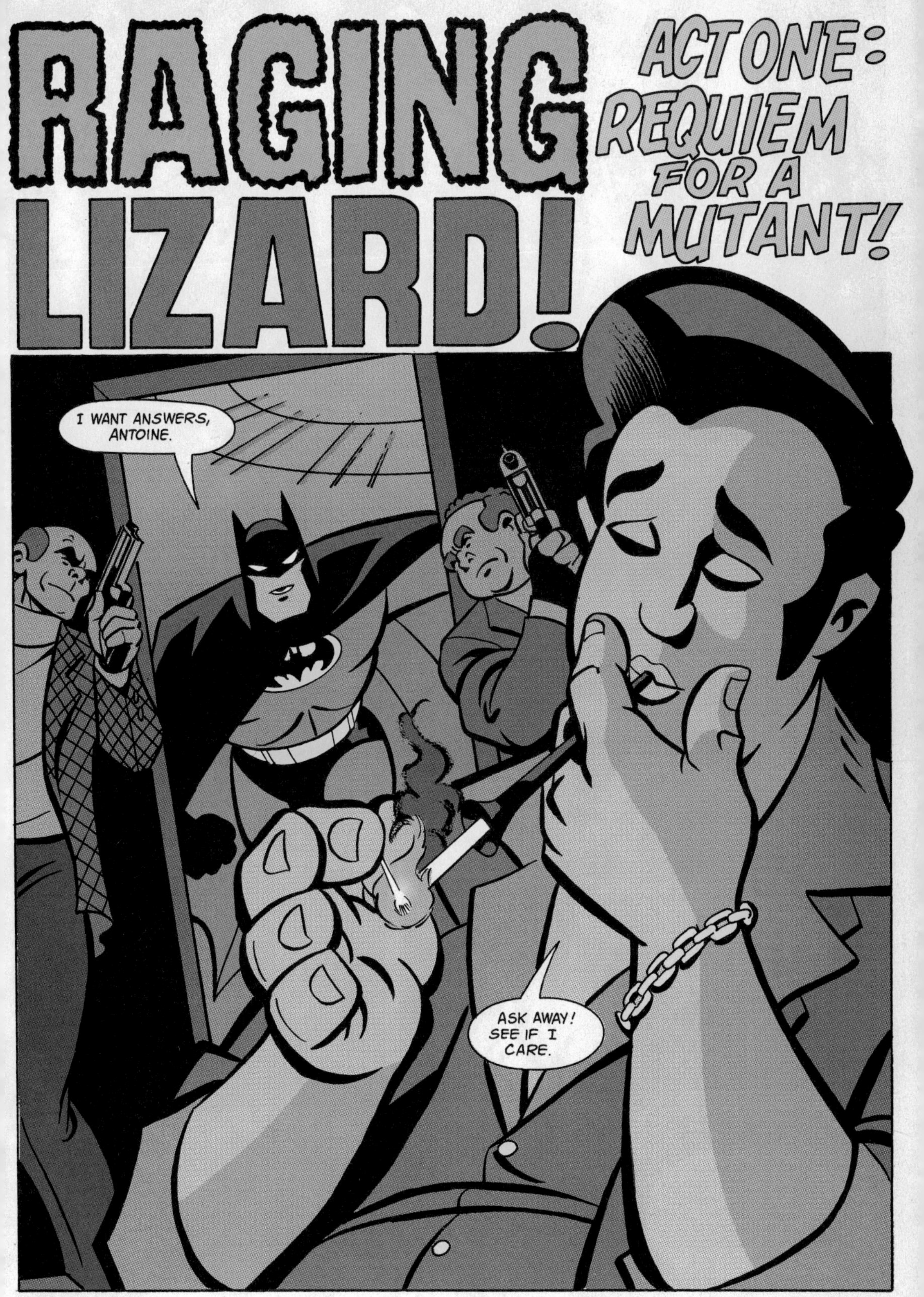
I WANT ANSWERS, ANTOINE.
ASK AWAY! SEE IF I CARE.

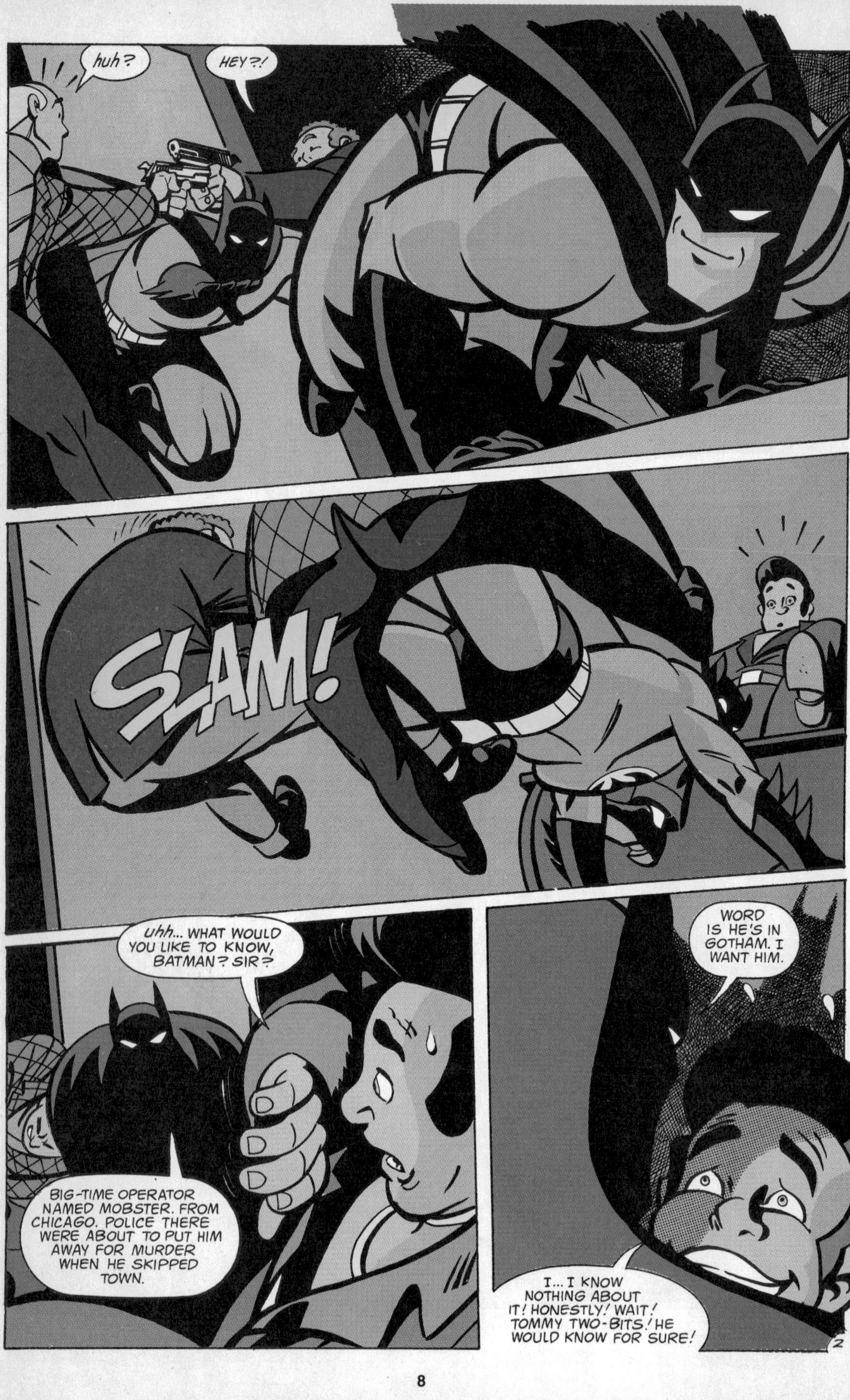
huh?
HEY?!
SLAM!
uhh... WHAT WOULD YOU LIKE TO KNOW, BATMAN? SIR?
BIG-TIME OPERATOR NAMED MOBSTER. FROM CHICAGO. POLICE THERE WERE ABOUT TO PUT HIM AWAY FOR MURDER WHEN HE SKIPPED TOWN.
WORD IS HE'S IN GOTHAM. I WANT HIM.
I... I KNOW NOTHING ABOUT IT! HONESTLY! WAIT! TOMMY TWO-BITS! HE WOULD KNOW FOR SURE!

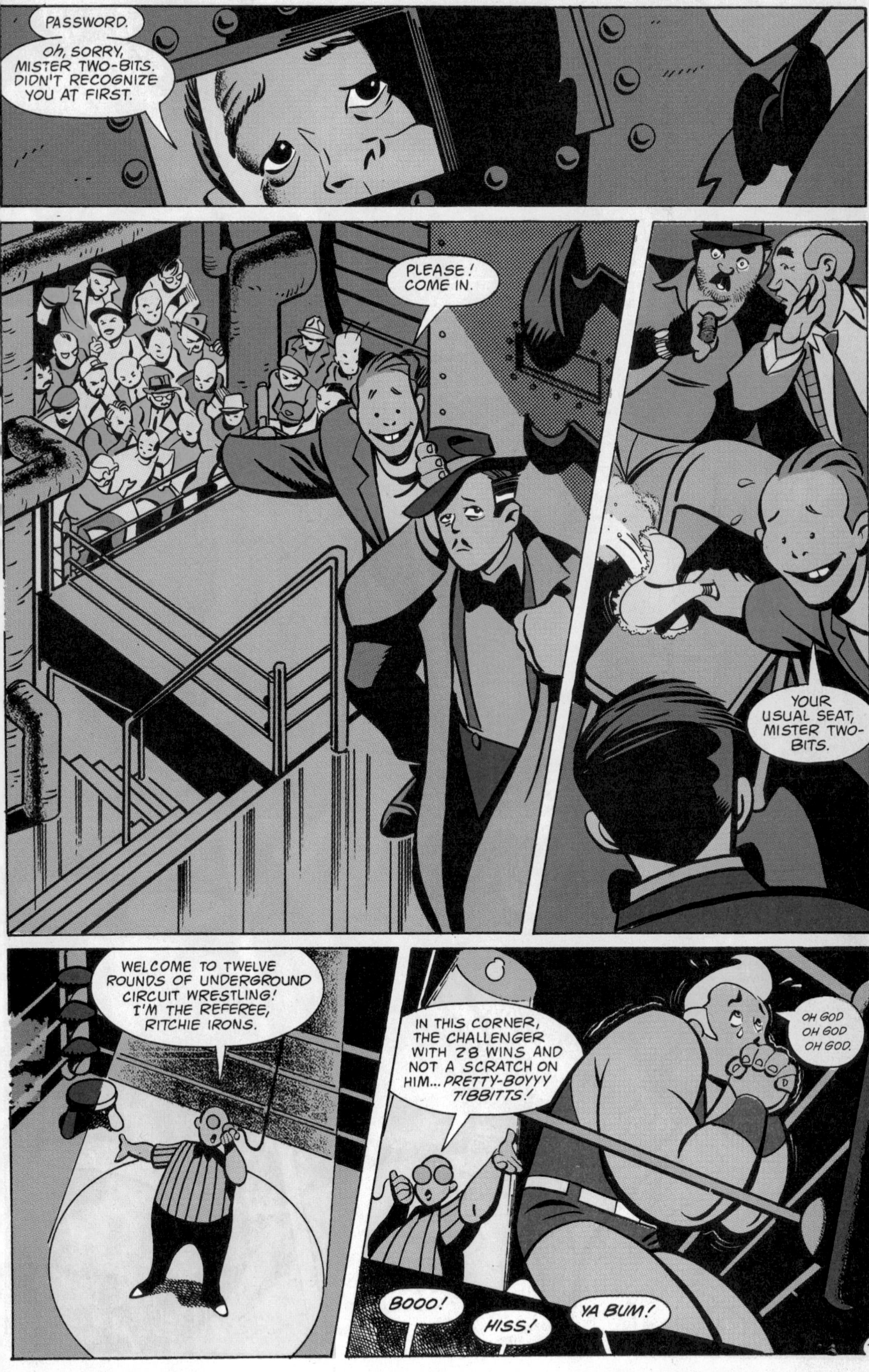
PASSWORD.
oh, SORRY, MISTER TWO-BITS. DIDN'T RECOGNIZE YOU AT FIRST.
PLEASE! COME IN.
YOUR USUAL SEAT, MISTER TWO-BITS.
WELCOME TO TWELVE ROUNDS OF UNDERGROUND CIRCUIT WRESTLING! I'M THE REFEREE, RITCHIE IRONS.
IN THIS CORNER, THE CHALLENGER WITH 28 WINS AND NOT A SCRATCH ON HIM... PRETTY-BOYYY TIBBITTS!
OH GOD OH GOD OH GOD.
BOOO!
HISS!
YA BUM!
3

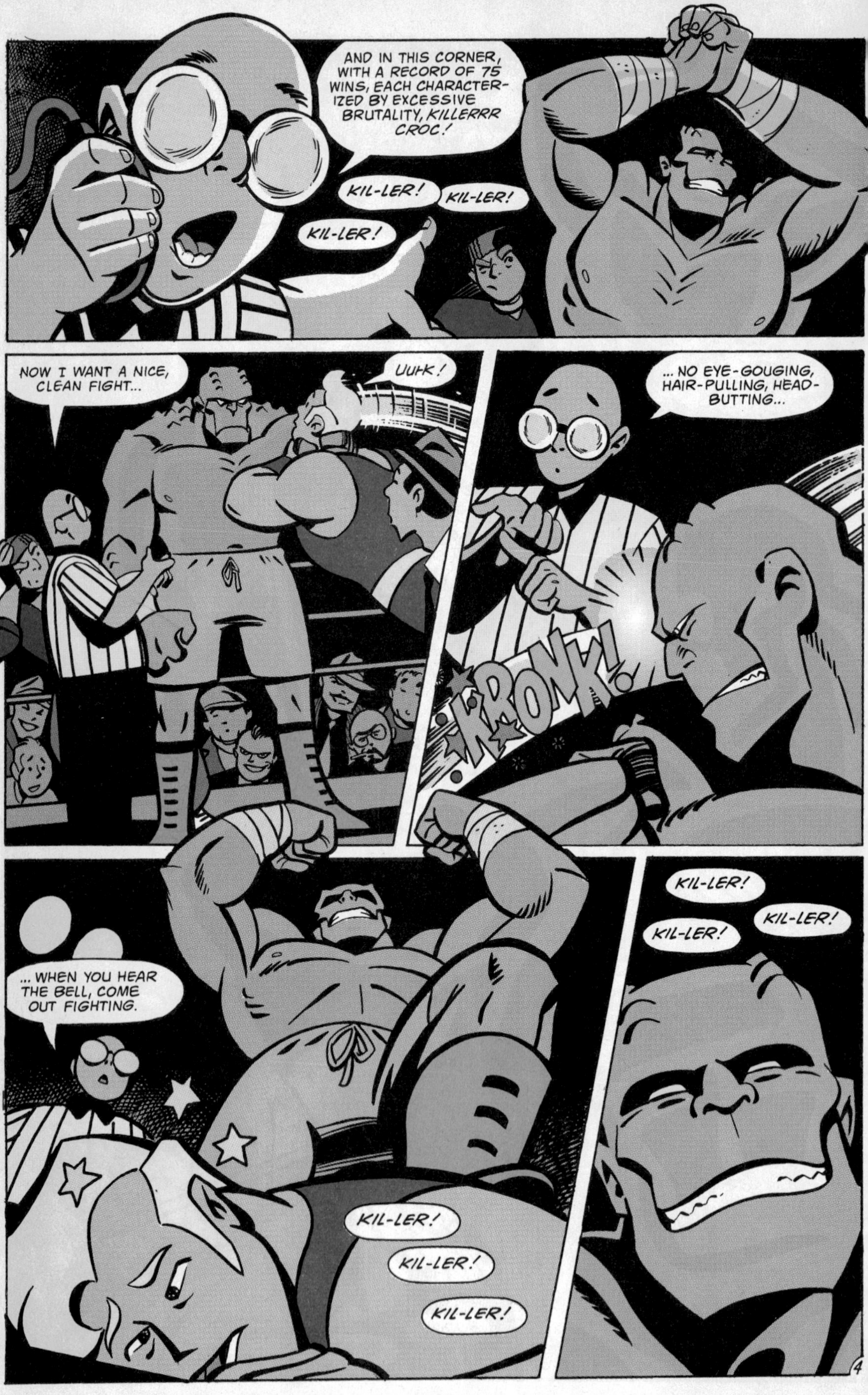
AND IN THIS CORNER, WITH A RECORD OF 75 WINS, EACH CHARACTERIZED BY EXCESSIVE BRUTALITY, KILLERRR CROC!
KIL-LER!
KIL-LER!
KIL-LER!
NOW I WANT A NICE, CLEAN FIGHT...
UUFK!
... NO EYE-GOUGING, HAIR-PULLING, HEAD-BUTTING...
KRONK!
... WHEN YOU HEAR THE BELL, COME OUT FIGHTING.
KIL-LER!
KIL-LER!
KIL-LER!
KIL-LER!
KIL-LER!
KIL-LER!
4

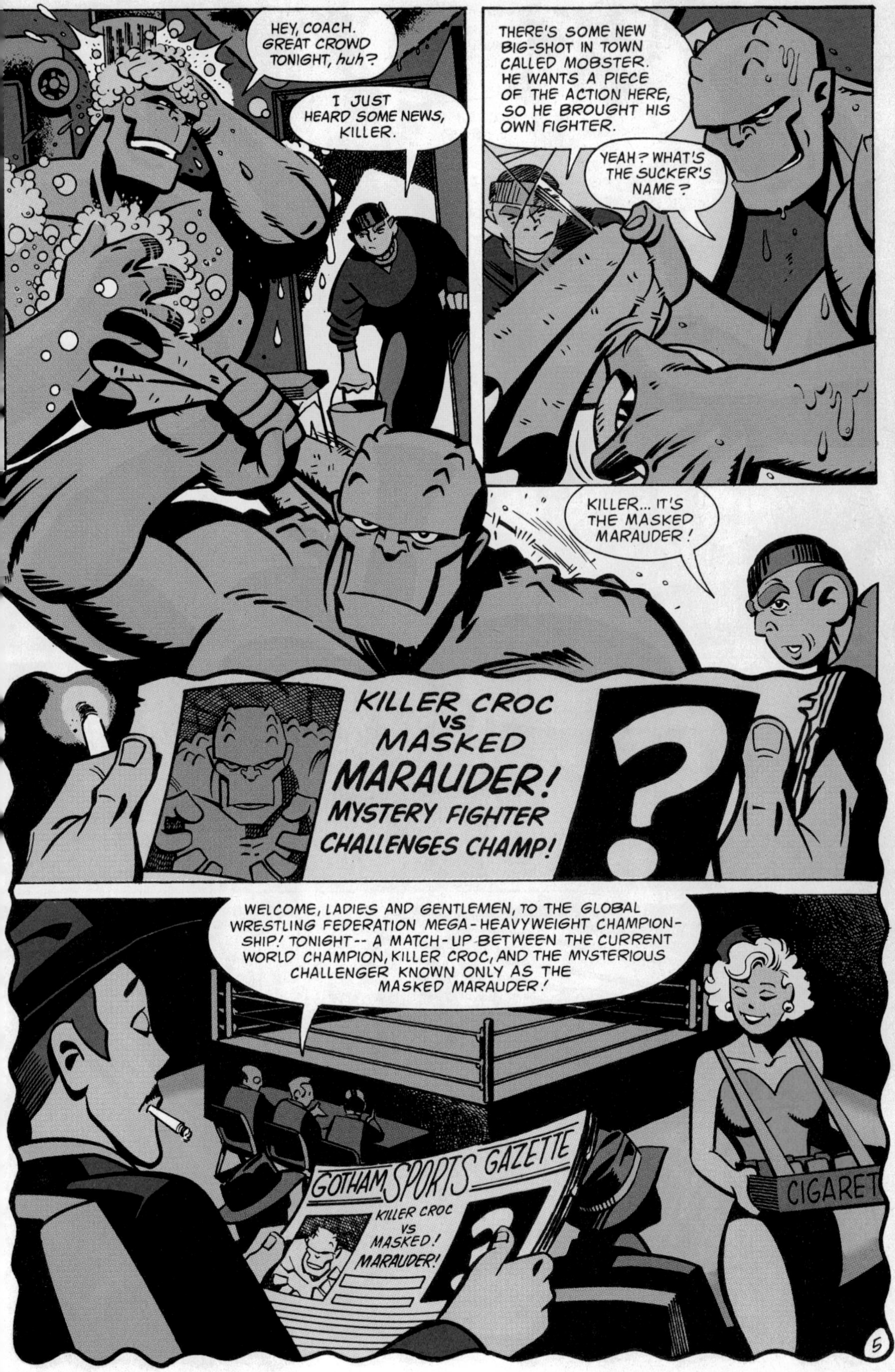
HEY, COACH. GREAT CROWD TONIGHT, huh?
I JUST HEARD SOME NEWS, KILLER.
THERE'S SOME NEW BIG-SHOT IN TOWN CALLED MOBSTER. HE WANTS A PIECE OF THE ACTION HERE, SO HE BROUGHT HIS OWN FIGHTER.
YEAH? WHAT'S THE SUCKER'S NAME?
KILLER... IT'S THE MASKED MARAUDER!
KILLER CROC VS MASKED MARAUDER! MYSTERY FIGHTER CHALLENGES CHAMP!
?
WELCOME, LADIES AND GENTLEMEN, TO THE GLOBAL WRESTLING FEDERATION MEGA-HEAVYWEIGHT CHAMPIONSHIP! TONIGHT-- A MATCH-UP BETWEEN THE CURRENT WORLD CHAMPION, KILLER CROC, AND THE MYSTERIOUS CHALLENGER KNOWN ONLY AS THE MASKED MARAUDER!
GOTHAM SPORTS GAZETTE
KILLER CROC VS MASKED! MARAUDER!
CIGARET
5

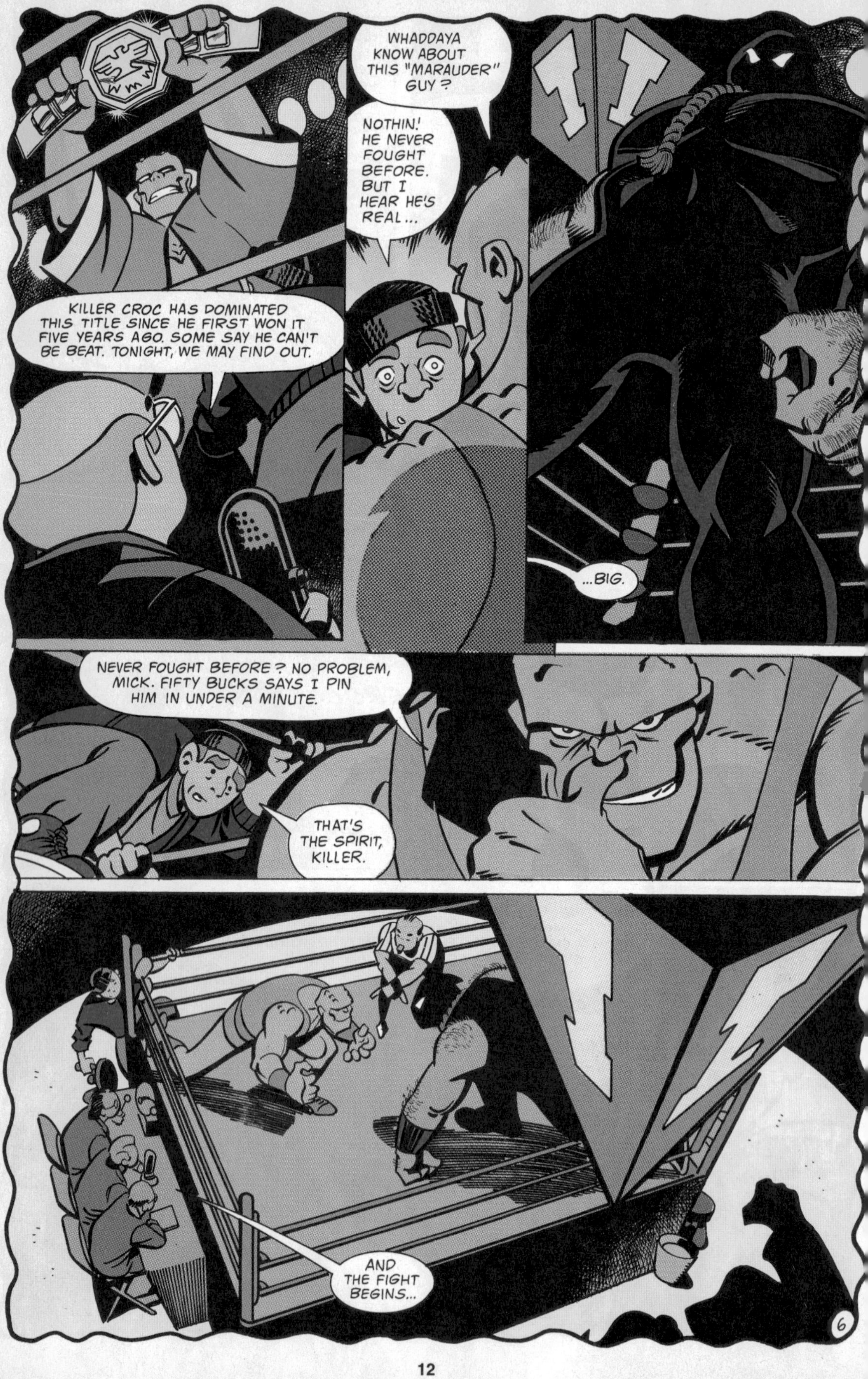
WHADDAYA KNOW ABOUT THIS "MARAUDER" GUY ?
NOTHIN'! HE NEVER FOUGHT BEFORE. BUT I HEAR HE'S REAL...
...BIG.
KILLER CROC HAS DOMINATED THIS TITLE SINCE HE FIRST WON IT FIVE YEARS AGO. SOME SAY HE CAN'T BE BEAT. TONIGHT, WE MAY FIND OUT.
NEVER FOUGHT BEFORE? NO PROBLEM, MICK. FIFTY BUCKS SAYS I PIN HIM IN UNDER A MINUTE.
THAT'S THE SPIRIT, KILLER.
AND THE FIGHT BEGINS...
6

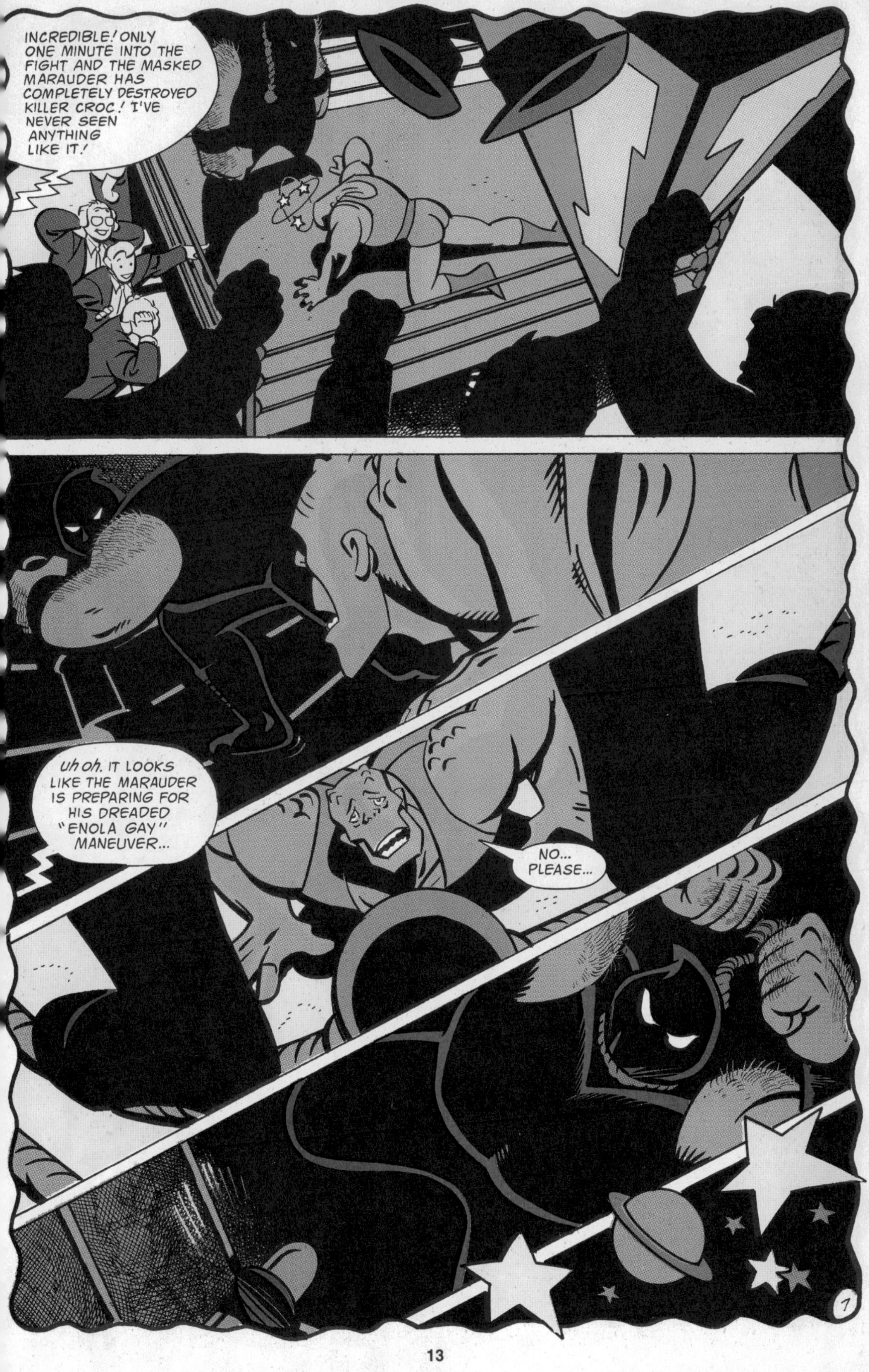
INCREDIBLE! ONLY ONE MINUTE INTO THE FIGHT AND THE MASKED MARAUDER HAS COMPLETELY DESTROYED KILLER CROC! I'VE NEVER SEEN ANYTHING LIKE IT!
uh oh. IT LOOKS LIKE THE MARAUDER IS PREPARING FOR HIS DREADED "ENOLA GAY" MANEUVER...
NO... PLEASE...
7

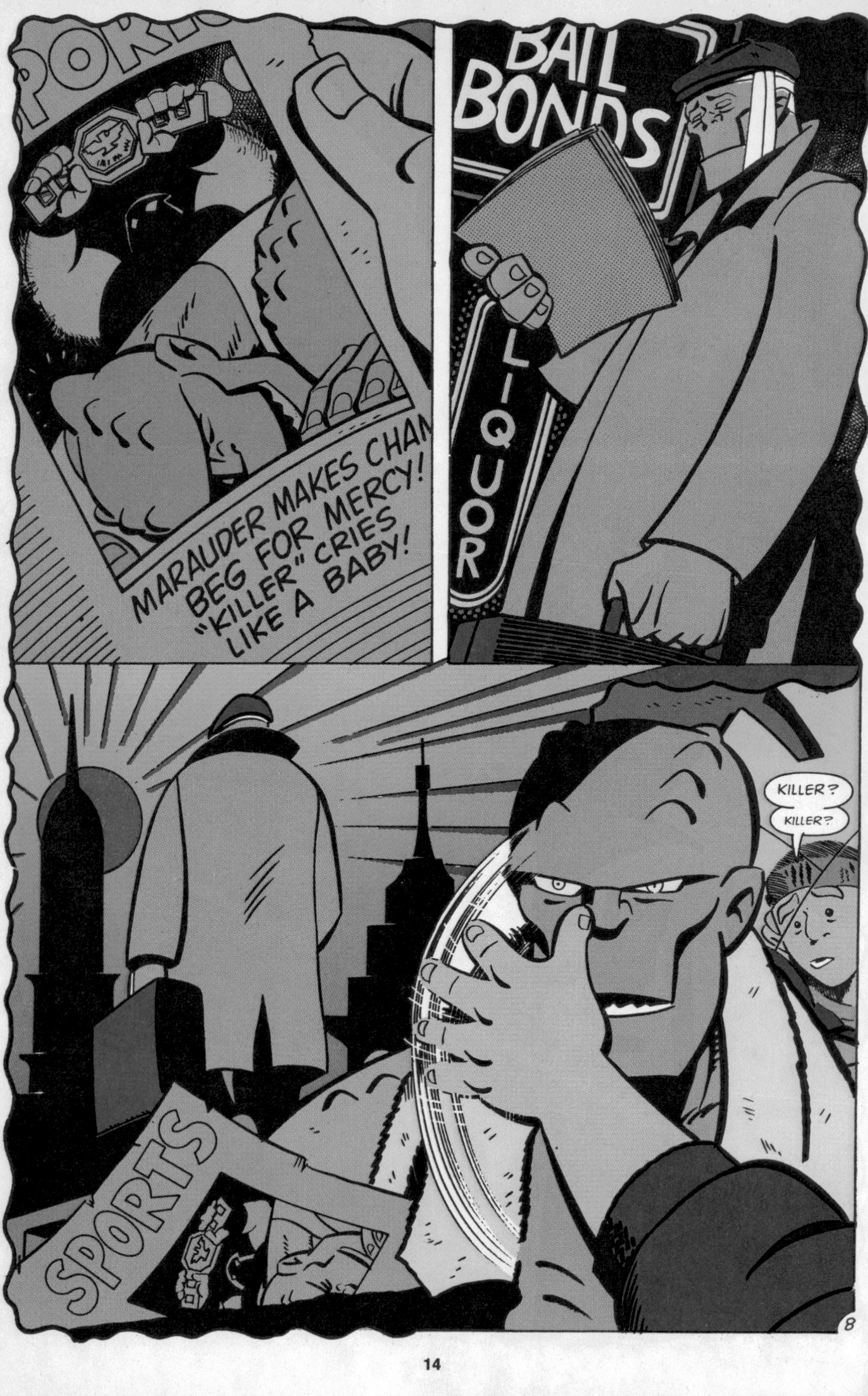
SPORTS
MARAUDER MAKES CHAM
BEG FOR MERCY!
"KILLER" CRIES
LIKE A BABY!
BAIL BONDS
LIQUOR
KILLER?
KILLER?
SPORTS
8

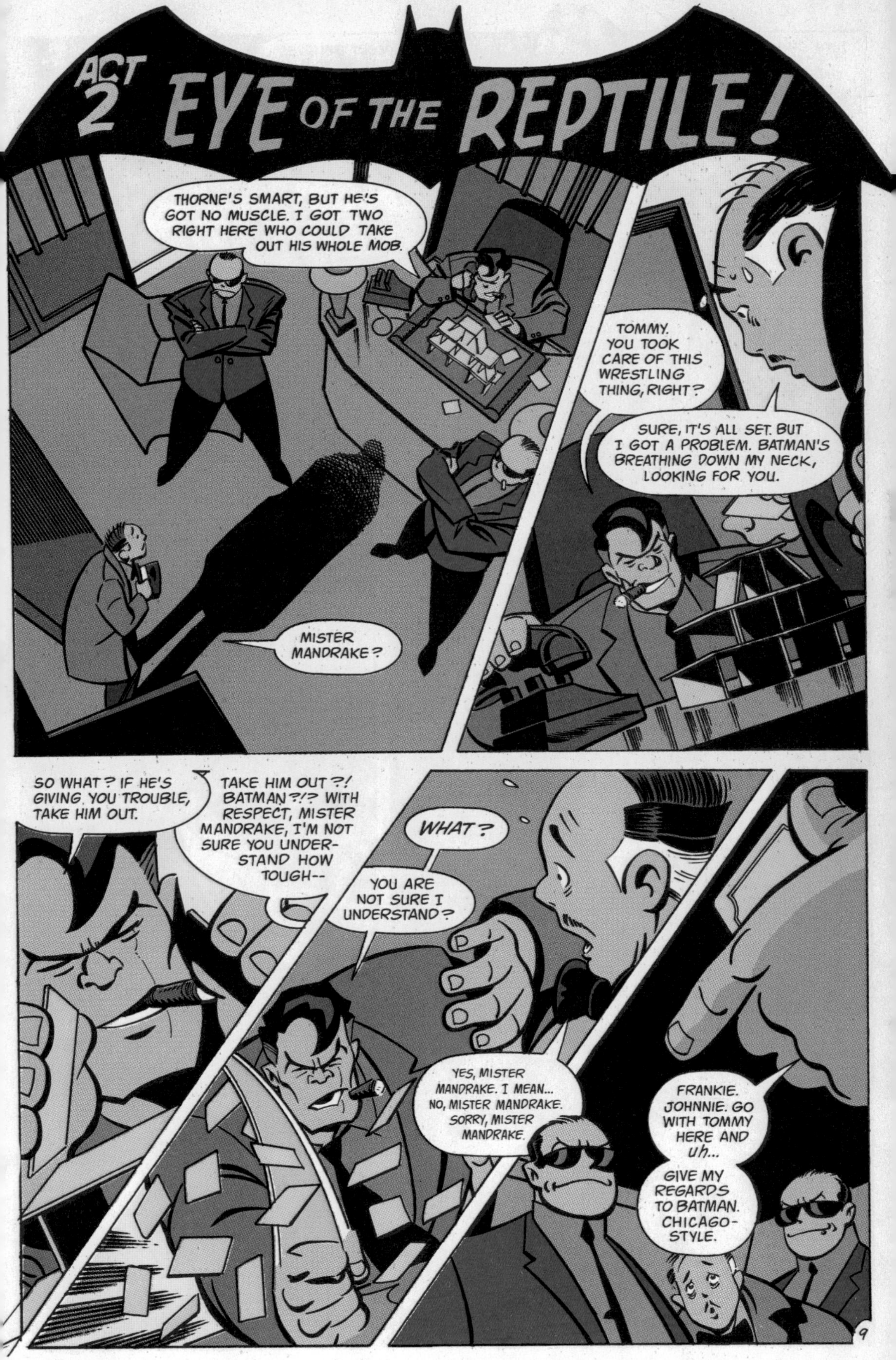
ACT 2
EYE OF THE REPTILE!
THORNE'S SMART, BUT HE'S GOT NO MUSCLE. I GOT TWO RIGHT HERE WHO COULD TAKE OUT HIS WHOLE MOB.
MISTER MANDRAKE?
TOMMY. YOU TOOK CARE OF THIS WRESTLING THING, RIGHT?
SURE, IT'S ALL SET. BUT I GOT A PROBLEM. BATMAN'S BREATHING DOWN MY NECK, LOOKING FOR YOU.
SO WHAT? IF HE'S GIVING YOU TROUBLE, TAKE HIM OUT.
TAKE HIM OUT?! BATMAN?!? WITH RESPECT, MISTER MANDRAKE, I'M NOT SURE YOU UNDERSTAND HOW TOUGH--
WHAT?
YOU ARE NOT SURE I UNDERSTAND?
YES, MISTER MANDRAKE. I MEAN... NO, MISTER MANDRAKE. SORRY, MISTER MANDRAKE.
FRANKIE. JOHNNIE. GO WITH TOMMY HERE AND uh...
GIVE MY REGARDS TO BATMAN. CHICAGO-STYLE.
9

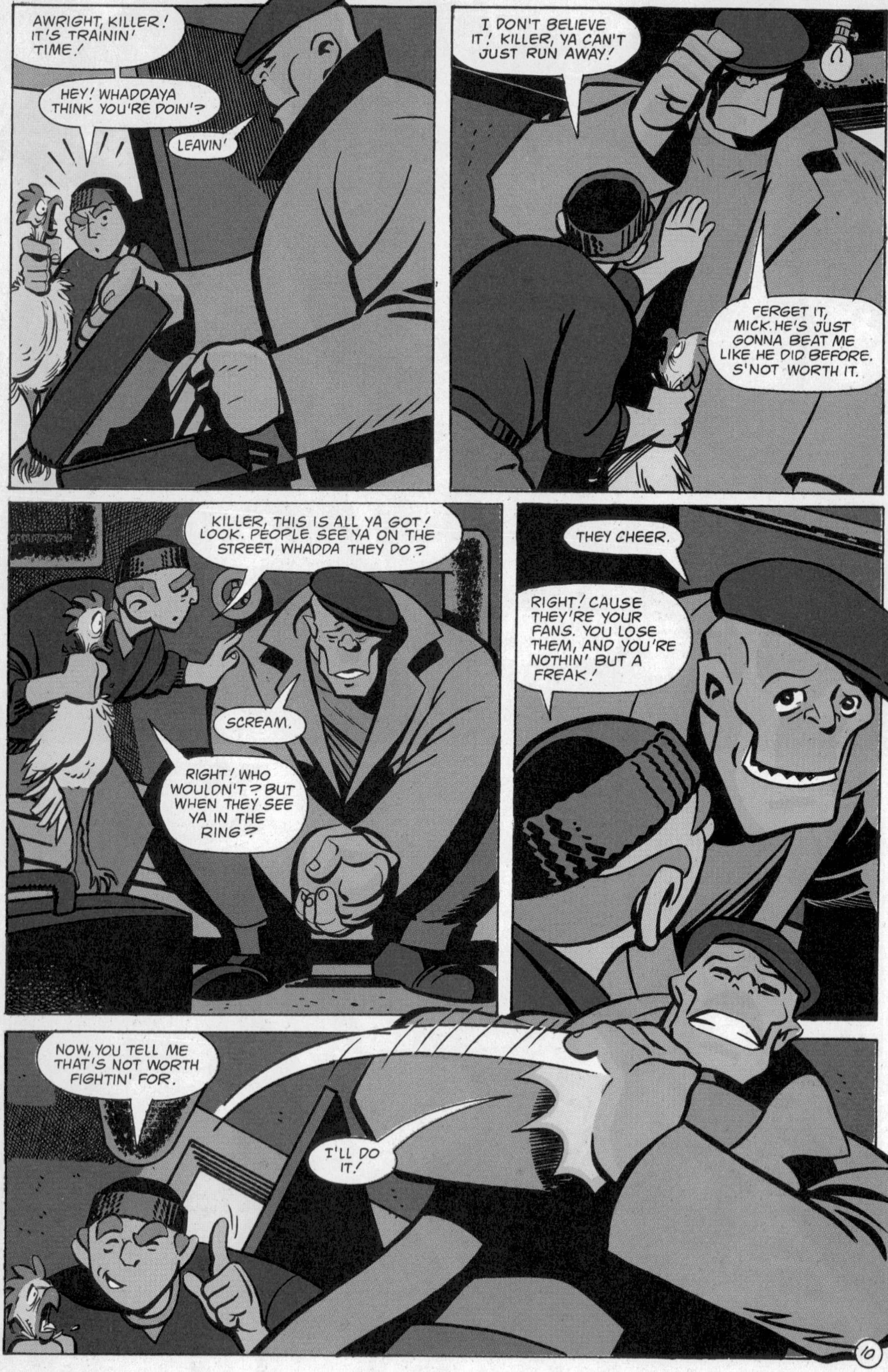
AWRIGHT, KILLER! IT'S TRAININ' TIME!
HEY! WHADDAYA THINK YOU'RE DOIN'?
LEAVIN'
I DON'T BELIEVE IT! KILLER, YA CAN'T JUST RUN AWAY!
FERGET IT, MICK. HE'S JUST GONNA BEAT ME LIKE HE DID BEFORE. S'NOT WORTH IT.
KILLER, THIS IS ALL YA GOT! LOOK. PEOPLE SEE YA ON THE STREET, WHADDA THEY DO?
SCREAM.
RIGHT! WHO WOULDN'T? BUT WHEN THEY SEE YA IN THE RING?
THEY CHEER.
RIGHT! CAUSE THEY'RE YOUR FANS. YOU LOSE THEM, AND YOU'RE NOTHIN' BUT A FREAK!
NOW, YOU TELL ME THAT'S NOT WORTH FIGHTIN' FOR.
I'LL DO IT!
10

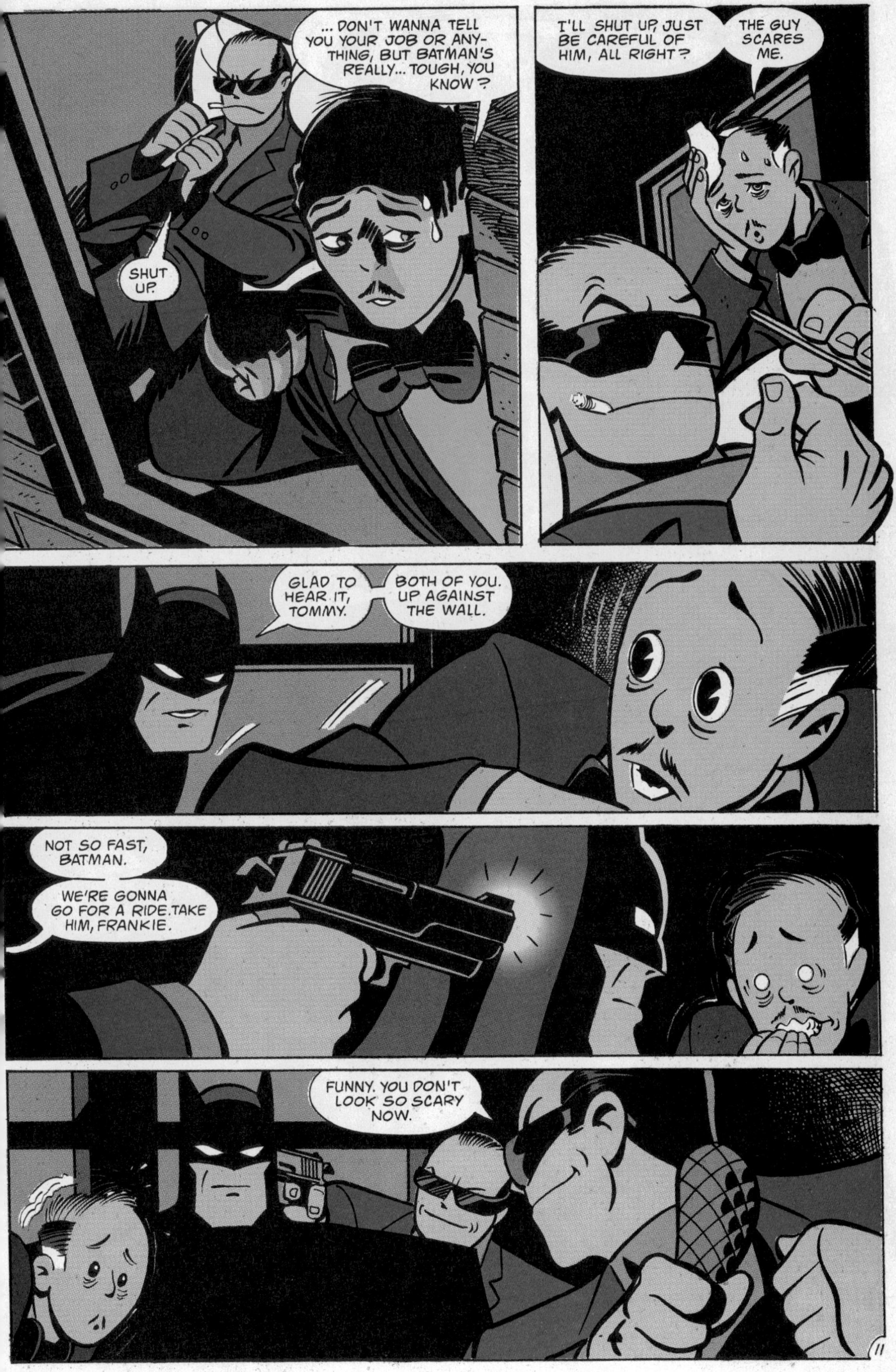
... DON'T WANNA TELL YOU YOUR JOB OR ANYTHING, BUT BATMAN'S REALLY... TOUGH, YOU KNOW?
SHUT UP.
I'LL SHUT UP, JUST BE CAREFUL OF HIM, ALL RIGHT?
THE GUY SCARES ME.
GLAD TO HEAR IT, TOMMY.
BOTH OF YOU. UP AGAINST THE WALL.
NOT SO FAST, BATMAN.
WE'RE GONNA GO FOR A RIDE. TAKE HIM, FRANKIE.
FUNNY. YOU DON'T LOOK SO SCARY NOW.
11

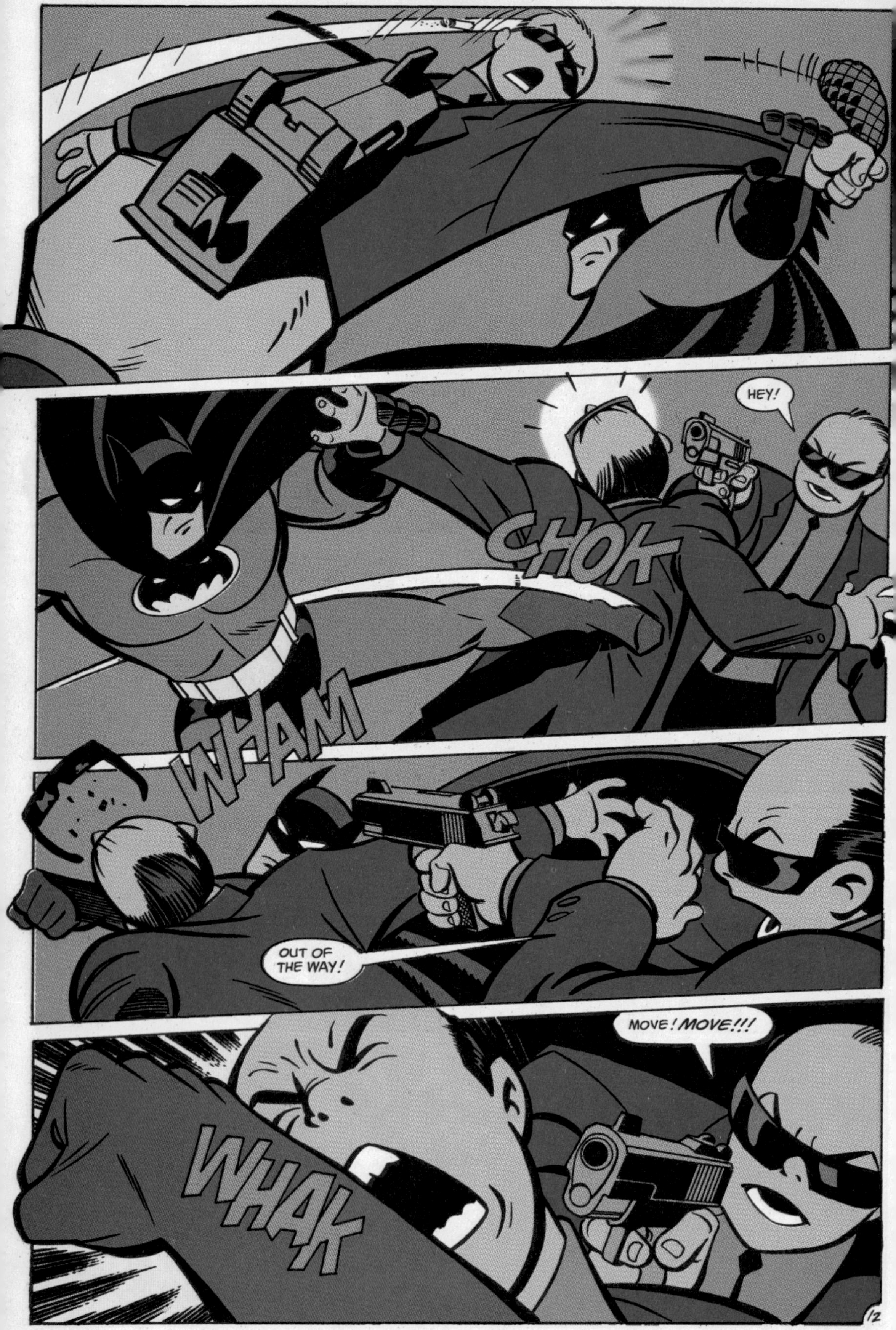
HEY!
CHOK
WHAM
OUT OF THE WAY!
MOVE! MOVE!!!
WHAK
12

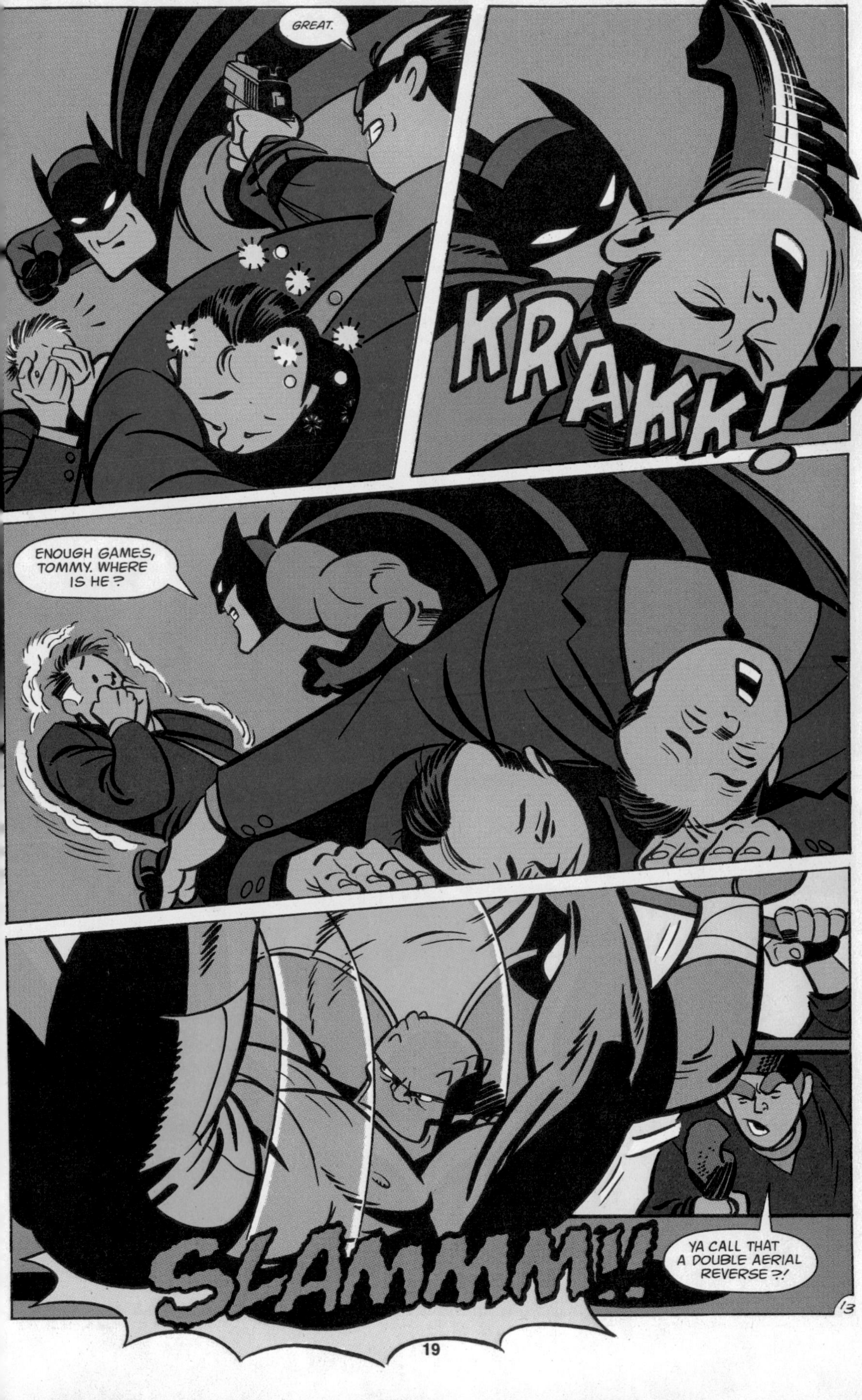
GREAT.
KRAKK!
ENOUGH GAMES, TOMMY. WHERE IS HE?
SLAMMM!
YA CALL THAT A DOUBLE AERIAL REVERSE?!

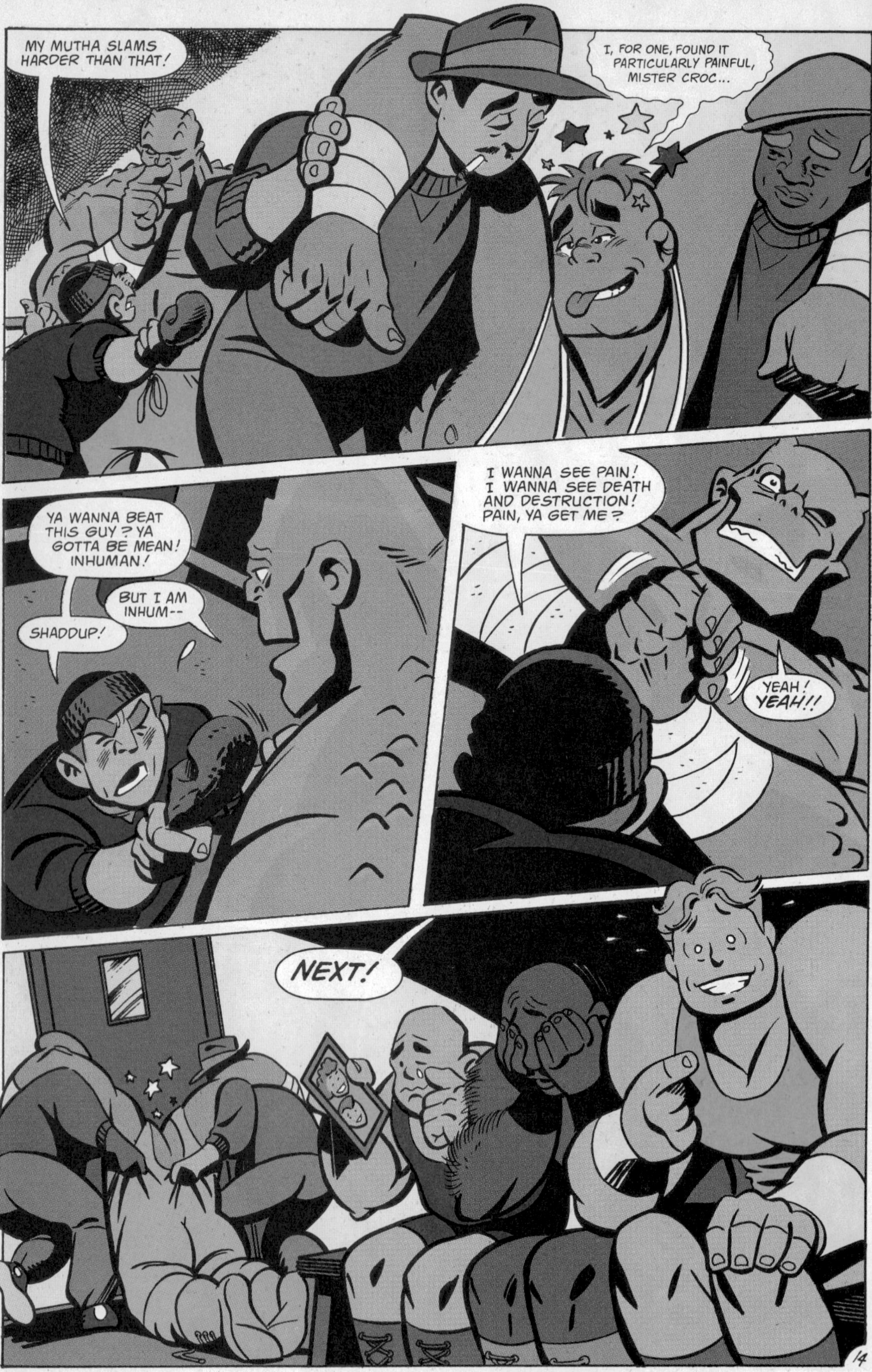
MY MUTHA SLAMS HARDER THAN THAT!
I, FOR ONE, FOUND IT PARTICULARLY PAINFUL, MISTER CROC...
YA WANNA BEAT THIS GUY? YA GOTTA BE MEAN! INHUMAN!
BUT I AM INHUM--
SHADDUP!
I WANNA SEE PAIN! I WANNA SEE DEATH AND DESTRUCTION! PAIN, YA GET ME?
YEAH! YEAH!!
NEXT!
14

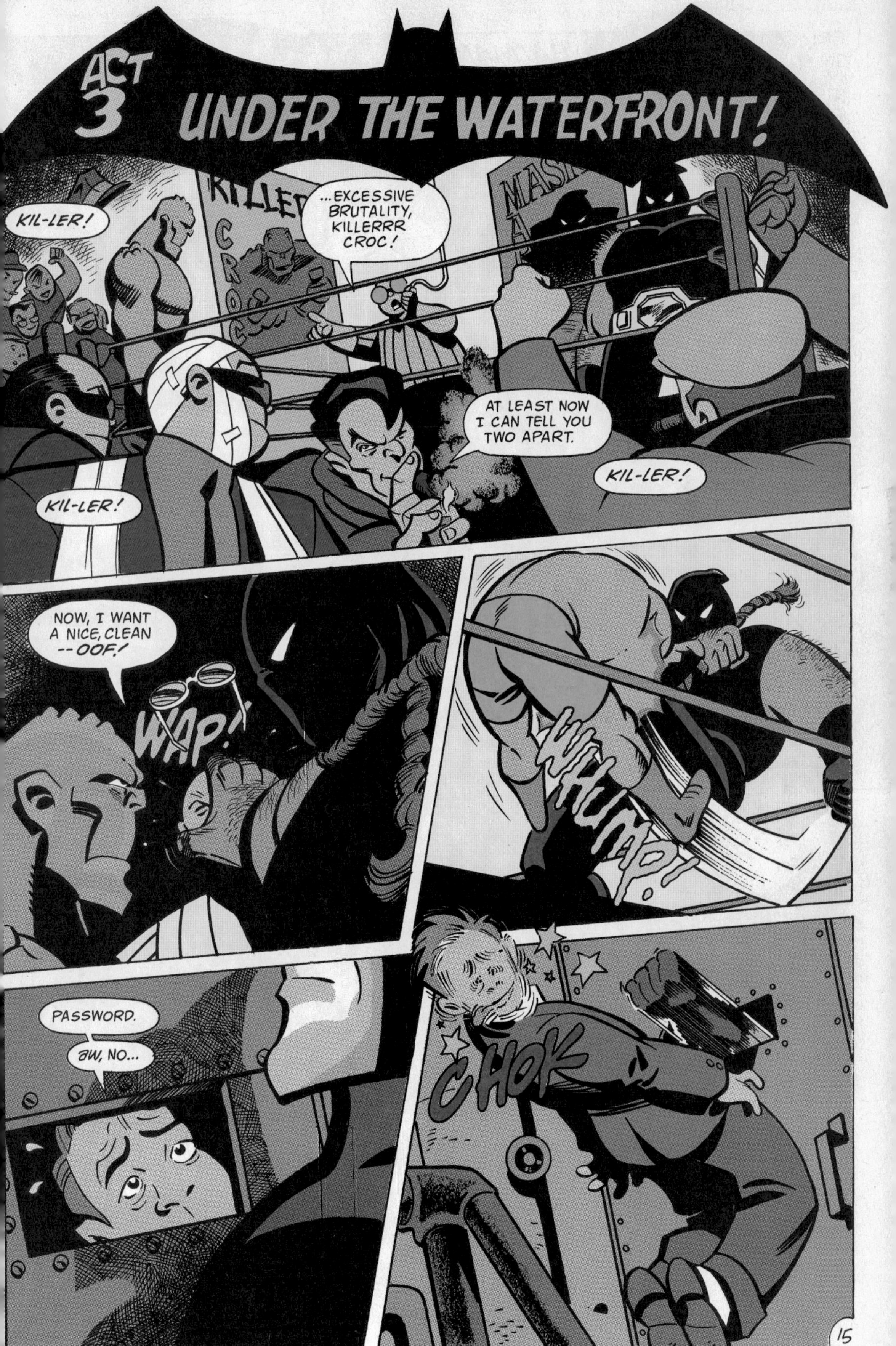
ACT 3
UNDER THE WATERFRONT!
KIL-LER!
...EXCESSIVE BRUTALITY, KILLERRR CROC!
KILLER CROC
AT LEAST NOW I CAN TELL YOU TWO APART.
KIL-LER!
KIL-LER!
NOW, I WANT A NICE, CLEAN --OOF!
WAP!
WHUMP!
PASSWORD.
aw, NO...
CHOK
15

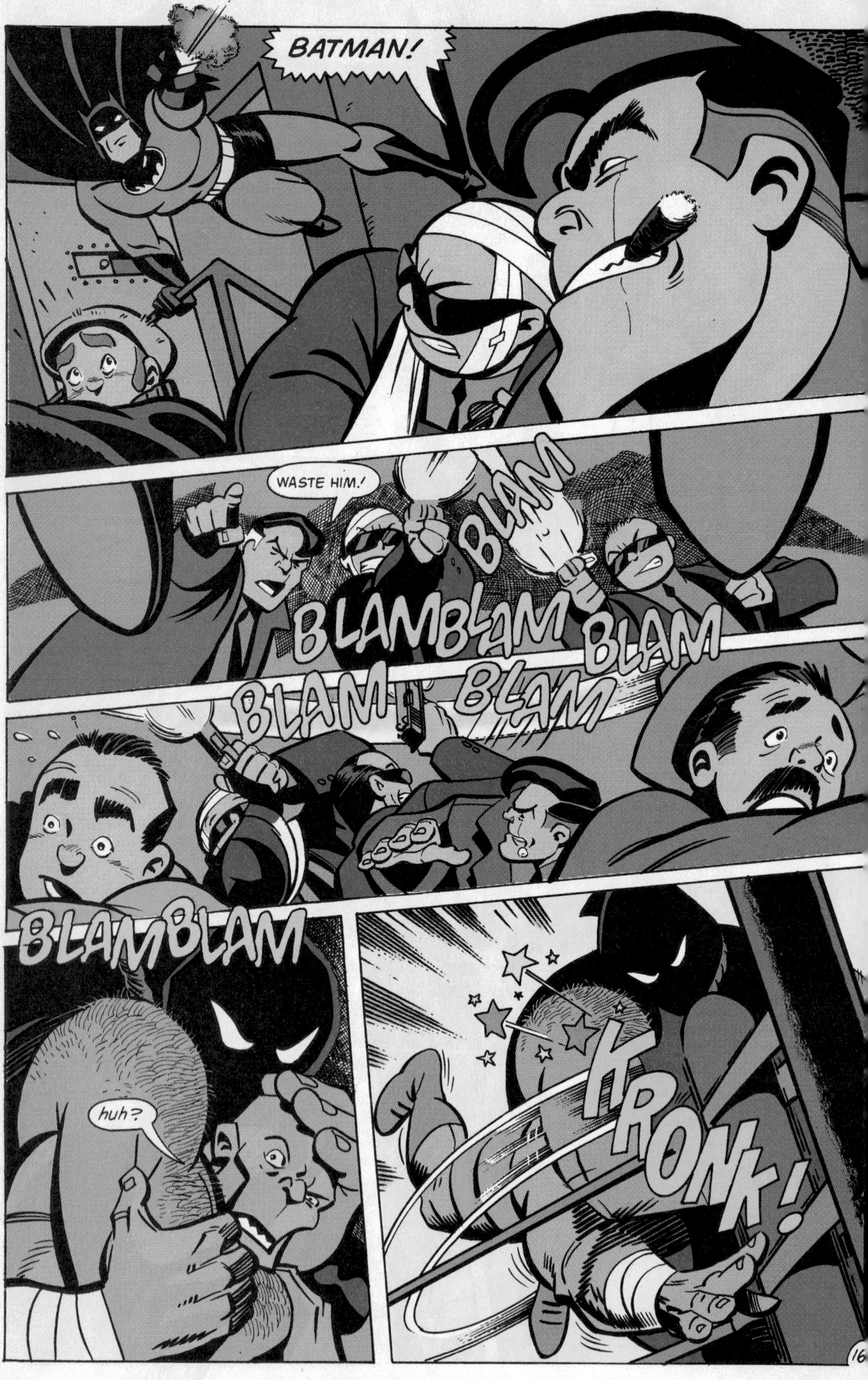
BATMAN!
WASTE HIM!
BLAM
BLAM
BLAMBLAM
BLAM
BLAM
BLAM
BLAM
BLAMBLAM
huh?
KRONK!
16

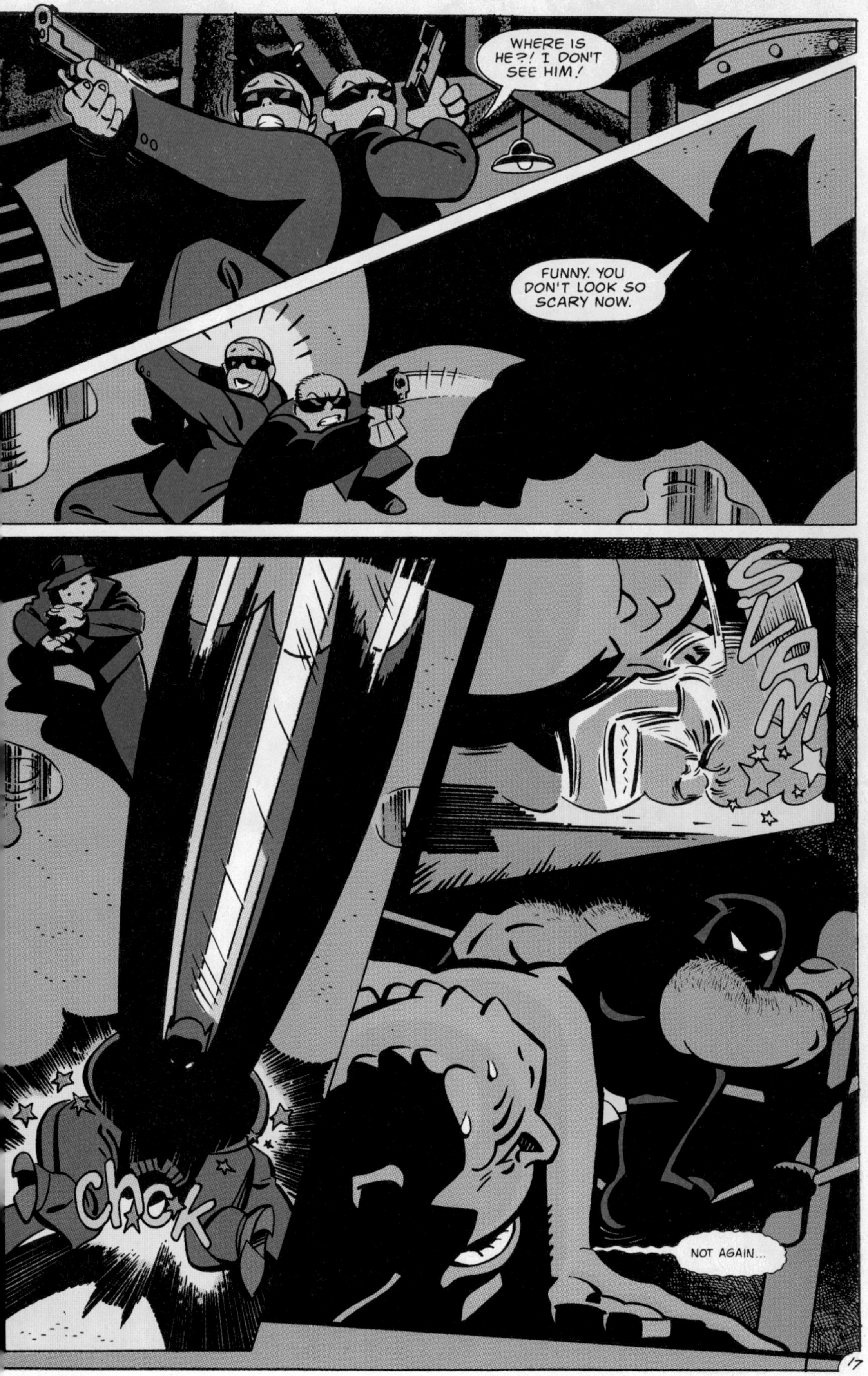
WHERE IS HE?! I DON'T SEE HIM!
FUNNY. YOU DON'T LOOK SO SCARY NOW.
SLAM
CHOK
NOT AGAIN...
17

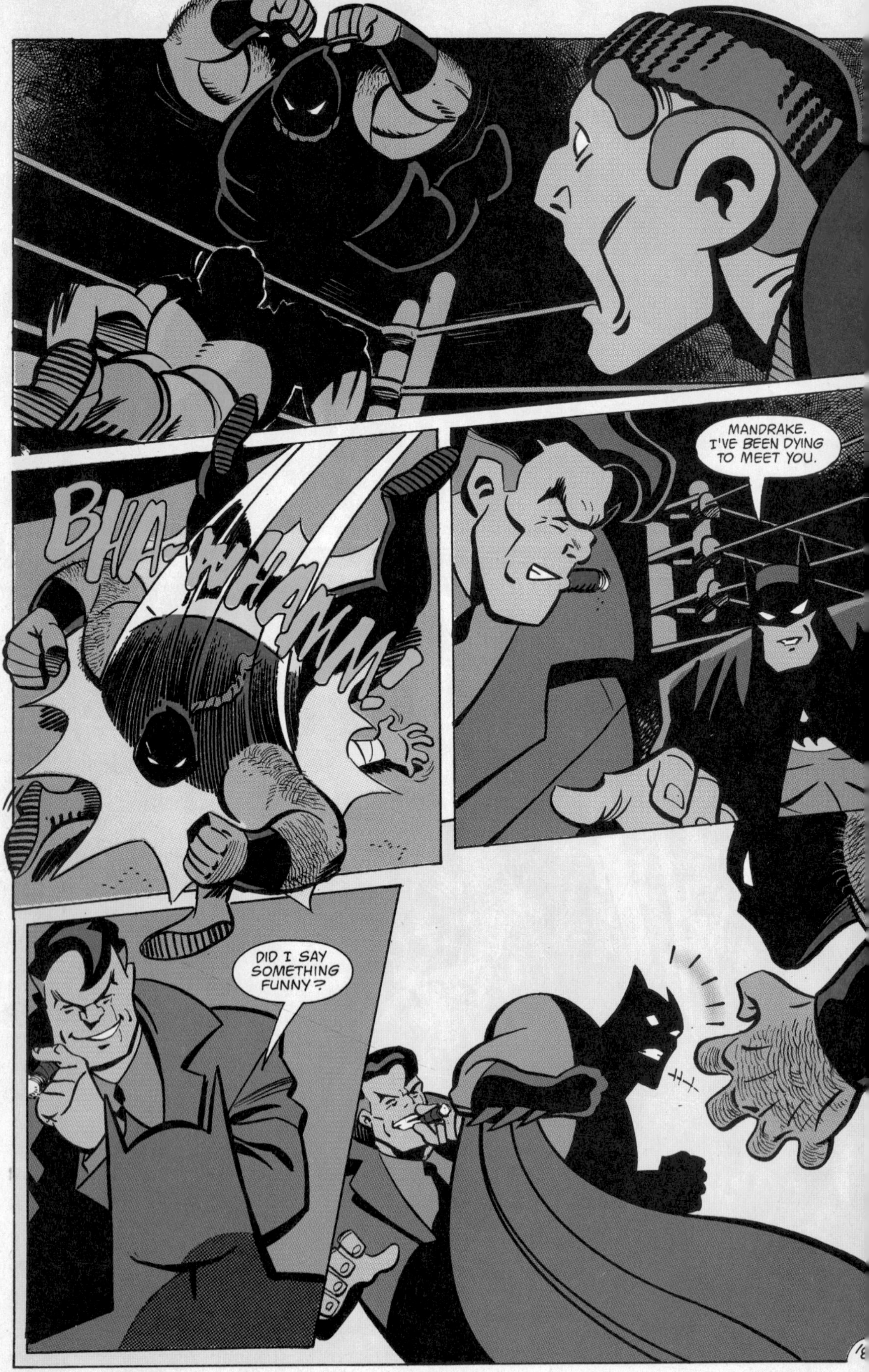

BHA-WHAMM!
MANDRAKE. I'VE BEEN DYING TO MEET YOU.
DID I SAY SOMETHING FUNNY?

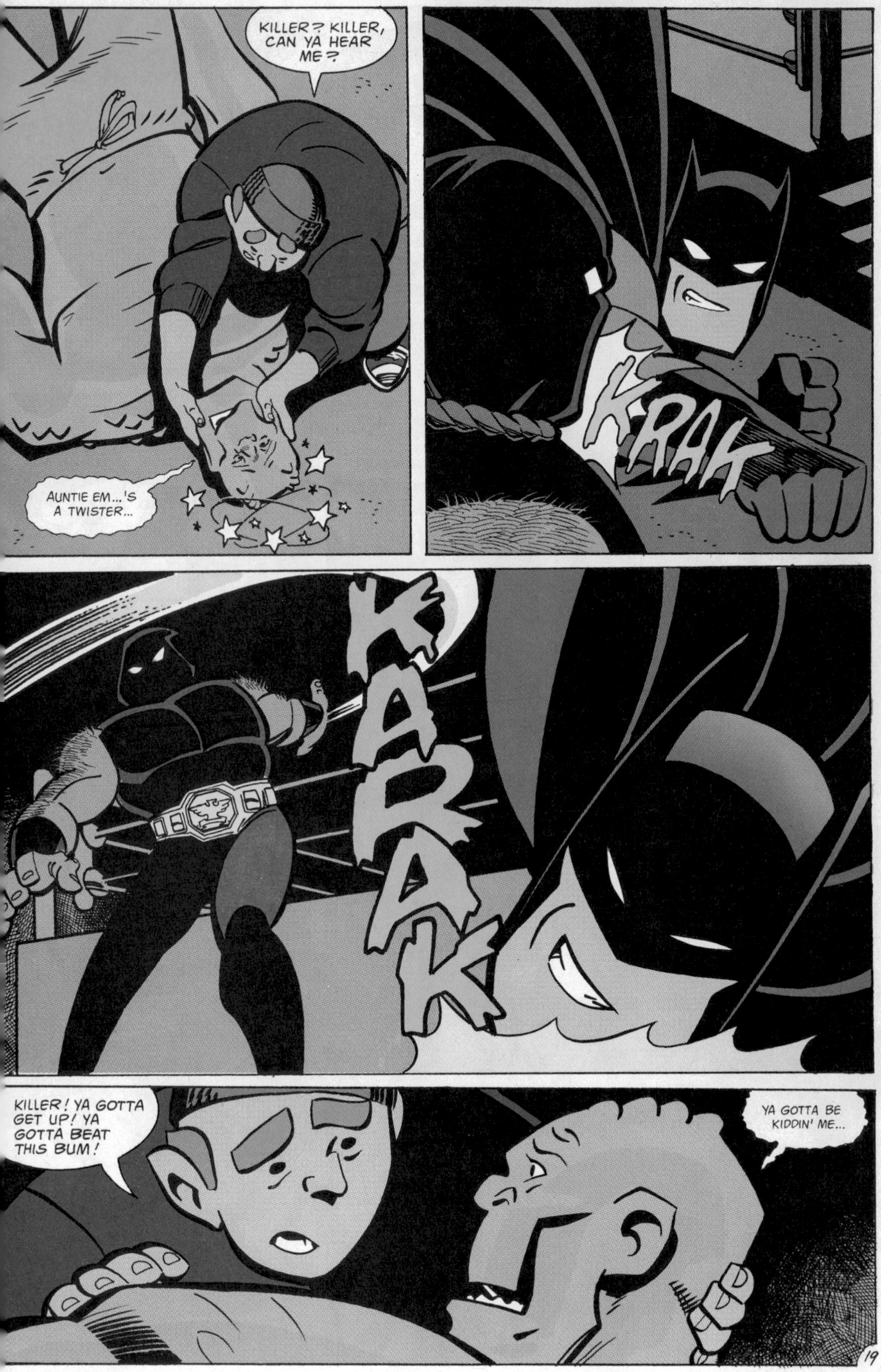
KILLER? KILLER, CAN YA HEAR ME?
AUNTIE EM...'S A TWISTER...
KRAK
KARAK
KILLER! YA GOTTA GET UP! YA GOTTA BEAT THIS BUM!
YA GOTTA BE KIDDIN' ME...
19

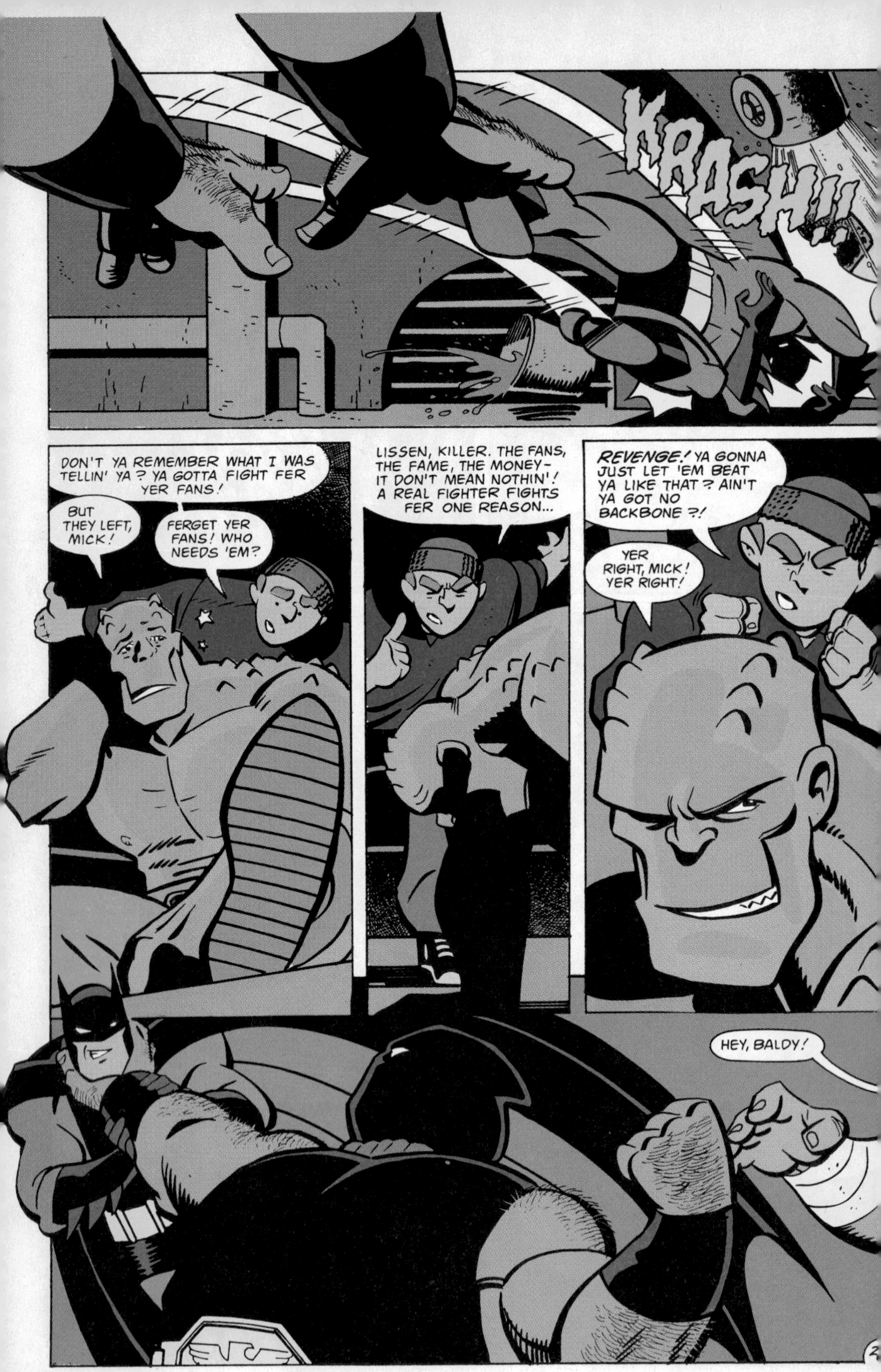
KRASH!!!
DON'T YA REMEMBER WHAT I WAS TELLIN' YA? YA GOTTA FIGHT FER YER FANS!
BUT THEY LEFT, MICK!
FERGET YER FANS! WHO NEEDS 'EM?
LISSEN, KILLER. THE FANS, THE FAME, THE MONEY- IT DON'T MEAN NOTHIN'! A REAL FIGHTER FIGHTS FER ONE REASON...
REVENGE! YA GONNA JUST LET 'EM BEAT YA LIKE THAT? AIN'T YA GOT NO BACKBONE?!
YER RIGHT, MICK! YER RIGHT!
HEY, BALDY!

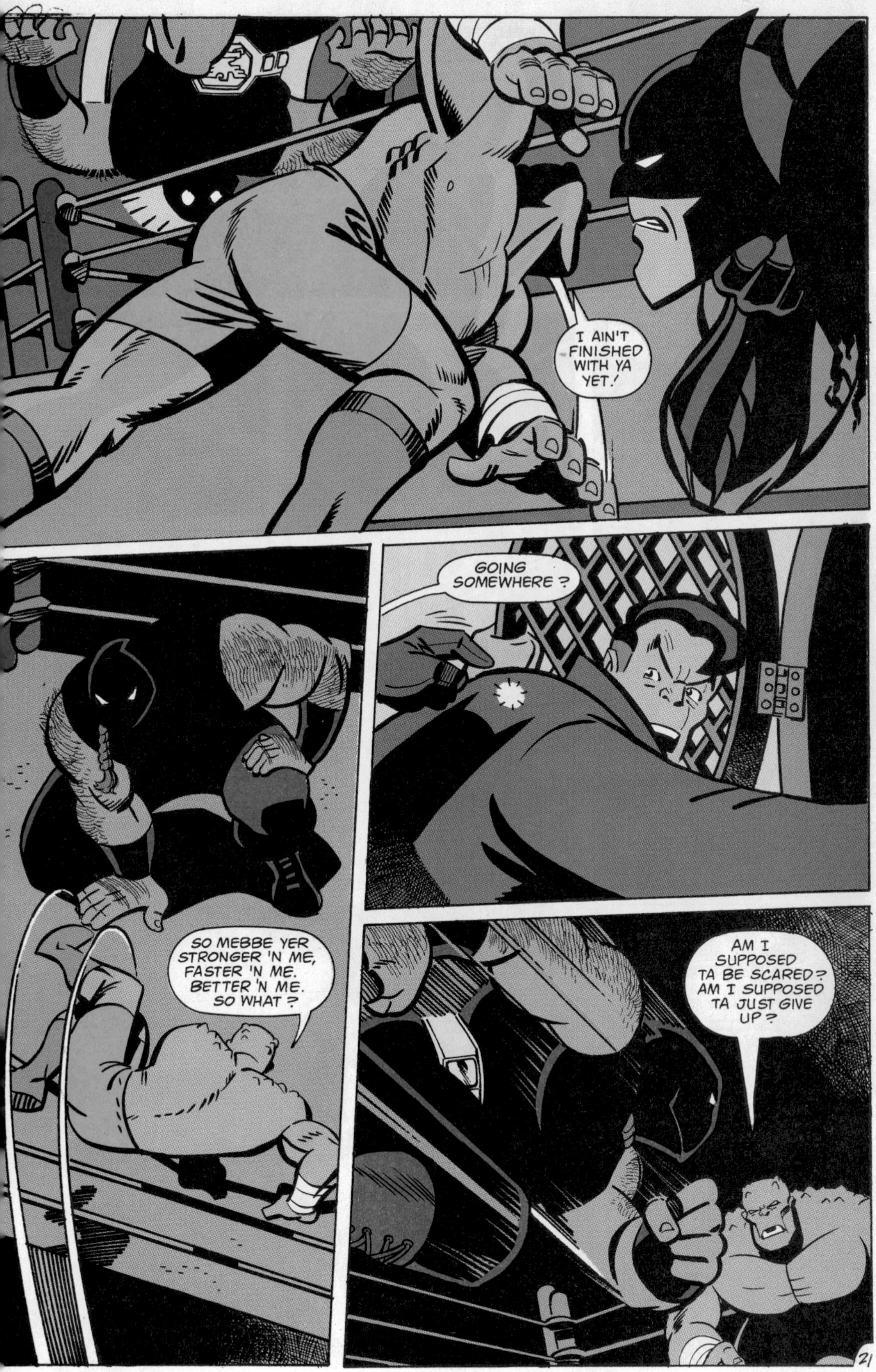
I AIN'T FINISHED WITH YA YET!
GOING SOMEWHERE?
SO MEBBE YER STRONGER 'N ME, FASTER 'N ME. BETTER 'N ME. SO WHAT?
AM I SUPPOSED TA BE SCARED? AM I SUPPOSED TA JUST GIVE UP?
21

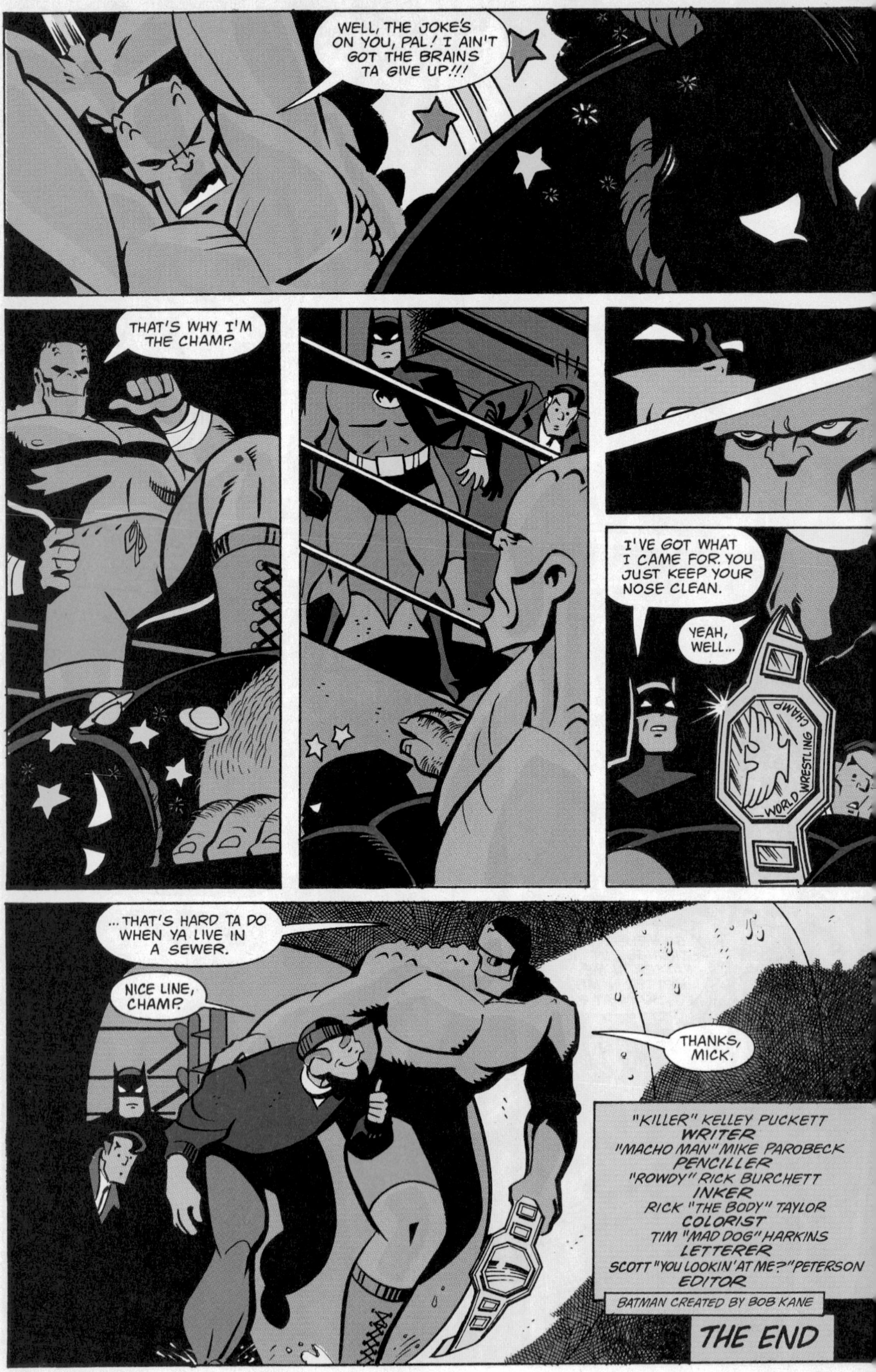
WELL, THE JOKE'S ON YOU, PAL! I AIN'T GOT THE BRAINS TA GIVE UP!!!
THAT'S WHY I'M THE CHAMP.
I'VE GOT WHAT I CAME FOR. YOU JUST KEEP YOUR NOSE CLEAN.
YEAH, WELL...
WORLD WRESTLING CHAMP
...THAT'S HARD TA DO WHEN YA LIVE IN A SEWER.
NICE LINE, CHAMP.
THANKS, MICK.
"KILLER" KELLEY PUCKETT
WRITER
"MACHO MAN" MIKE PAROBECK
PENCILLER
"ROWDY" RICK BURCHETT
INKER
RICK "THE BODY" TAYLOR
COLORIST
TIM "MAD DOG" HARKINS
LETTERER
SCOTT "YOU LOOKIN' AT ME?" PETERSON
EDITOR
BATMAN CREATED BY BOB KANE
THE END

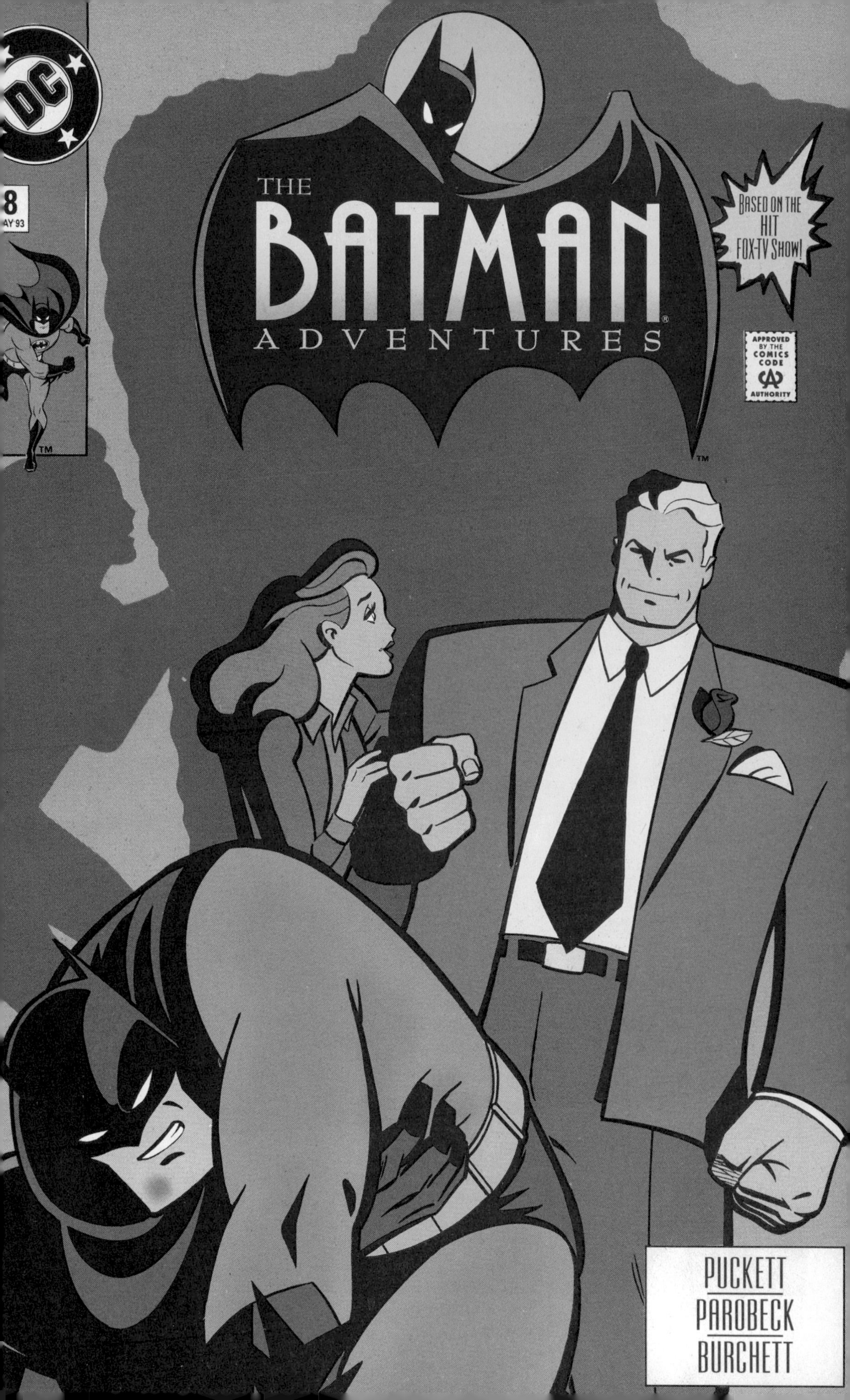
DC
8
AY'93
THE
BATMAN
ADVENTURES
BASED ON THE HIT FOX-TV SHOW!
APPROVED BY THE COMICS CODE AUTHORITY
PUCKETT
PAROBECK
BURCHETT

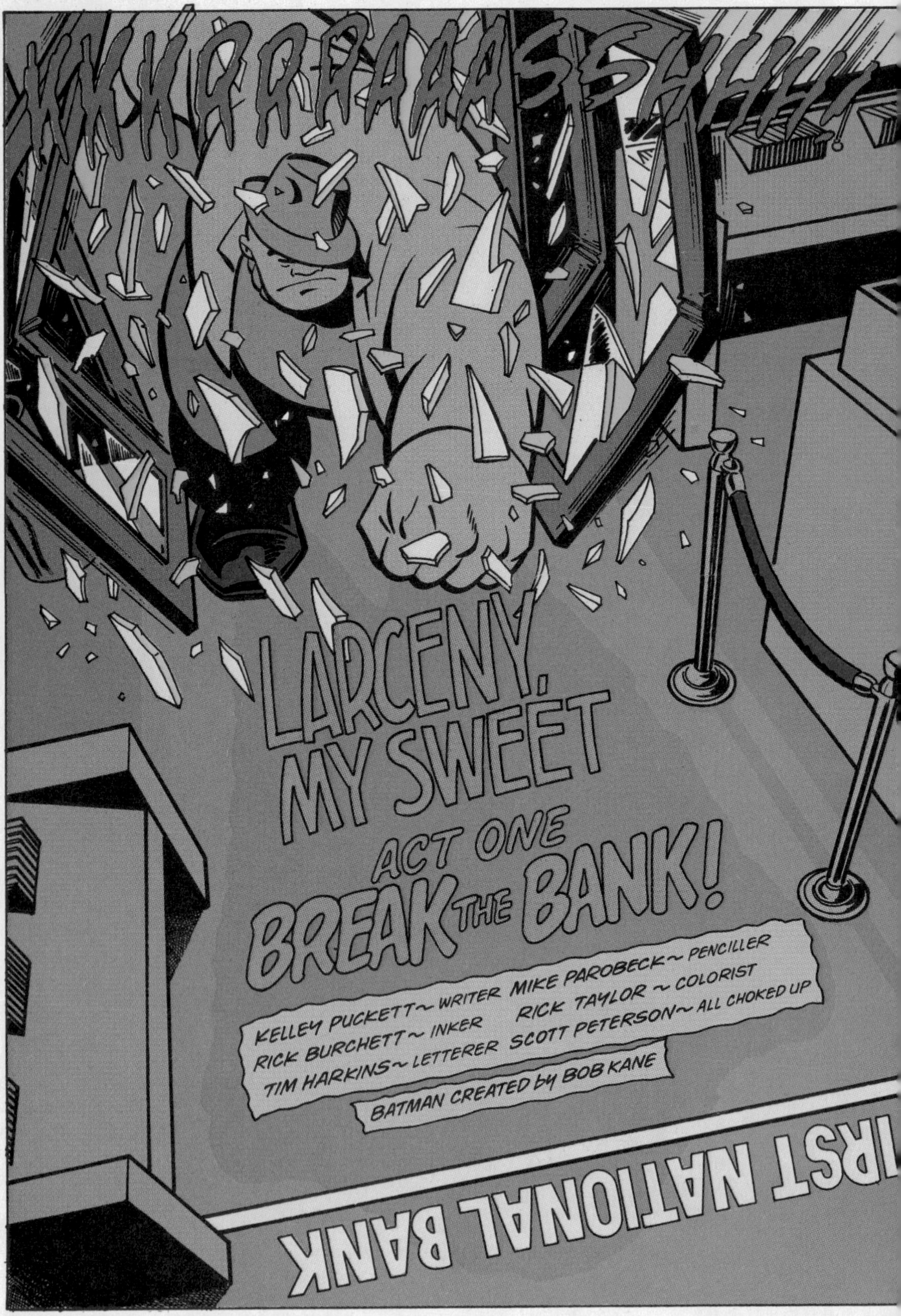
KKKRRRAAASSHHHH!
LARCENY, MY SWEET
ACT ONE
BREAK THE BANK!
KELLEY PUCKETT~WRITER MIKE PAROBECK~PENCILLER
RICK BURCHETT~INKER RICK TAYLOR~COLORIST
TIM HARKINS~LETTERER SCOTT PETERSON~ALL CHOKED UP
BATMAN CREATED BY BOB KANE
FIRST NATIONAL BANK

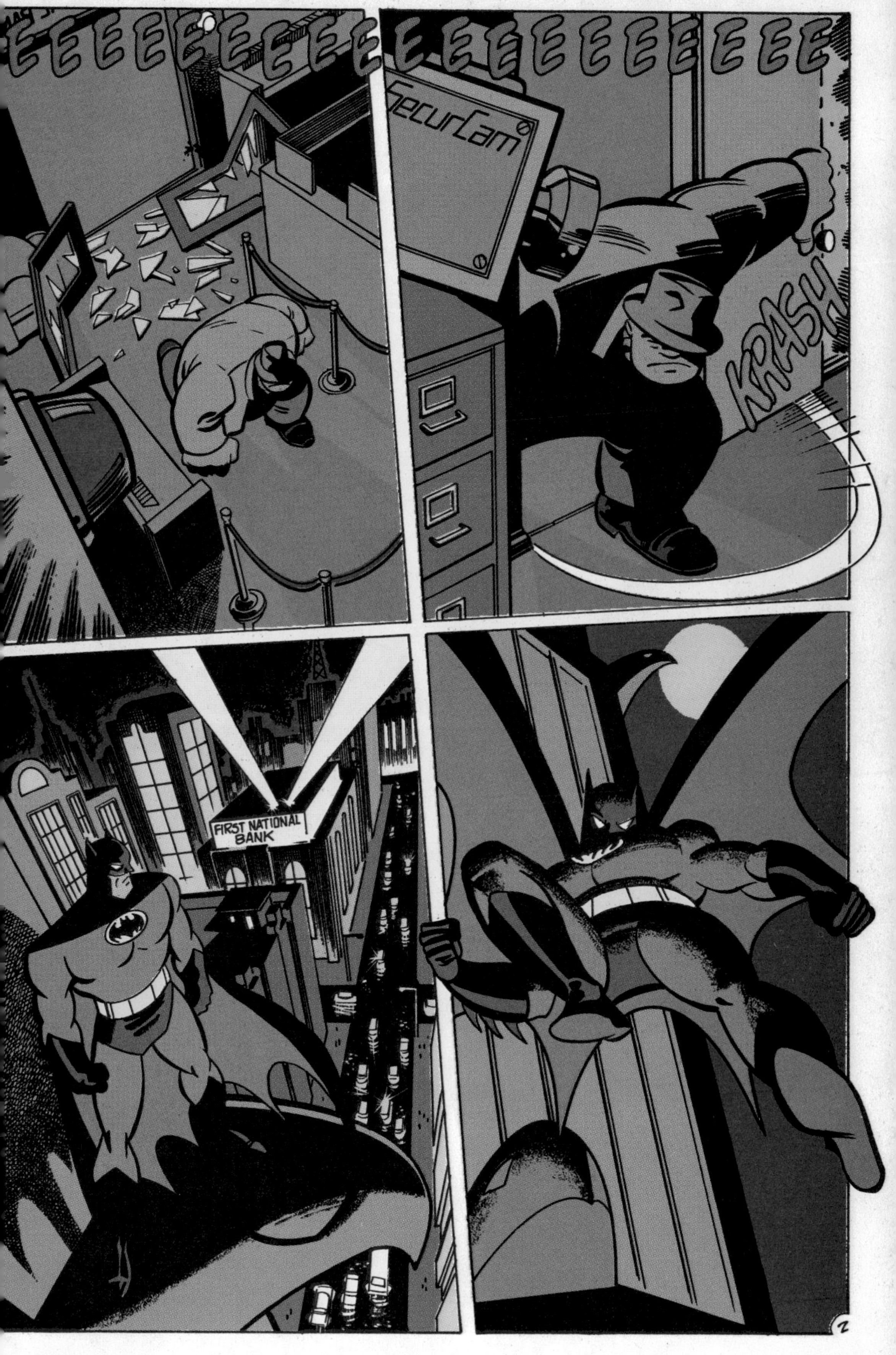
EEEEEEEEEEEEEEEEEEEE
SecurCam
KRASH
FIRST NATIONAL BANK

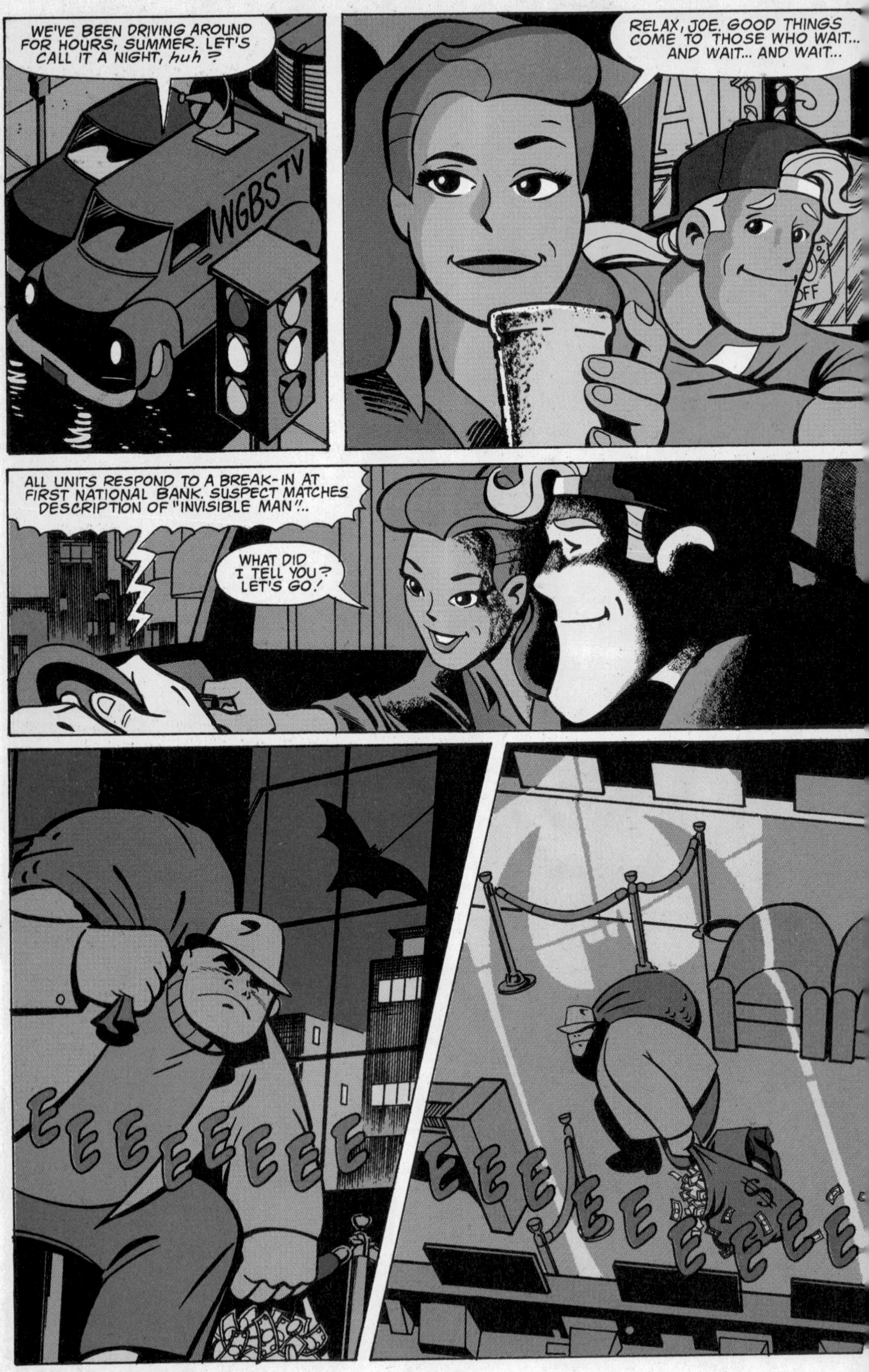
WE'VE BEEN DRIVING AROUND FOR HOURS, SUMMER. LET'S CALL IT A NIGHT, huh?
WGBS TV
RELAX, JOE. GOOD THINGS COME TO THOSE WHO WAIT... AND WAIT... AND WAIT...
ALL UNITS RESPOND TO A BREAK-IN AT FIRST NATIONAL BANK. SUSPECT MATCHES DESCRIPTION OF "INVISIBLE MAN"...
WHAT DID I TELL YOU? LET'S GO!
EEEEEEEEEEEEEEEEEE

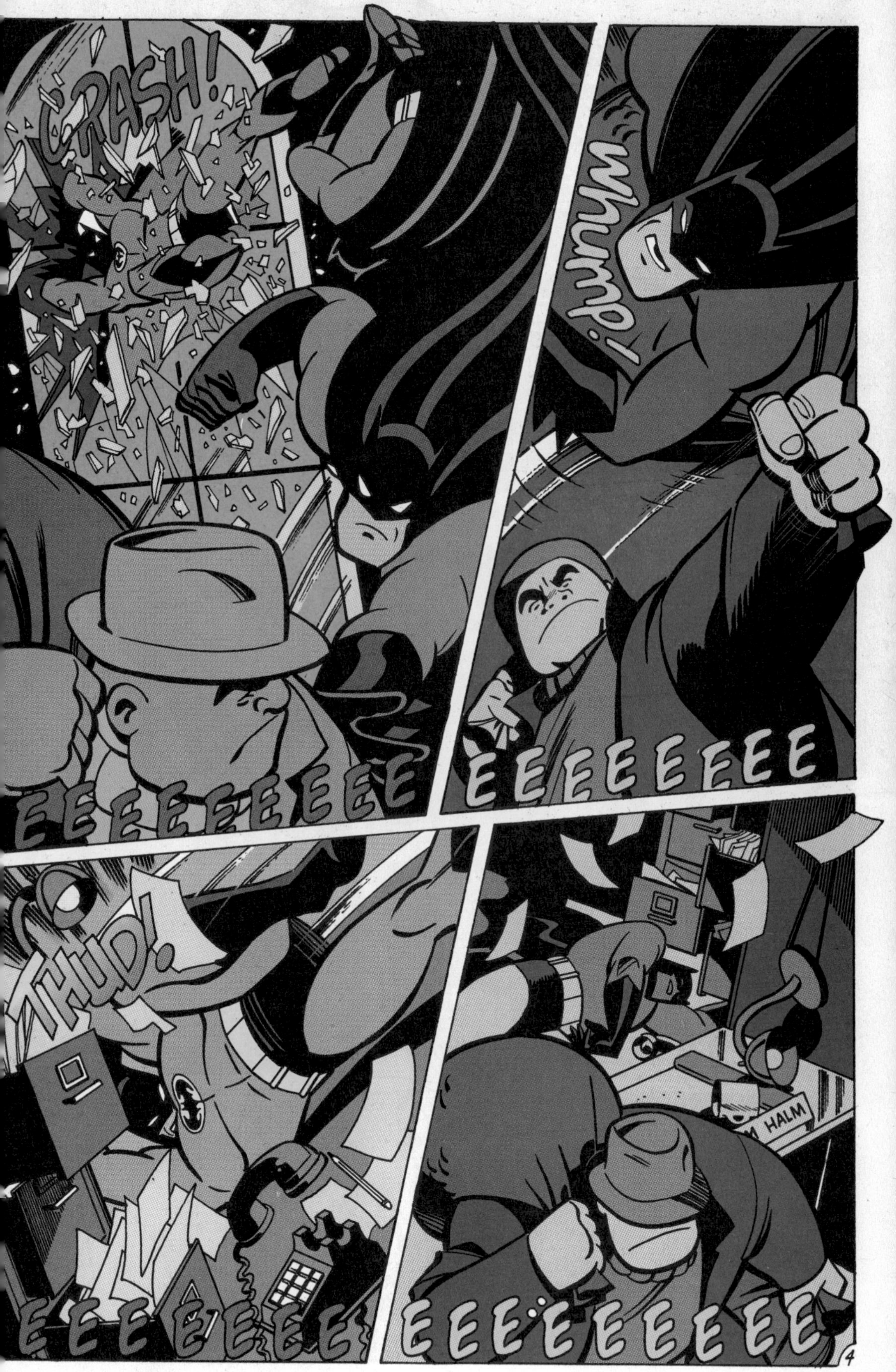
CRASH!
WHUMP!
EEEEEEEEEE
EEEEEEEEE
THUD!
HALM
EEEEEEEEE
EEE..EEEEEEE
4

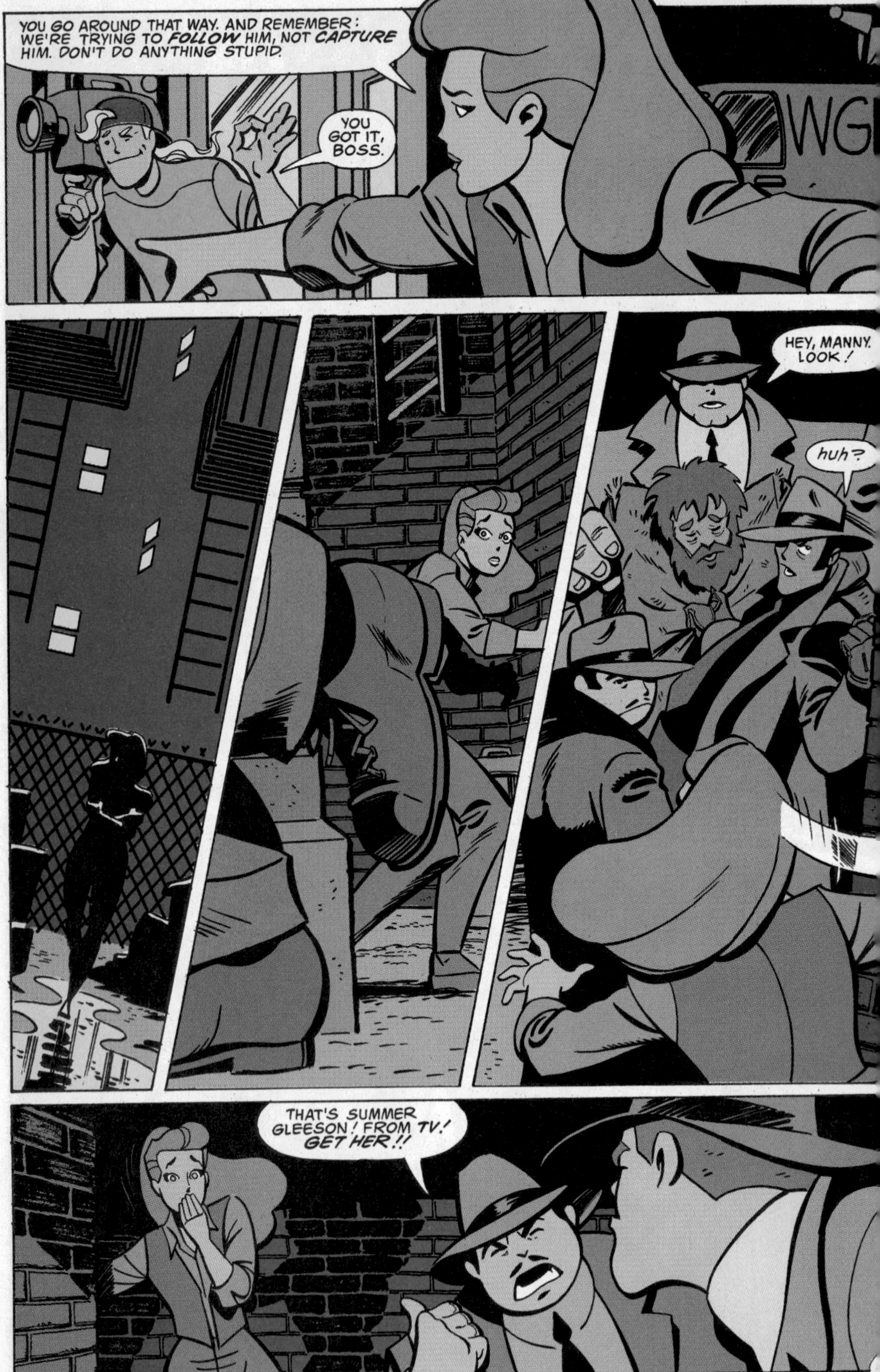
YOU GO AROUND THAT WAY. AND REMEMBER: WE'RE TRYING TO FOLLOW HIM, NOT CAPTURE HIM. DON'T DO ANYTHING STUPID.
YOU GOT IT, BOSS.
WG
HEY, MANNY. LOOK!
huh?
THAT'S SUMMER GLEESON! FROM TV! GET HER!!

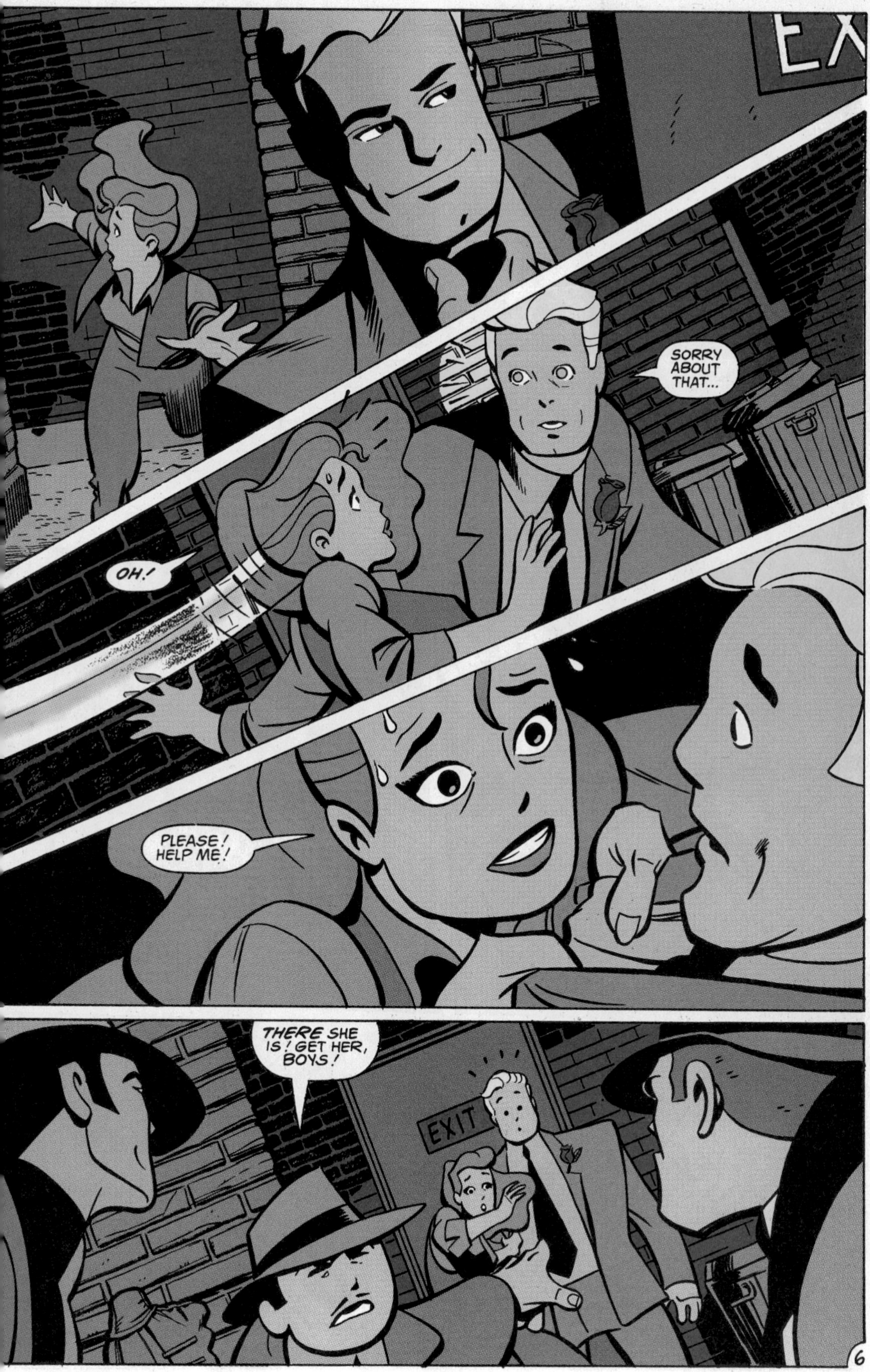
SORRY ABOUT THAT...
OH!
PLEASE! HELP ME!
THERE SHE IS! GET HER, BOYS!
EXIT
6

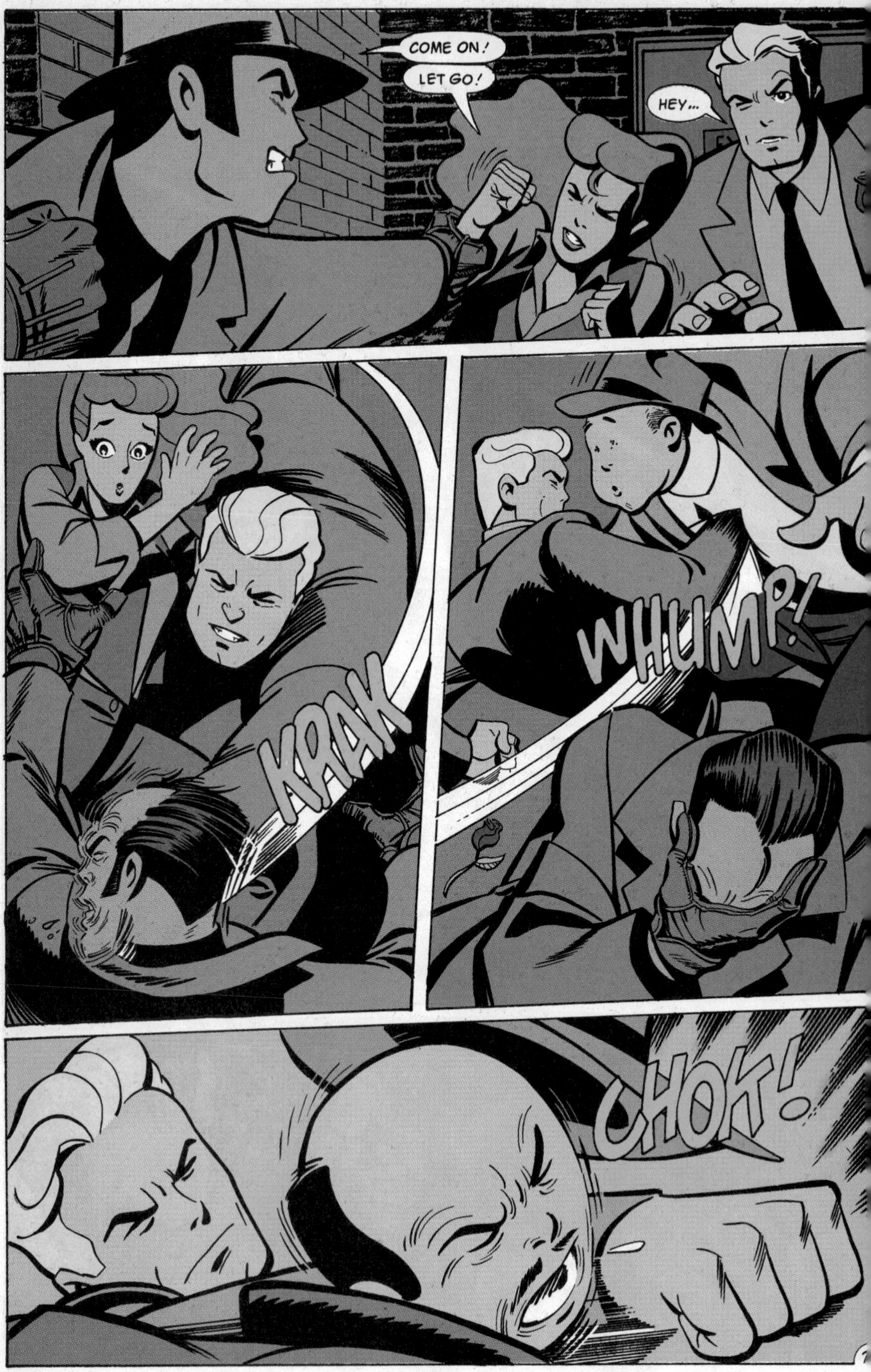
COME ON!
LET GO!
HEY...
KRAK
WHUMP!
CHOK!

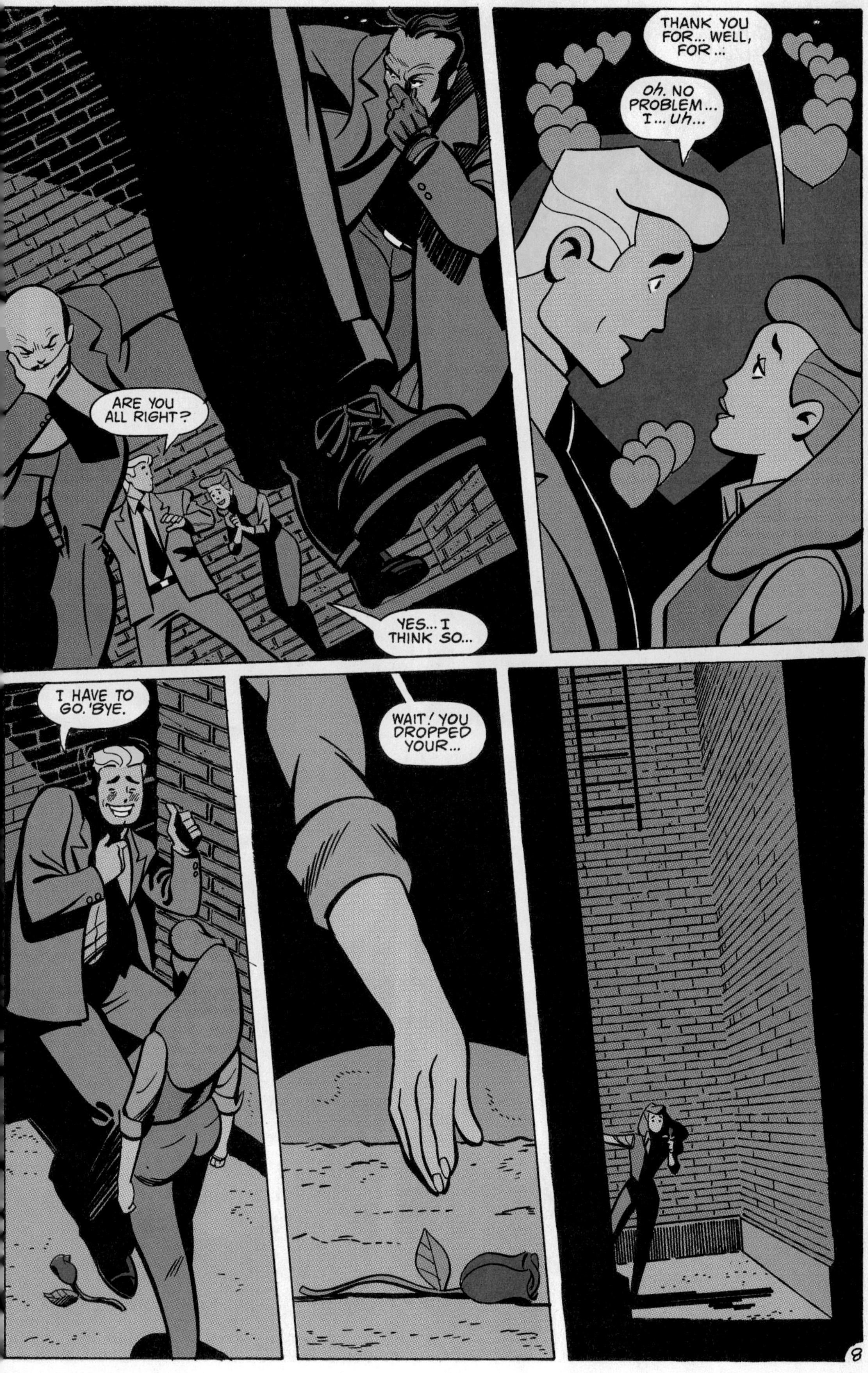
ARE YOU ALL RIGHT?
YES... I THINK SO...
THANK YOU FOR... WELL, FOR...
oh. NO PROBLEM... I... uh...
I HAVE TO GO. 'BYE.
WAIT! YOU DROPPED YOUR...
8

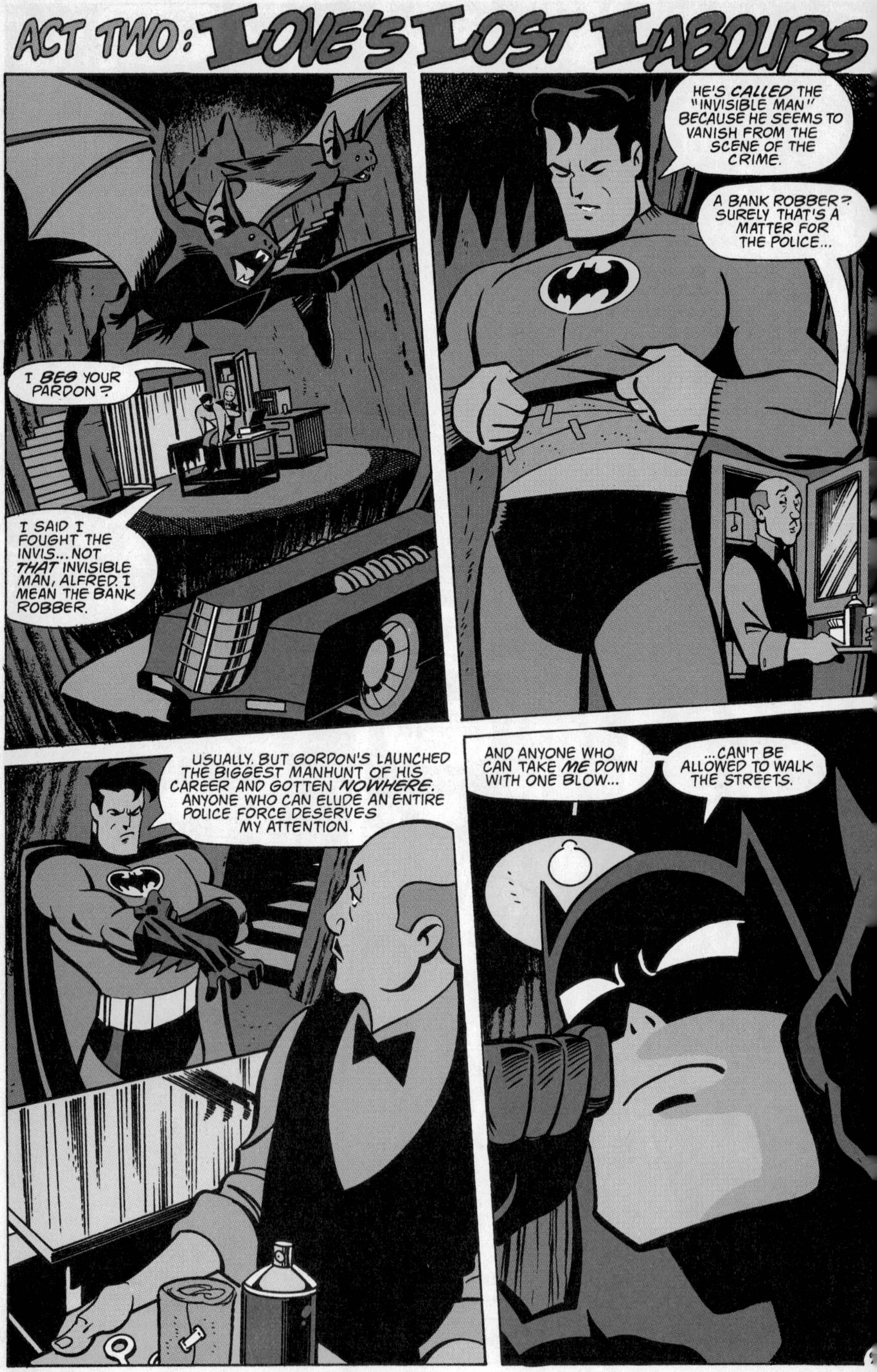
ACT TWO: LOVE'S LOST LABOURS
I BEG YOUR PARDON?
I SAID I FOUGHT THE INVIS... NOT THAT INVISIBLE MAN, ALFRED. I MEAN THE BANK ROBBER.
HE'S CALLED THE "INVISIBLE MAN" BECAUSE HE SEEMS TO VANISH FROM THE SCENE OF THE CRIME.
A BANK ROBBER? SURELY THAT'S A MATTER FOR THE POLICE...
USUALLY. BUT GORDON'S LAUNCHED THE BIGGEST MANHUNT OF HIS CAREER AND GOTTEN NOWHERE. ANYONE WHO CAN ELUDE AN ENTIRE POLICE FORCE DESERVES MY ATTENTION.
AND ANYONE WHO CAN TAKE ME DOWN WITH ONE BLOW...
...CAN'T BE ALLOWED TO WALK THE STREETS.

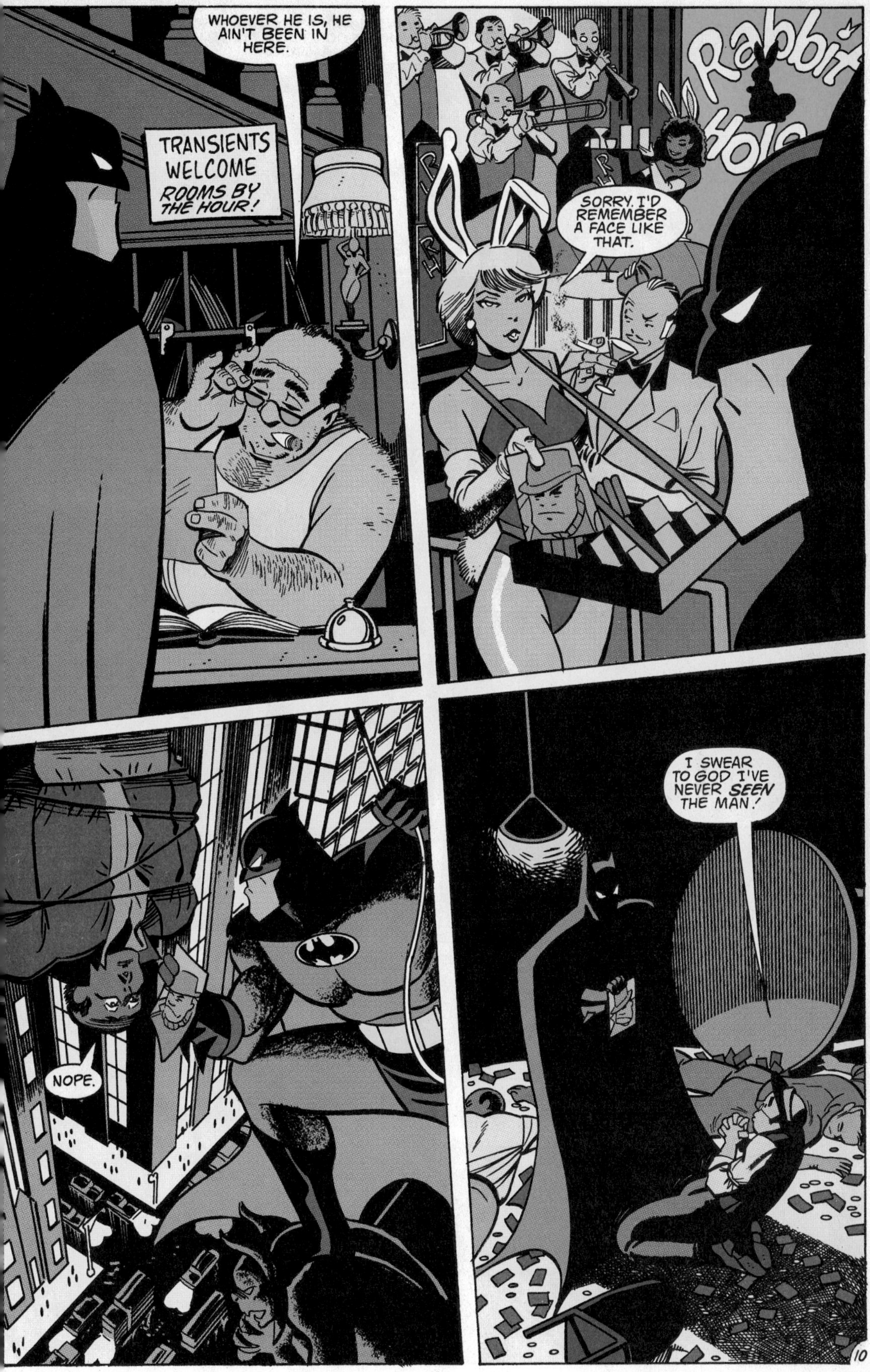
WHOEVER HE IS, HE AIN'T BEEN IN HERE.
TRANSIENTS WELCOME ROOMS BY THE HOUR!
Rabbit Hole
SORRY. I'D REMEMBER A FACE LIKE THAT.
NOPE.
I SWEAR TO GOD I'VE NEVER SEEN THE MAN!
10

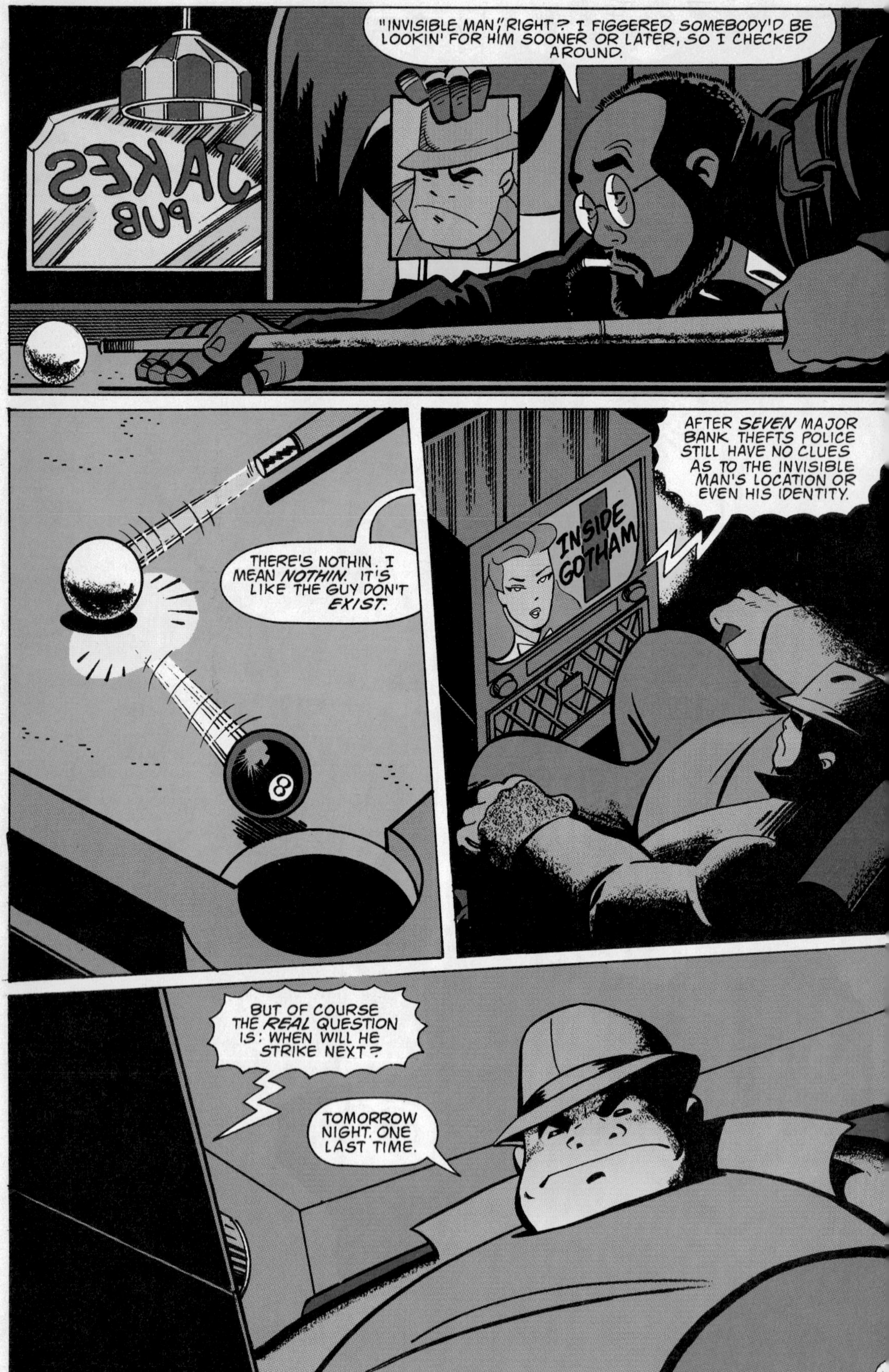
"INVISIBLE MAN," RIGHT? I FIGGERED SOMEBODY'D BE LOOKIN' FOR HIM SOONER OR LATER, SO I CHECKED AROUND.
JAKES PUB
THERE'S NOTHIN. I MEAN *NOTHIN.* IT'S LIKE THE GUY DON'T *EXIST.*
AFTER *SEVEN* MAJOR BANK THEFTS POLICE STILL HAVE NO CLUES AS TO THE INVISIBLE MAN'S LOCATION OR EVEN HIS IDENTITY.
INSIDE GOTHAM
BUT OF COURSE THE *REAL* QUESTION IS: WHEN WILL HE STRIKE NEXT?
TOMORROW NIGHT. ONE LAST TIME.

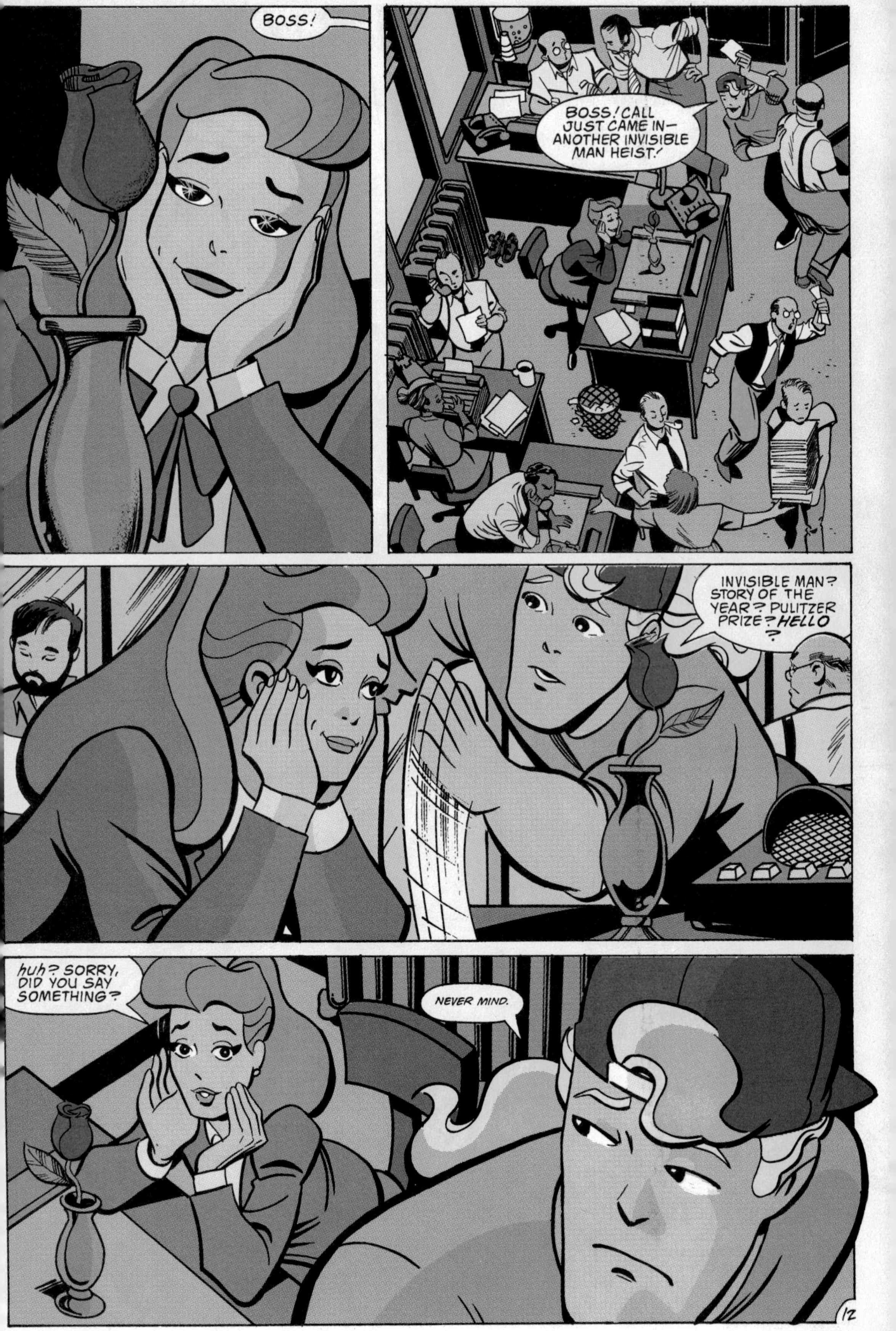
BOSS!
BOSS! CALL JUST CAME IN-- ANOTHER INVISIBLE MAN HEIST!
INVISIBLE MAN? STORY OF THE YEAR? PULITZER PRIZE? HELLO?
huh? SORRY, DID YOU SAY SOMETHING?
NEVER MIND.
12

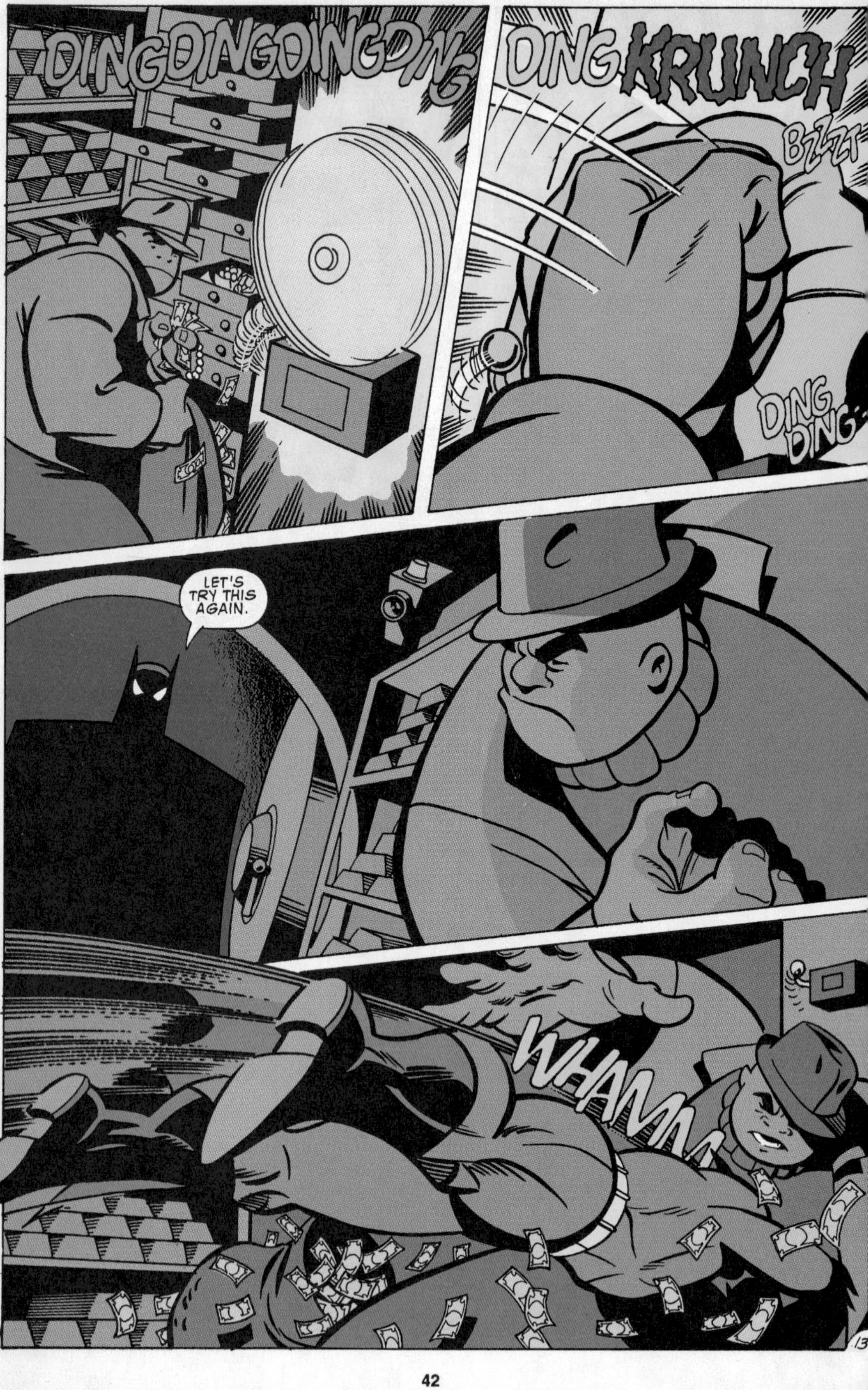
DINGDINGDINGDINGDING
DING KRUNCH
BZZZT
DING DING
LET'S TRY THIS AGAIN.
WHAM
13

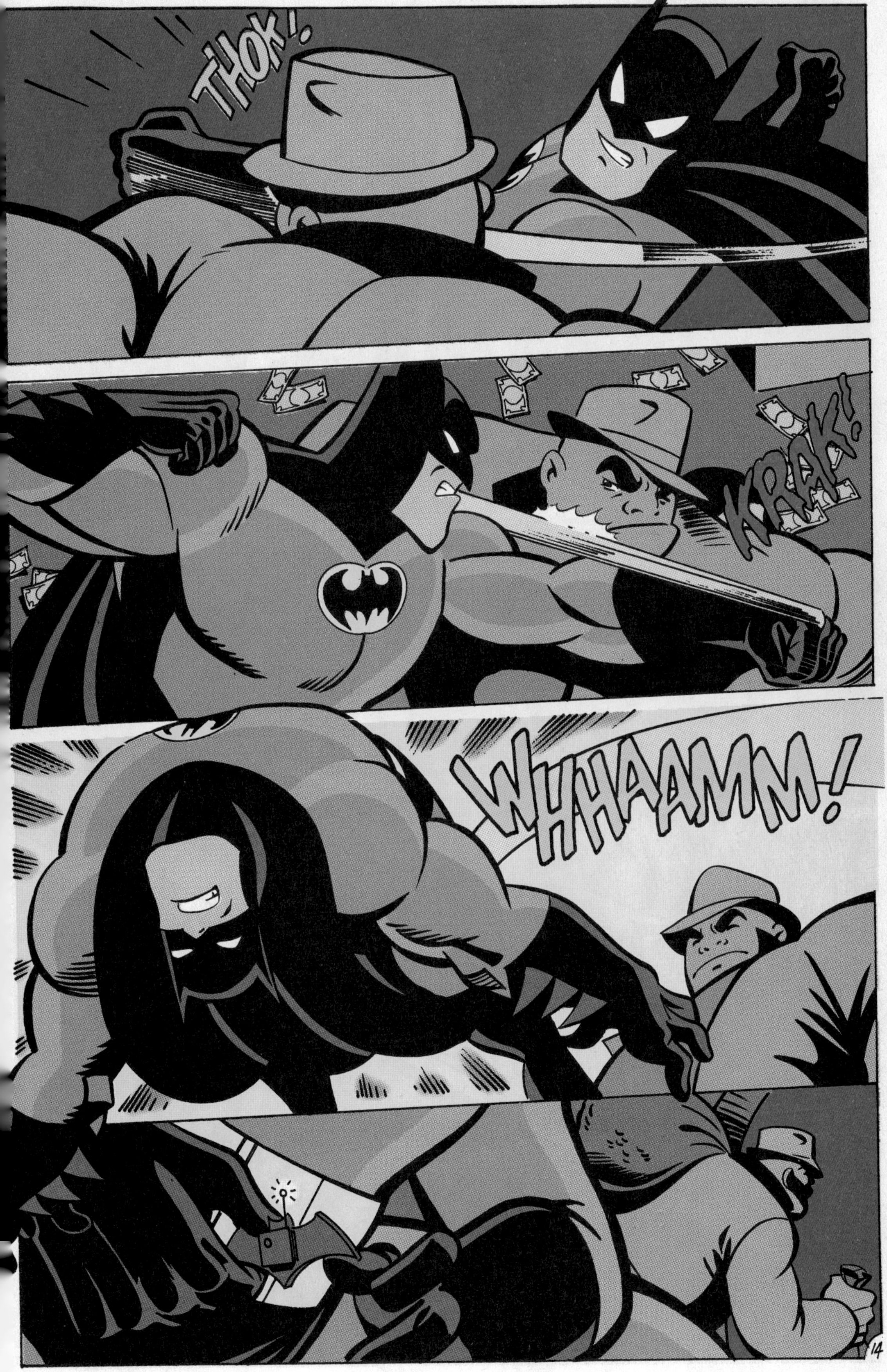
THOK!
KRAK!
WHHAAMM!
14

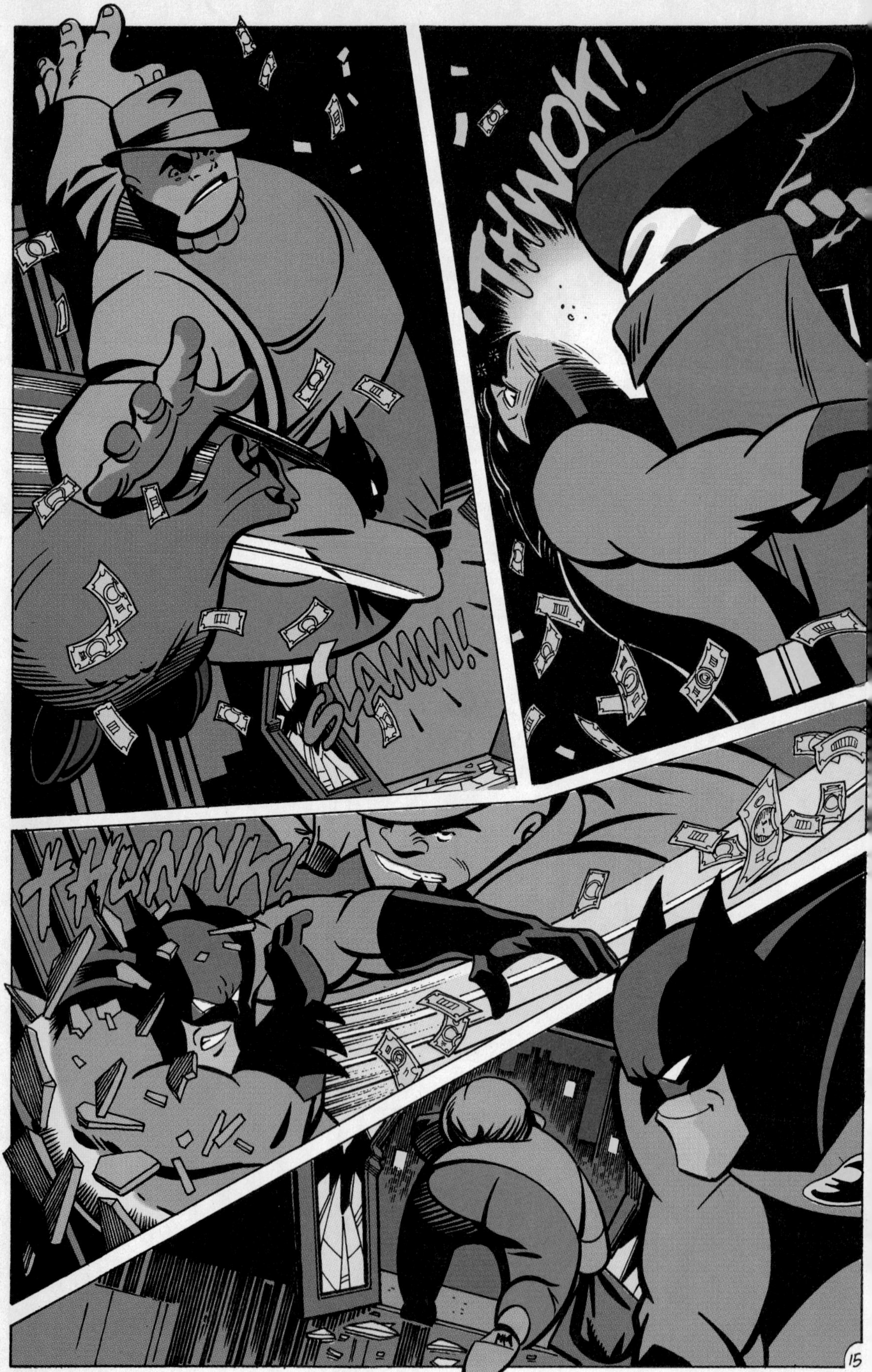
SLAMM!
THWOK!
THUNNK!
15

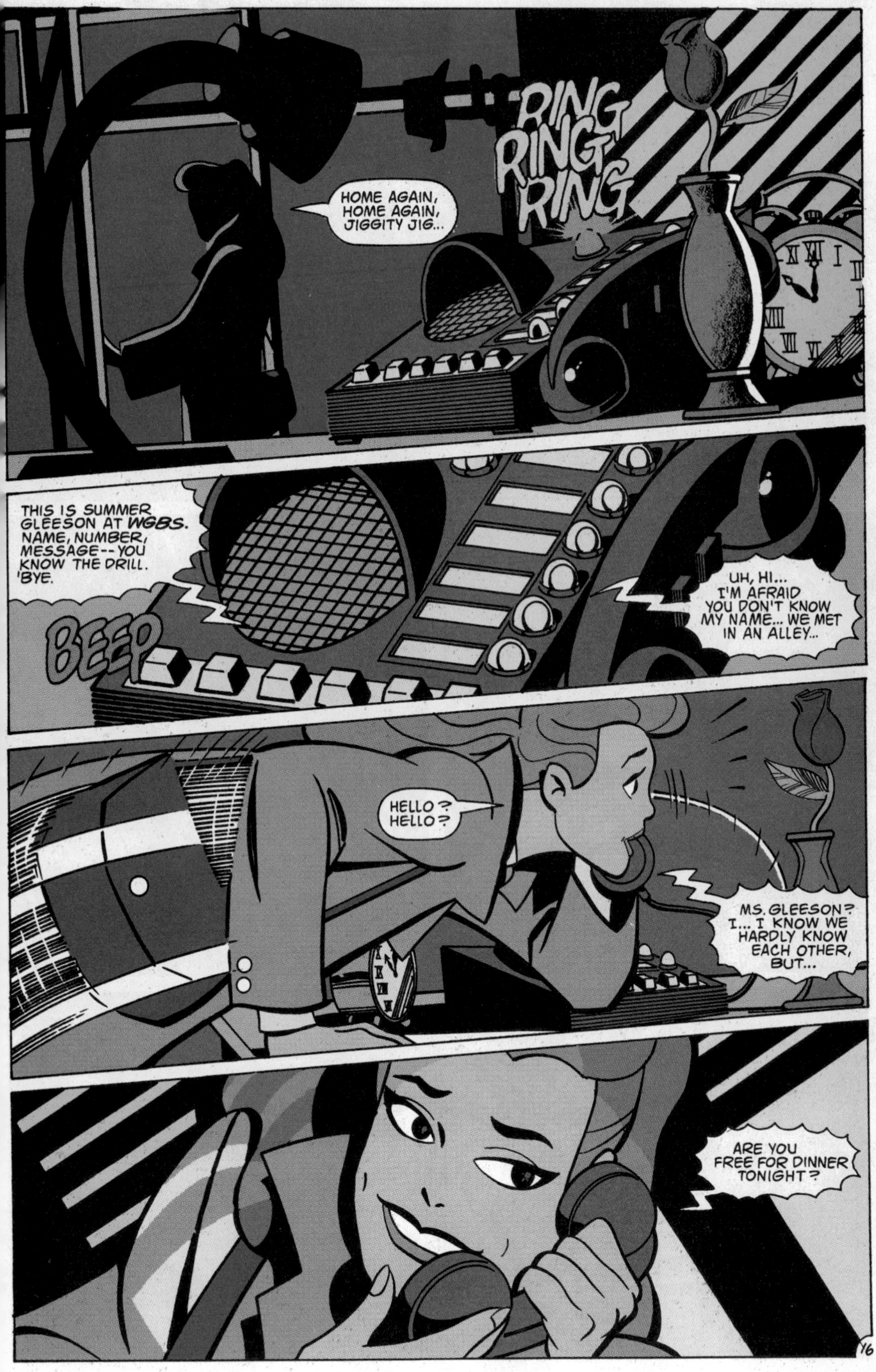
RING
RING
RING
HOME AGAIN, HOME AGAIN, JIGGITY JIG...
THIS IS SUMMER GLEESON AT WGBS. NAME, NUMBER, MESSAGE-- YOU KNOW THE DRILL. 'BYE.
BEEP
UH, HI... I'M AFRAID YOU DON'T KNOW MY NAME... WE MET IN AN ALLEY...
HELLO? HELLO?
MS. GLEESON? I... I KNOW WE HARDLY KNOW EACH OTHER, BUT...
ARE YOU FREE FOR DINNER TONIGHT?
16

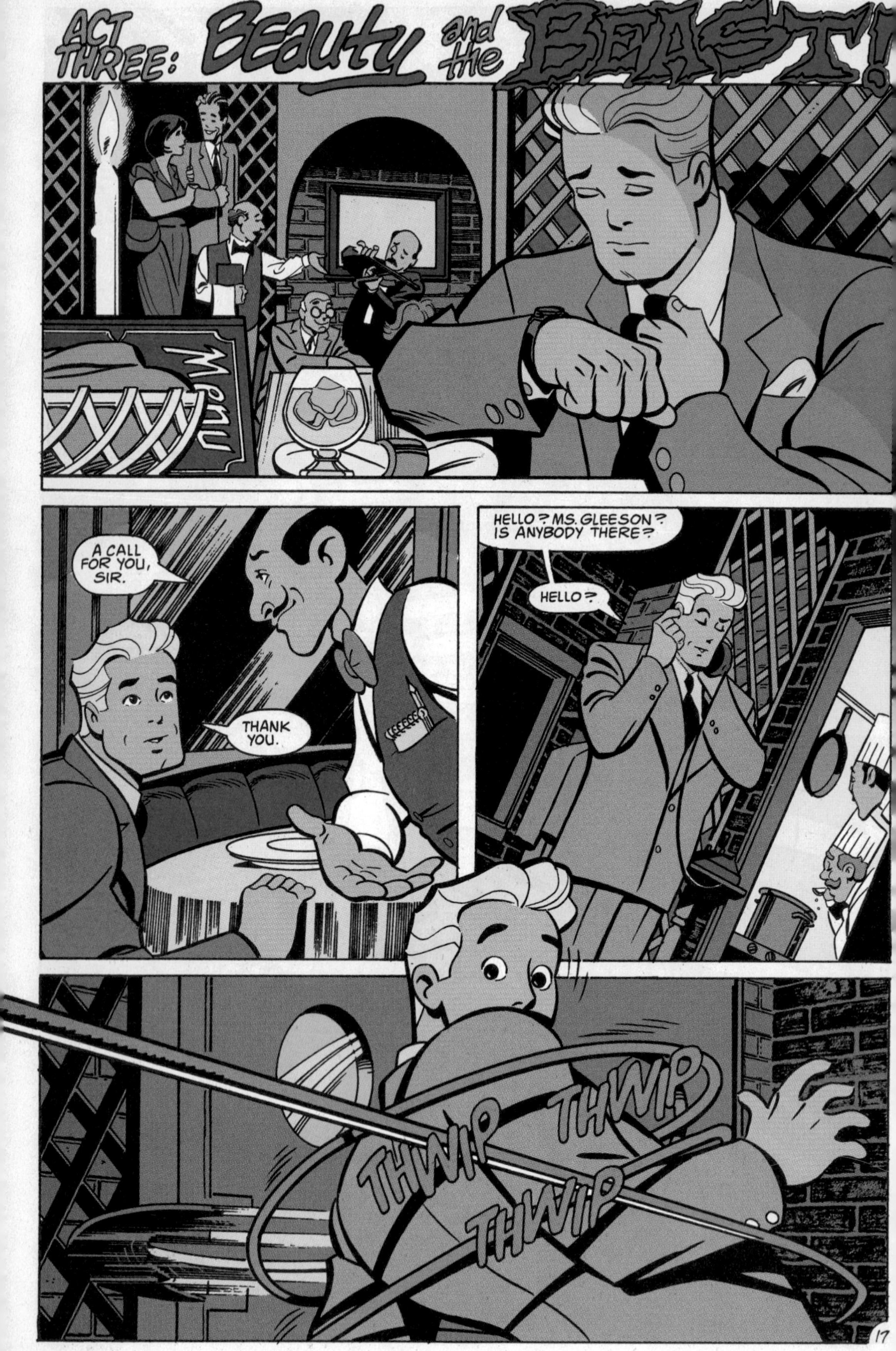
ACT THREE: Beauty and the BEAST!
Menu
A CALL FOR YOU, SIR.
THANK YOU.
HELLO? MS. GLEESON? IS ANYBODY THERE?
HELLO?
THWIP
THWIP
THWIP
17

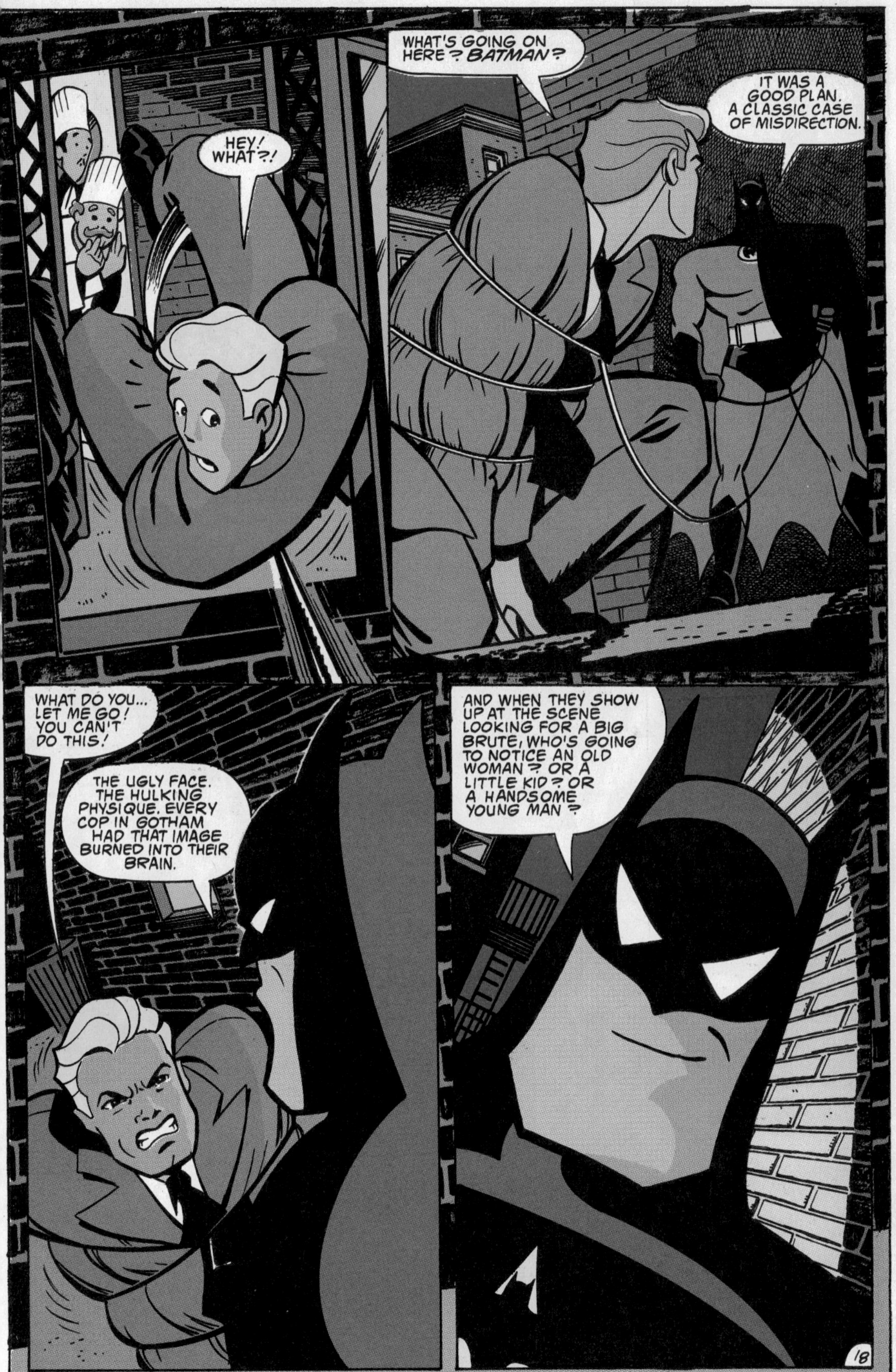
HEY! WHAT?!
WHAT'S GOING ON HERE? BATMAN?
IT WAS A GOOD PLAN. A CLASSIC CASE OF MISDIRECTION.
WHAT DO YOU... LET ME GO! YOU CAN'T DO THIS!
THE UGLY FACE. THE HULKING PHYSIQUE. EVERY COP IN GOTHAM HAD THAT IMAGE BURNED INTO THEIR BRAIN.
AND WHEN THEY SHOW UP AT THE SCENE LOOKING FOR A BIG BRUTE, WHO'S GOING TO NOTICE AN OLD WOMAN? OR A LITTLE KID? OR A HANDSOME YOUNG MAN?
18

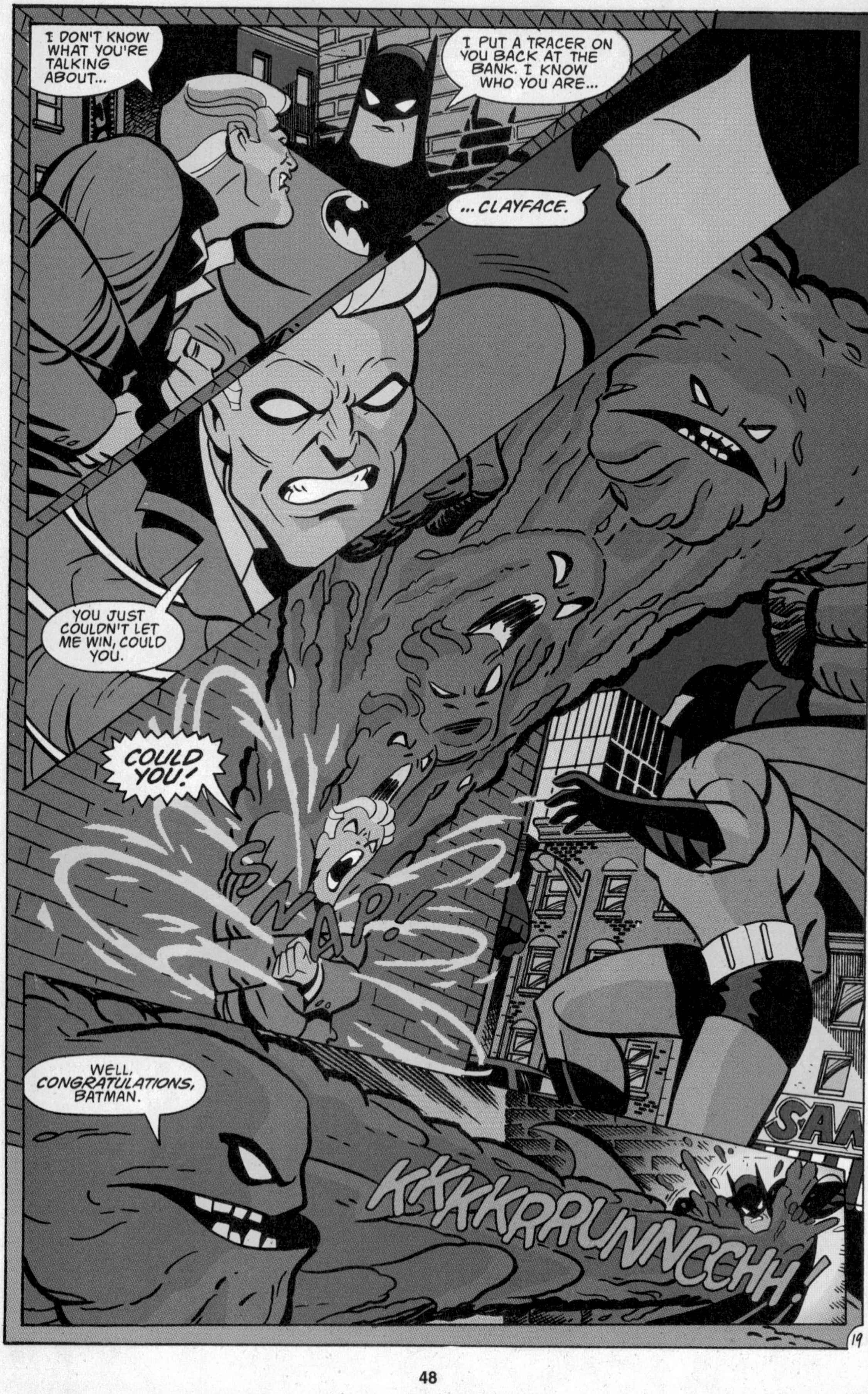
I DON'T KNOW WHAT YOU'RE TALKING ABOUT...
I PUT A TRACER ON YOU BACK AT THE BANK. I KNOW WHO YOU ARE...
...CLAYFACE.
YOU JUST COULDN'T LET ME WIN, COULD YOU.
COULD YOU!
SNAP!
WELL, CONGRATULATIONS, BATMAN.
KKKKRRRUNNCCHH!
19

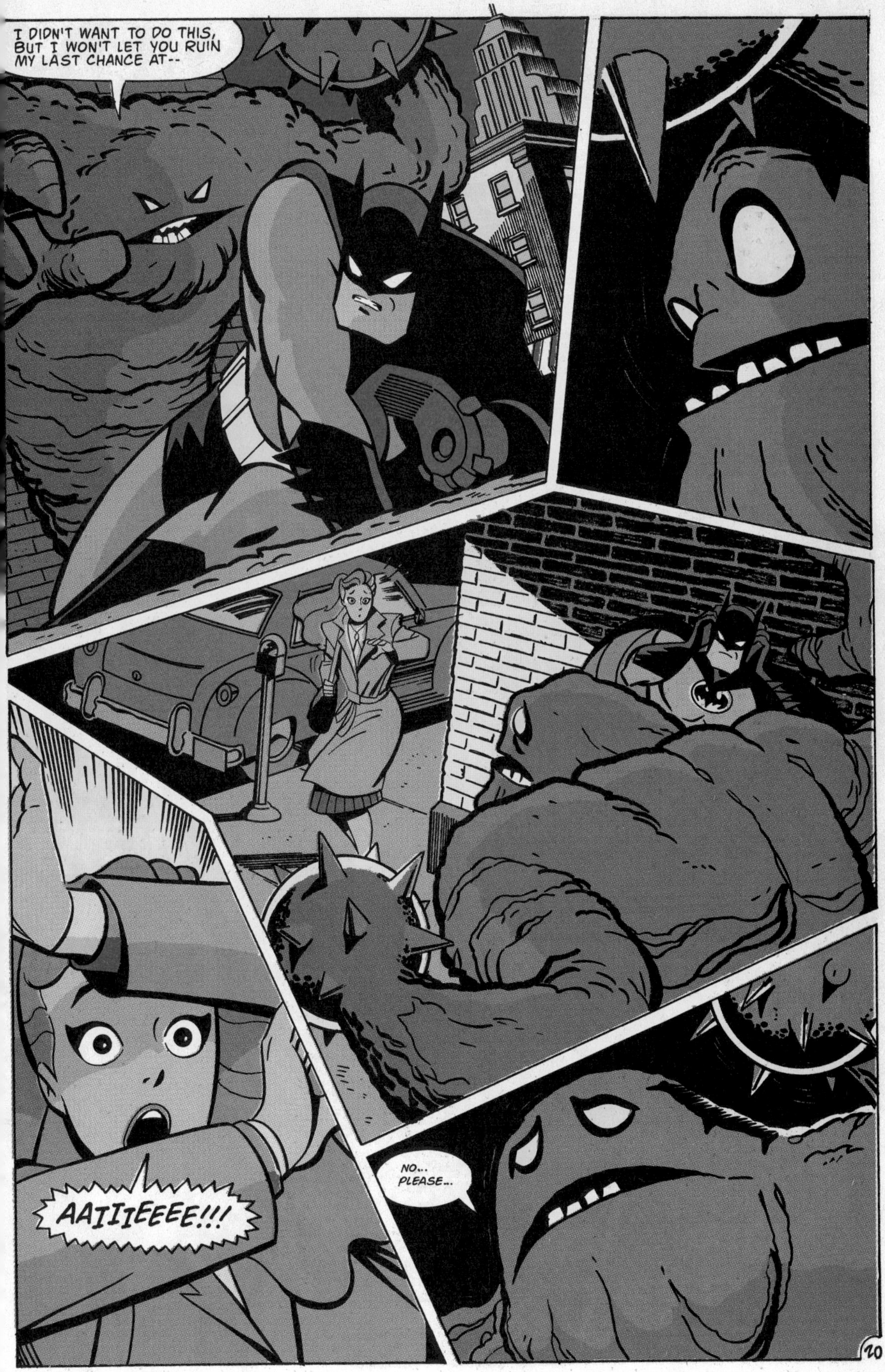
I DIDN'T WANT TO DO THIS, BUT I WON'T LET YOU RUIN MY LAST CHANCE AT--
AAIIIEEEE!!!
NO... PLEASE...
20

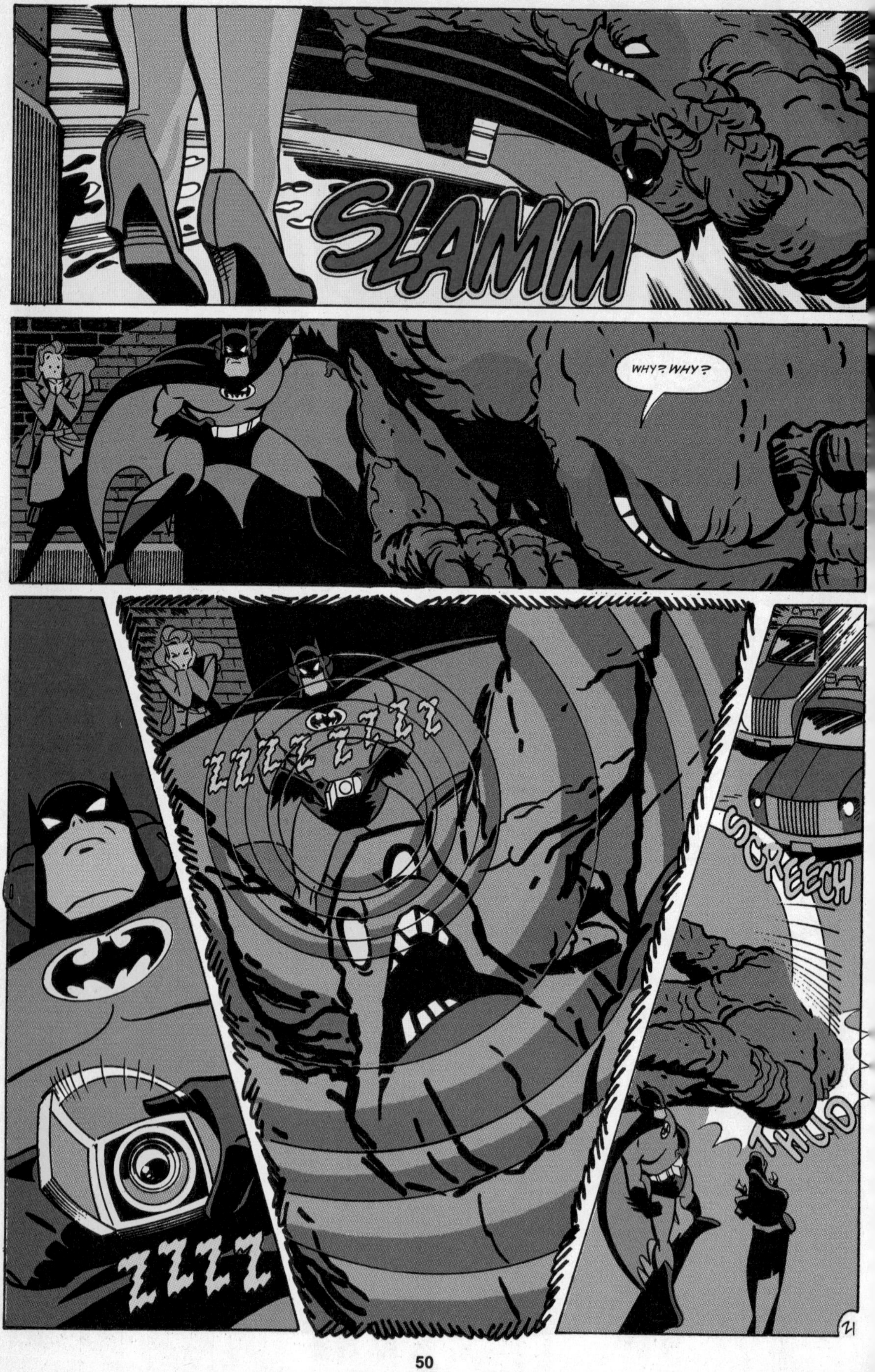
SLAMM
WHY? WHY?
ZZZZZZZZ
ZZZZ
SCKREECH
THUD
21

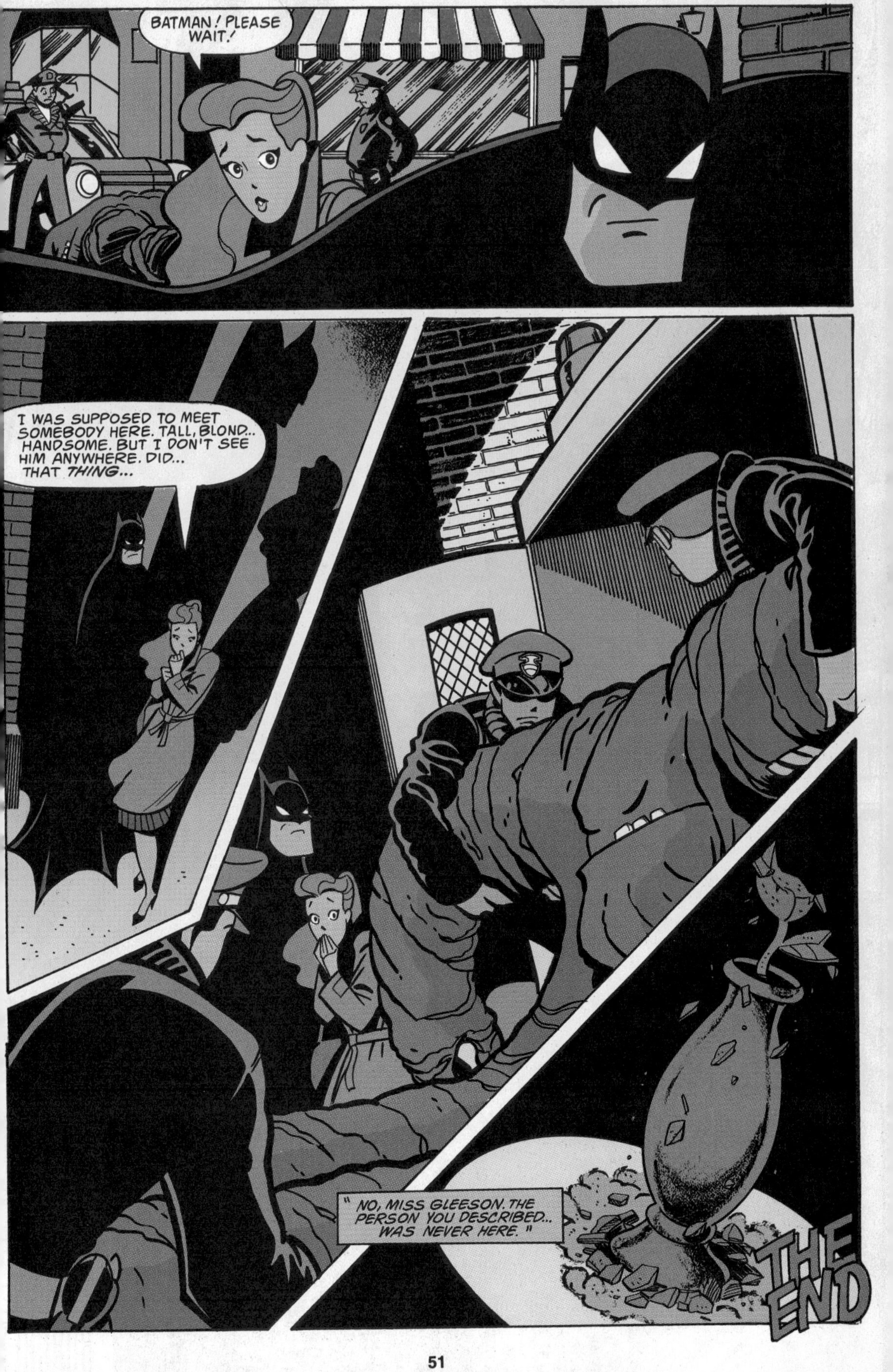
BATMAN! PLEASE WAIT!
I WAS SUPPOSED TO MEET SOMEBODY HERE. TALL, BLOND... HANDSOME. BUT I DON'T SEE HIM ANYWHERE. DID... THAT THING...
"NO, MISS GLEESON. THE PERSON YOU DESCRIBED... WAS NEVER HERE."
THE END

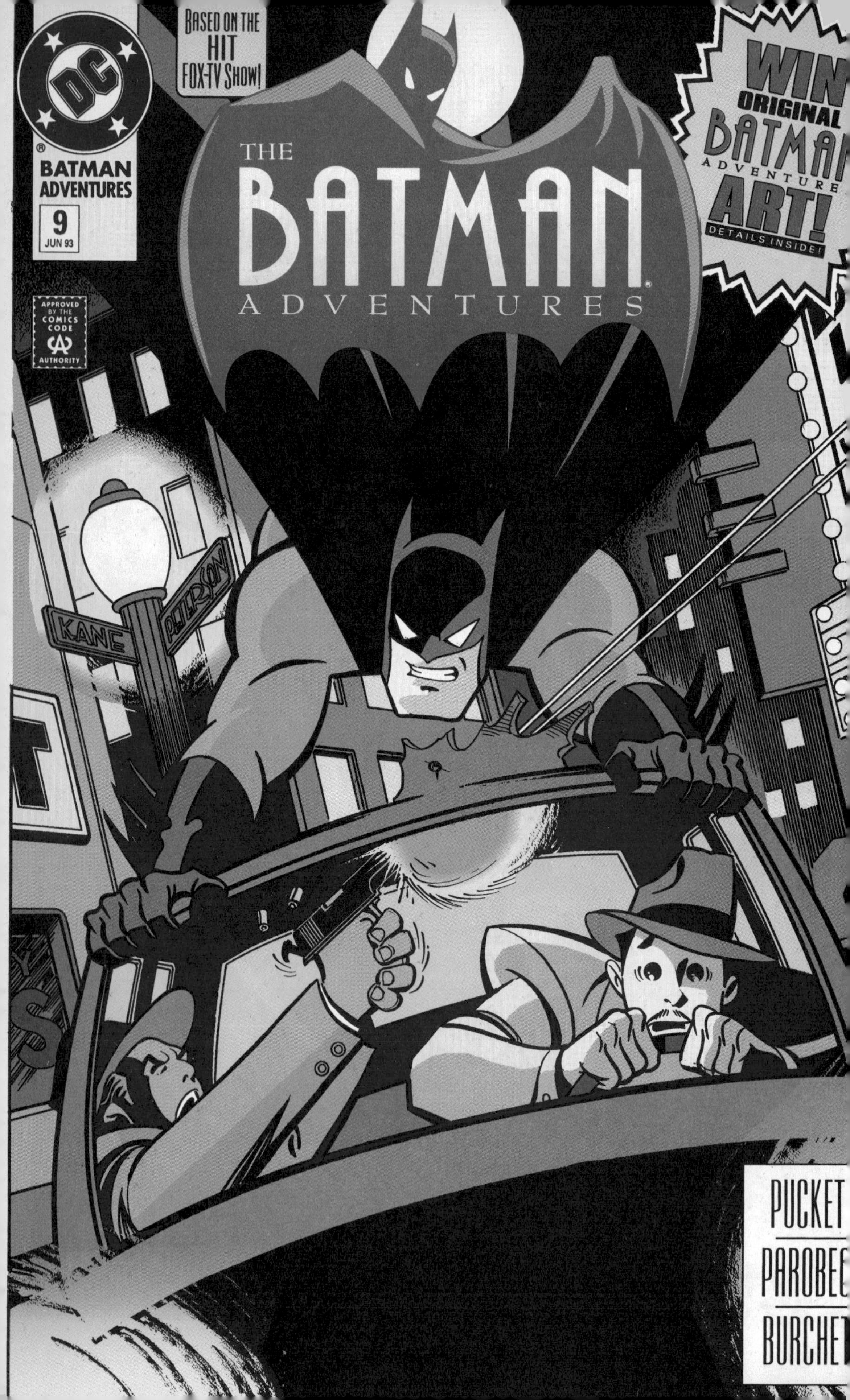
DC
BATMAN ADVENTURES
9
JUN 93
BASED ON THE HIT FOX-TV SHOW!
THE BATMAN ADVENTURES
WIN ORIGINAL BATMAN ADVENTURE ART!
DETAILS INSIDE!
APPROVED BY THE COMICS CODE AUTHORITY
KANE
PETERSON
PUCKET
PAROBEC
BURCHET

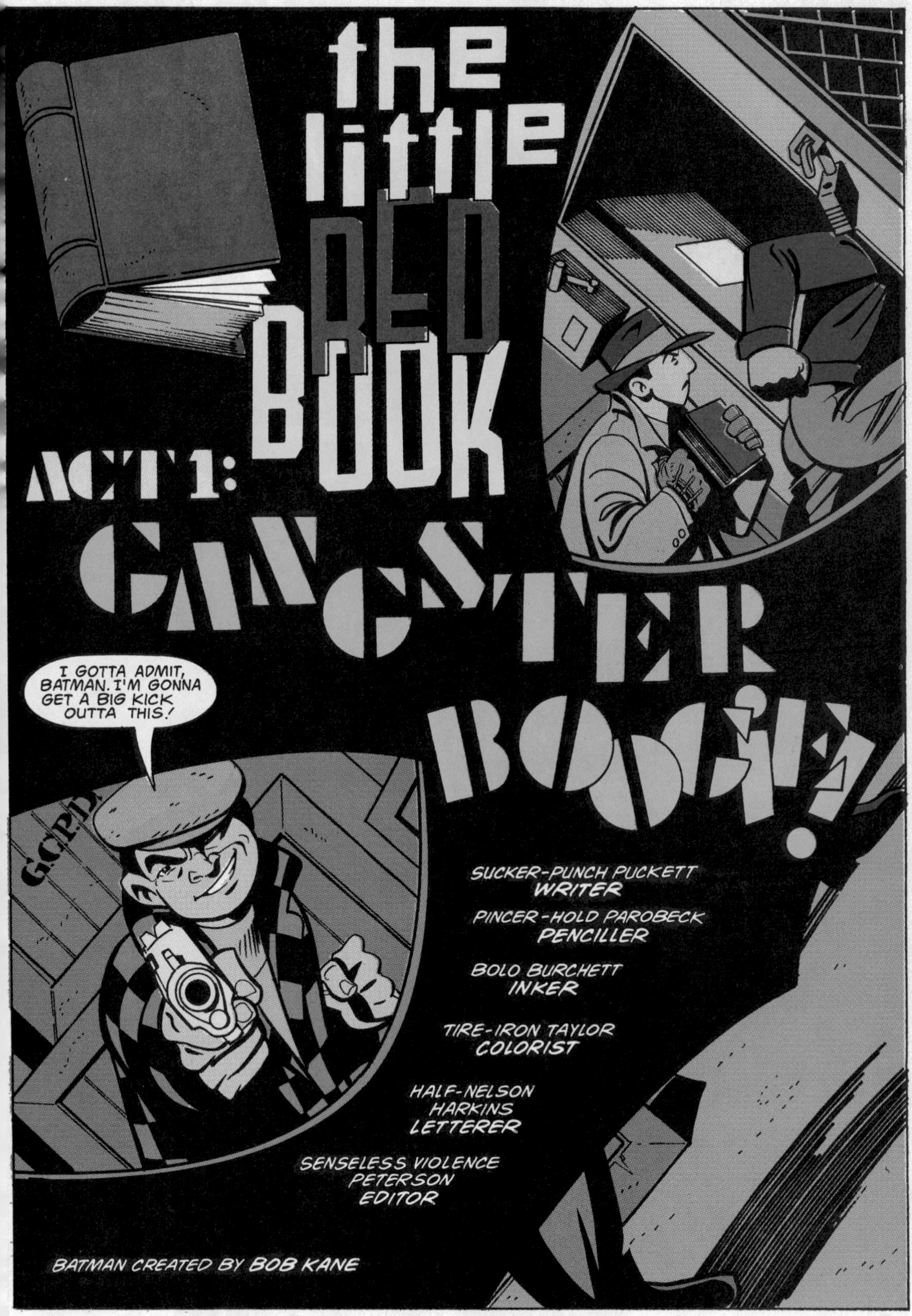
the little RED BOOK
ACT 1: GANGSTER BOOGIE!
I GOTTA ADMIT, BATMAN. I'M GONNA GET A BIG KICK OUTTA THIS!
G.C.P.D.
SUCKER-PUNCH PUCKETT WRITER
PINCER-HOLD PAROBECK PENCILLER
BOLO BURCHETT INKER
TIRE-IRON TAYLOR COLORIST
HALF-NELSON HARKINS LETTERER
SENSELESS VIOLENCE PETERSON EDITOR
BATMAN CREATED BY BOB KANE

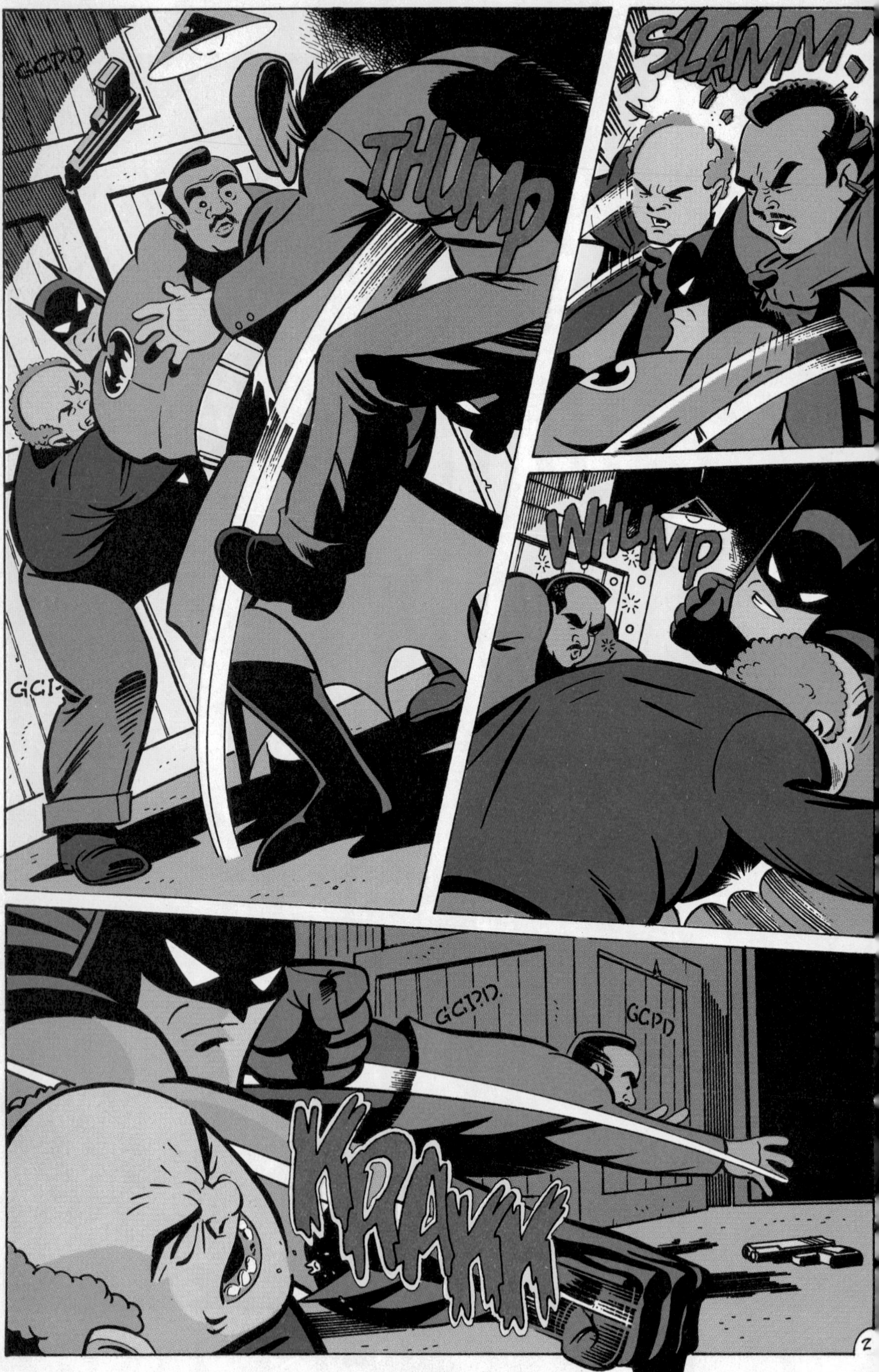
GCPD
THUMP
GCI-
SLAMM
WHUMP
GCPD
GCPD
KRAKK
2

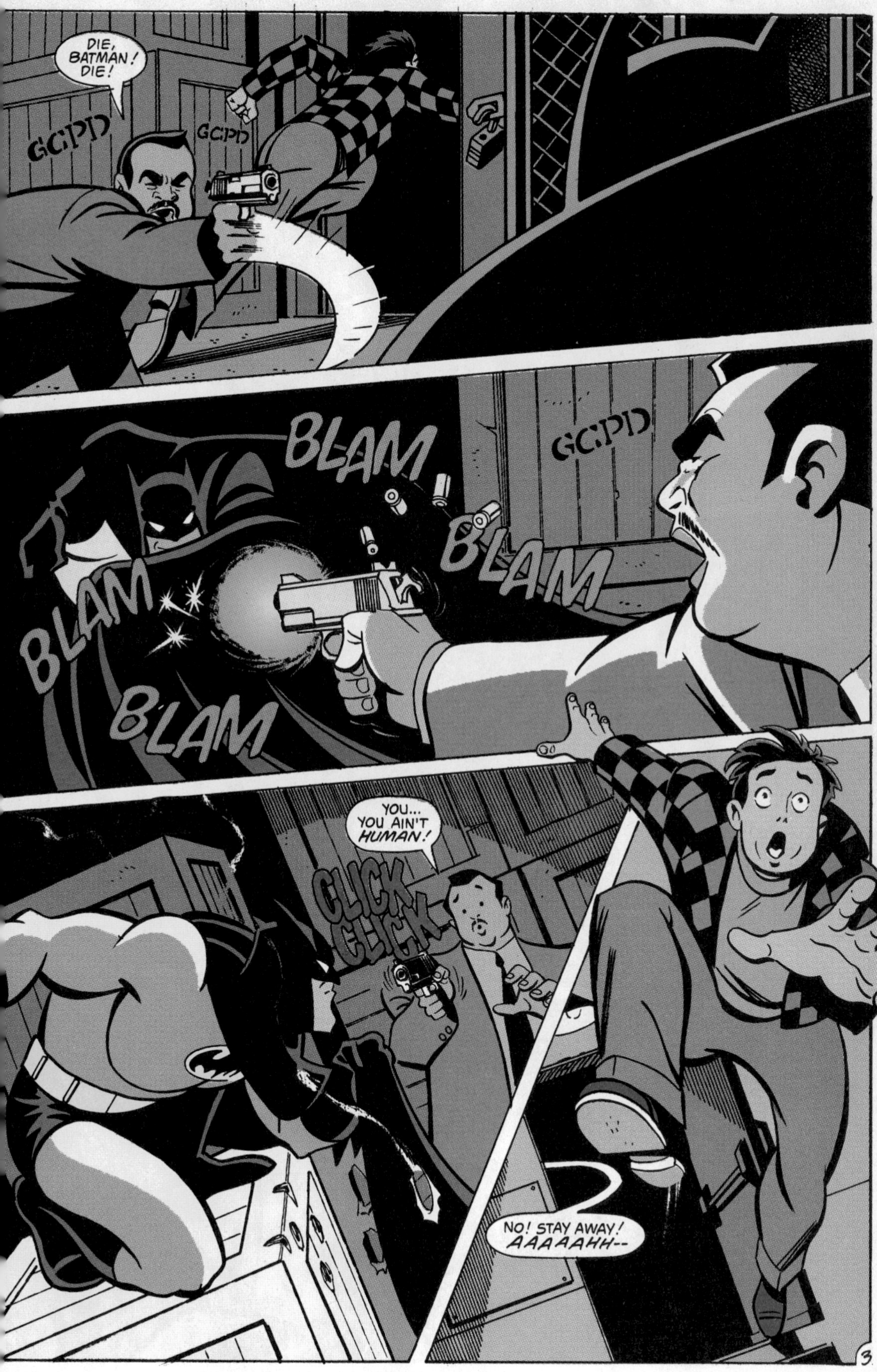
DIE, BATMAN! DIE!
GCPD
GCPD
BLAM
GCPD
BLAM
BLAM
BLAM
YOU... YOU AIN'T HUMAN!
CLICK CLICK
NO! STAY AWAY! AAAAAHH--
3

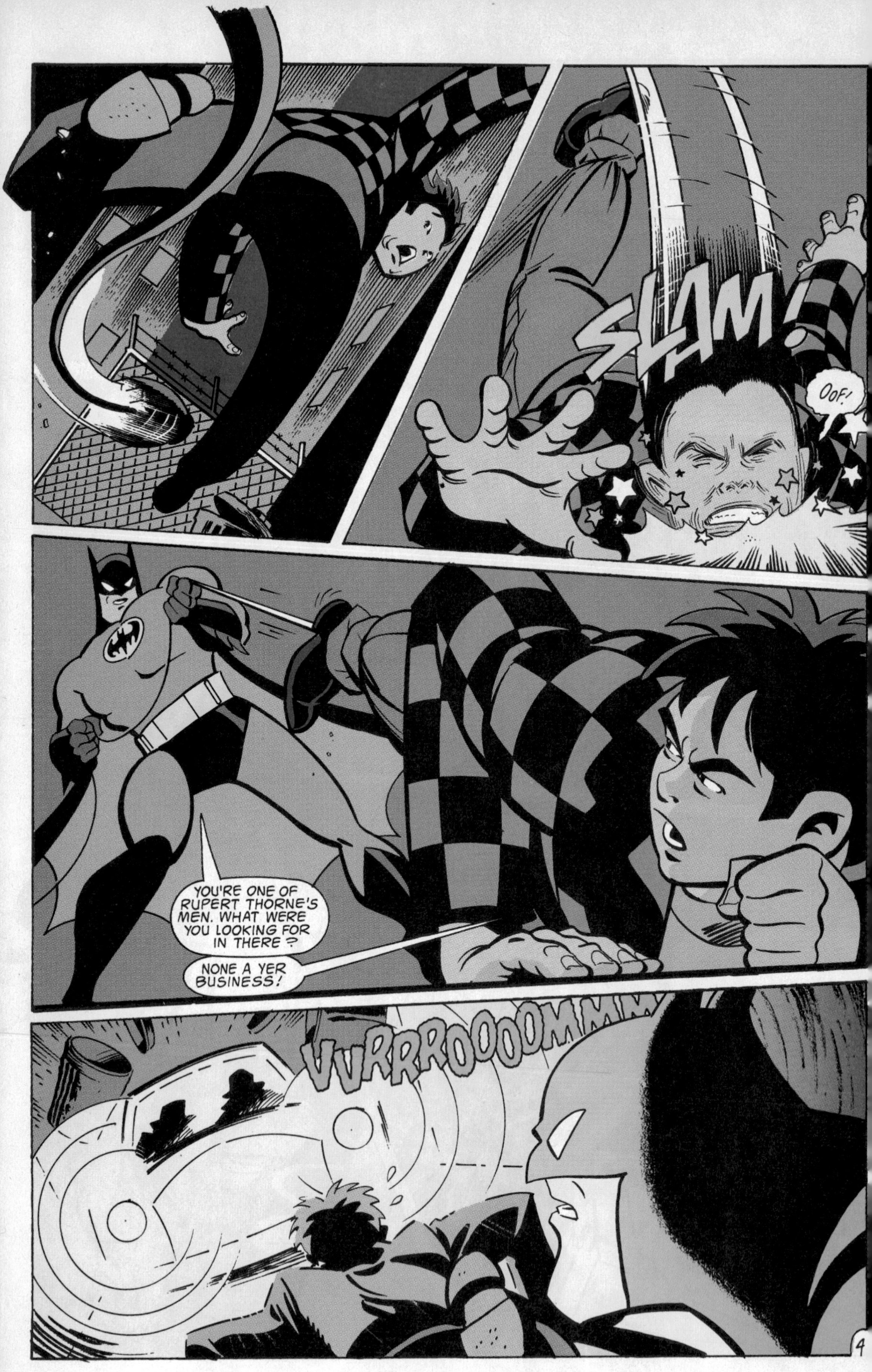
SLAM!
OOF!
YOU'RE ONE OF RUPERT THORNE'S MEN. WHAT WERE YOU LOOKING FOR IN THERE?
NONE A YER BUSINESS!
VVRRROOOOMMM
4

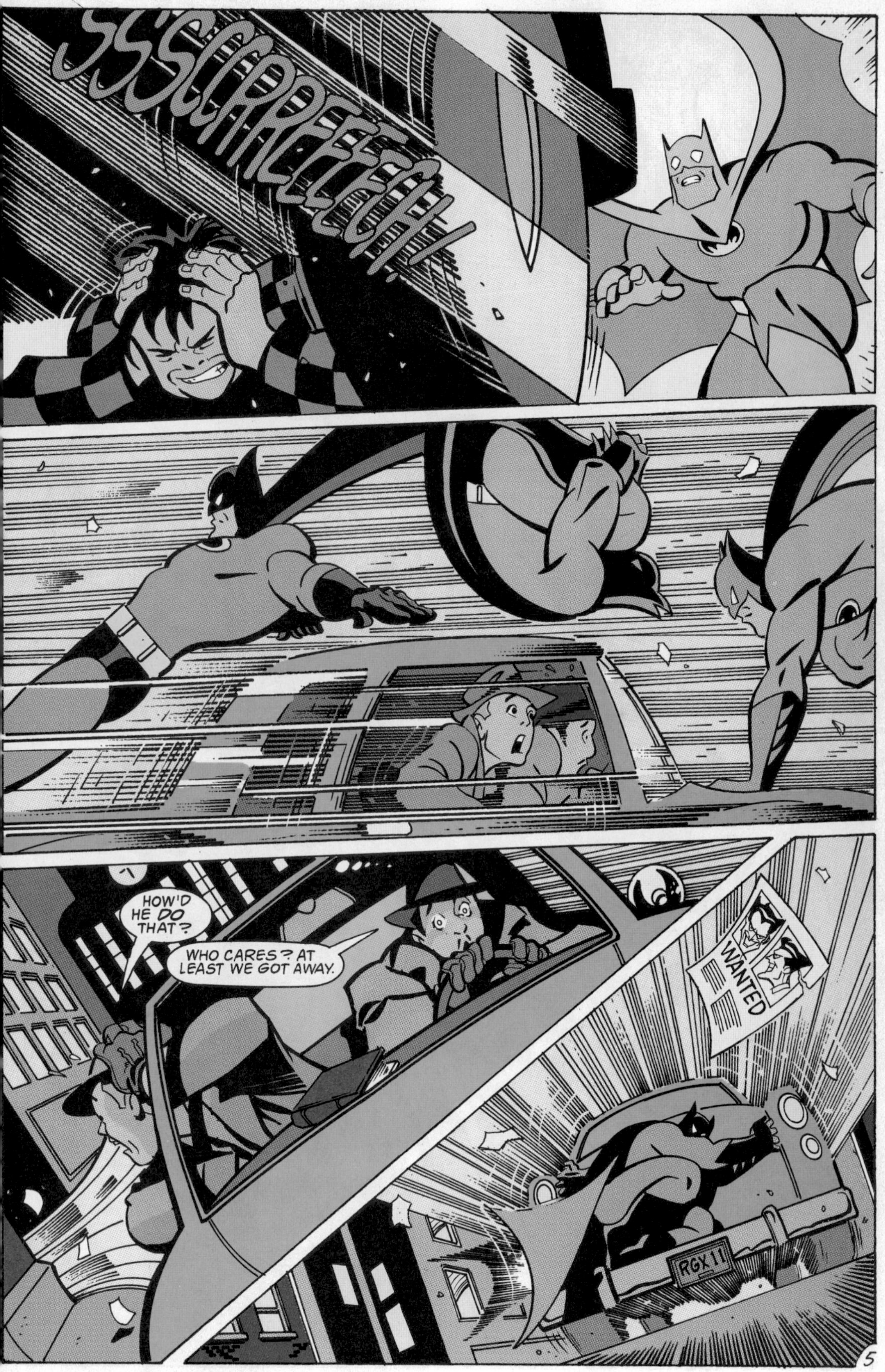
SSSCRREEECH!
HOW'D HE DO THAT?
WHO CARES? AT LEAST WE GOT AWAY.
WANTED
RGX 11
5

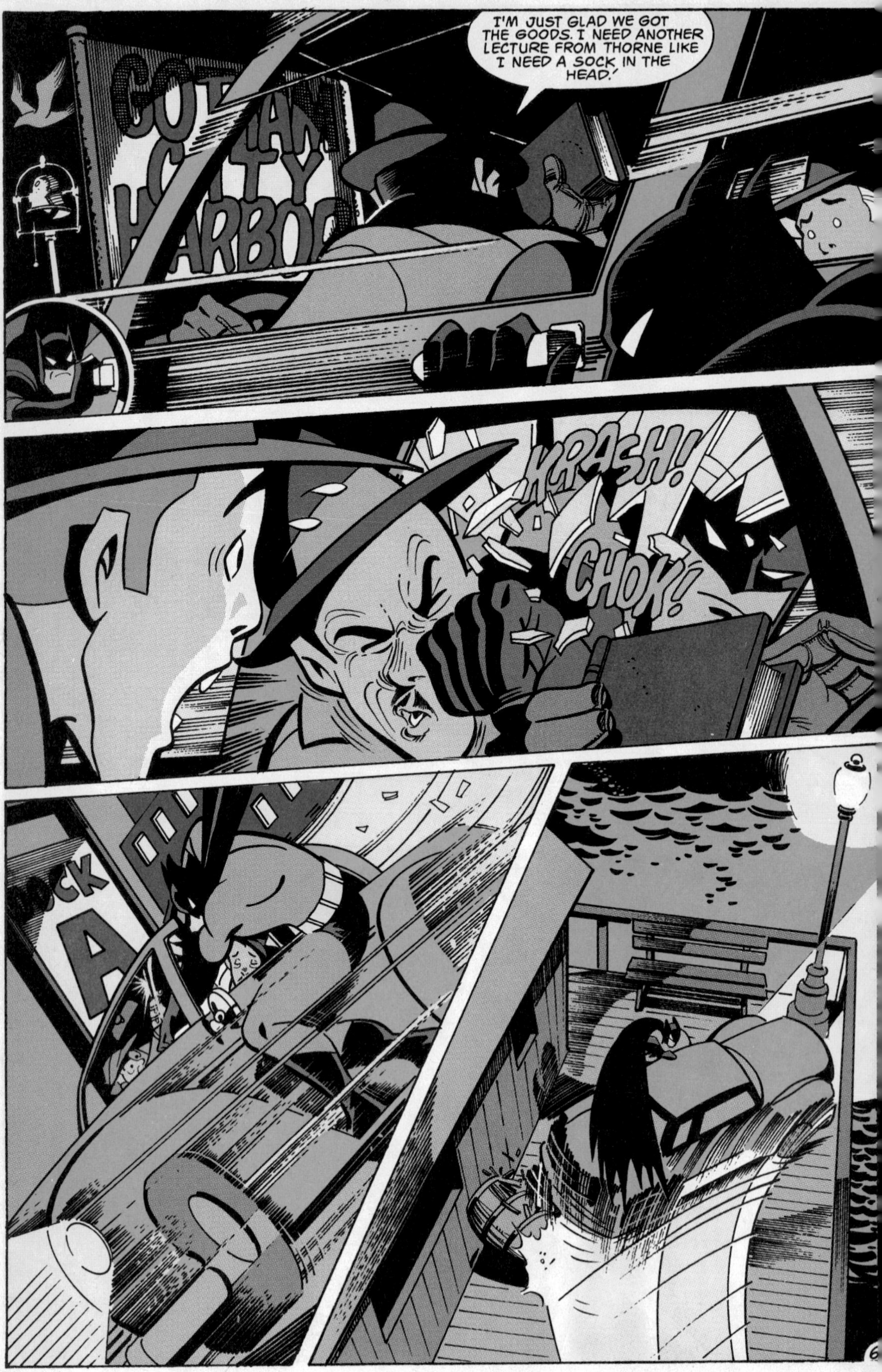
I'M JUST GLAD WE GOT THE GOODS. I NEED ANOTHER LECTURE FROM THORNE LIKE I NEED A SOCK IN THE HEAD.'
GOTHAM CITY HARBOR
K-RASH!
CHOK!
DOCK
A

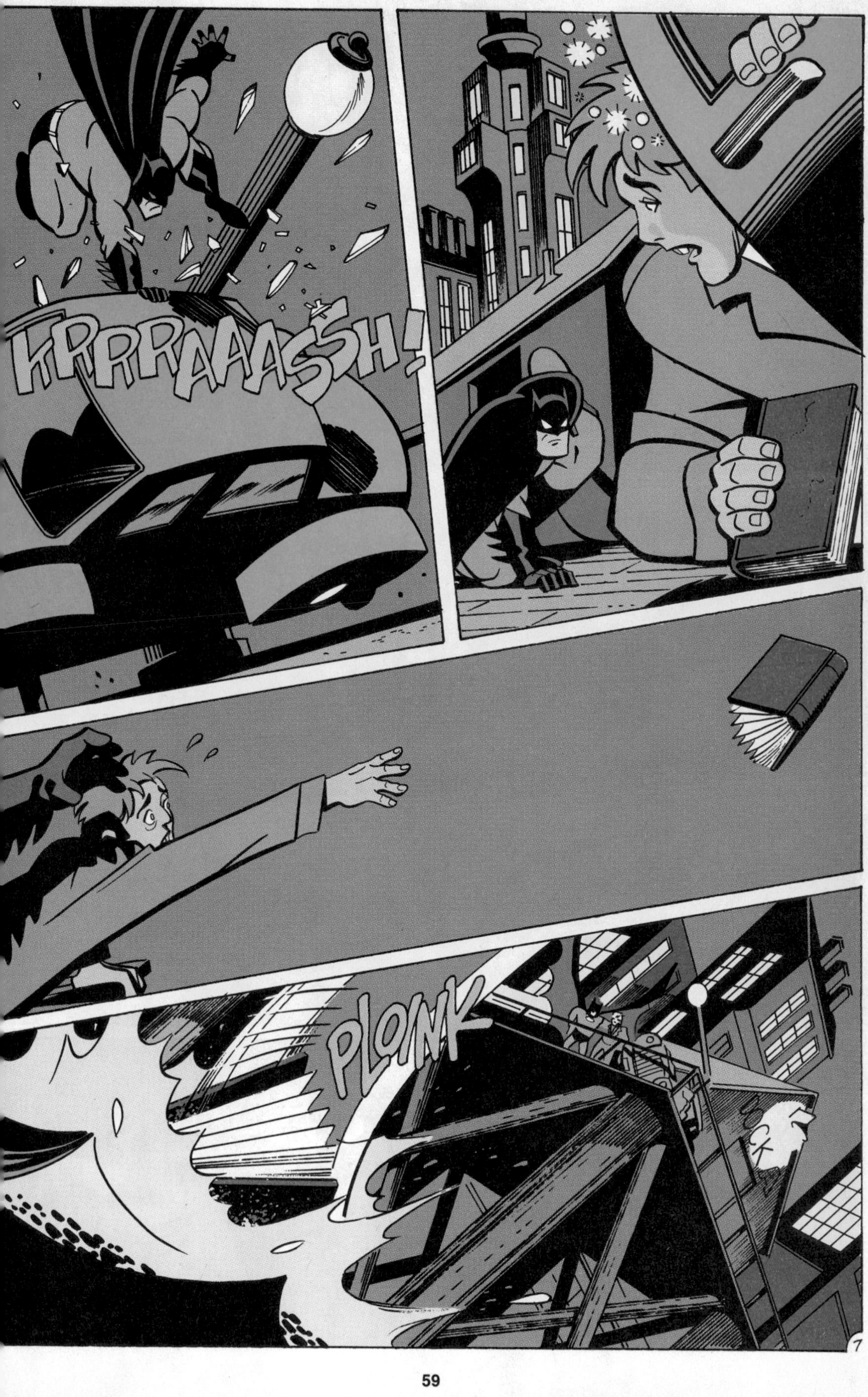
KRRRAAASSH!
PLONK
7

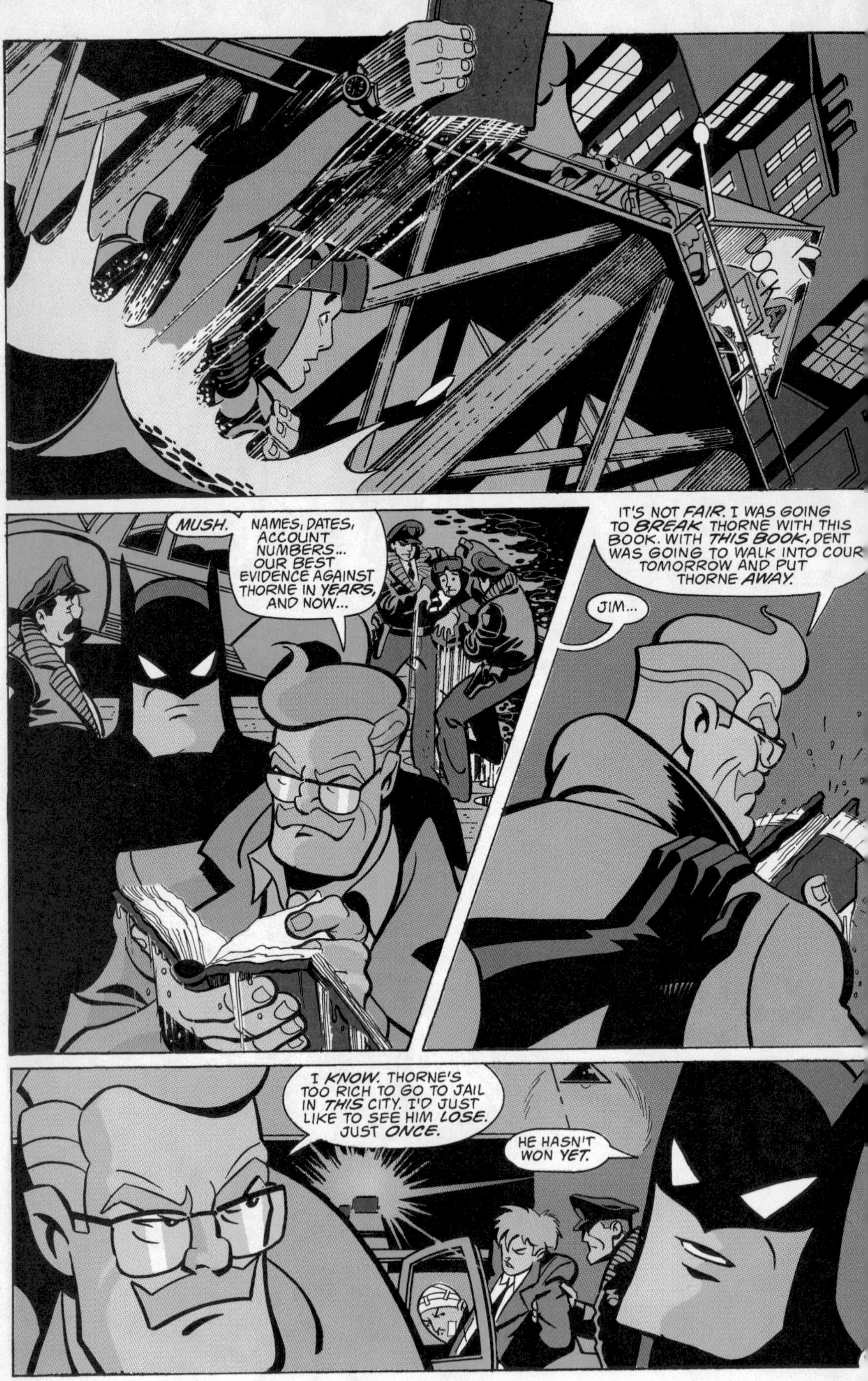
DOCK
MUSH.
NAMES, DATES, ACCOUNT NUMBERS... OUR BEST EVIDENCE AGAINST THORNE IN YEARS, AND NOW...
IT'S NOT FAIR. I WAS GOING TO BREAK THORNE WITH THIS BOOK. WITH THIS BOOK, DENT WAS GOING TO WALK INTO COUR TOMORROW AND PUT THORNE AWAY.
JIM...
I KNOW. THORNE'S TOO RICH TO GO TO JAIL IN THIS CITY. I'D JUST LIKE TO SEE HIM LOSE. JUST ONCE.
HE HASN'T WON YET.

ACT 2: the BIG BOSS

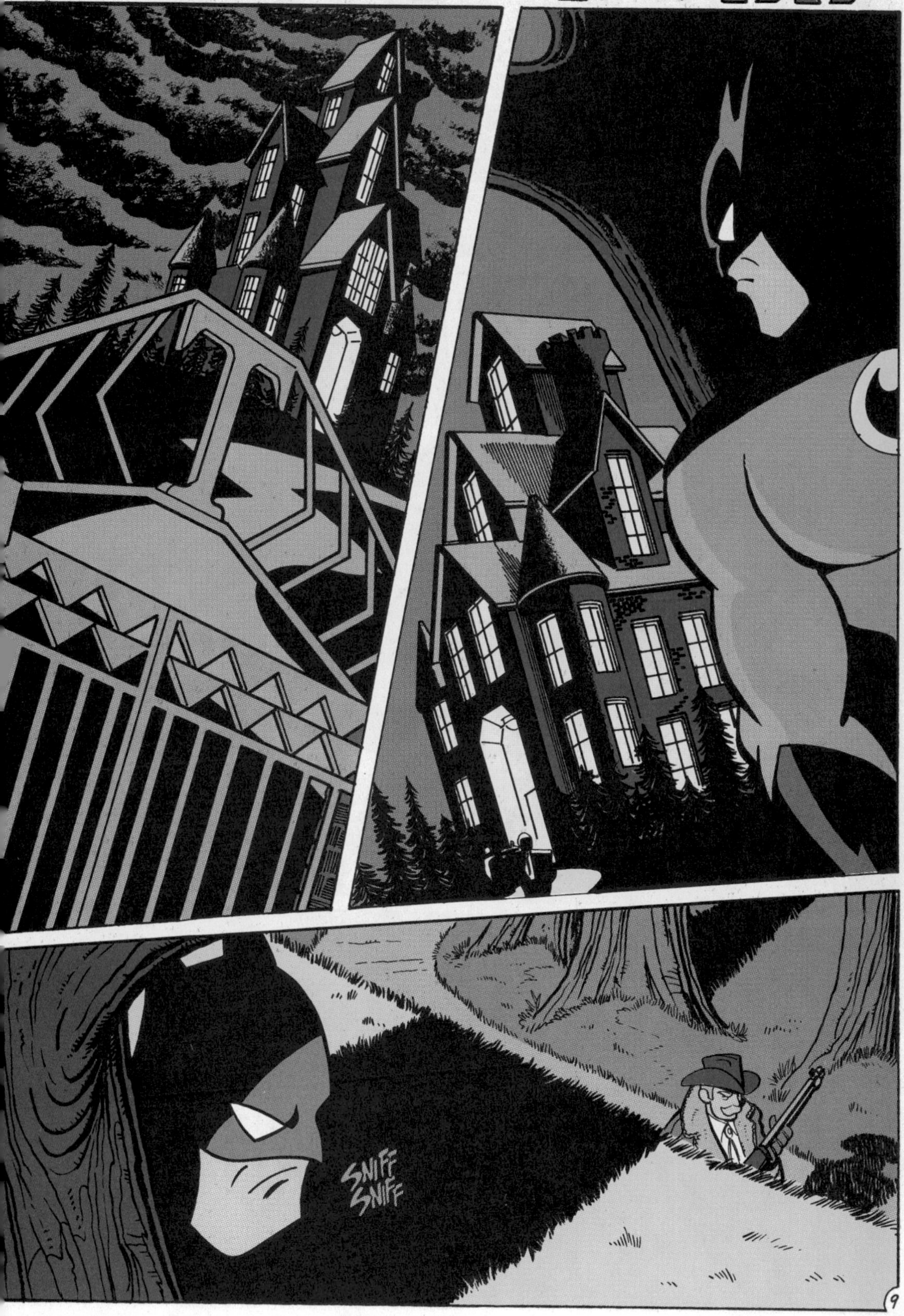
SNIFF
SNIFF
9

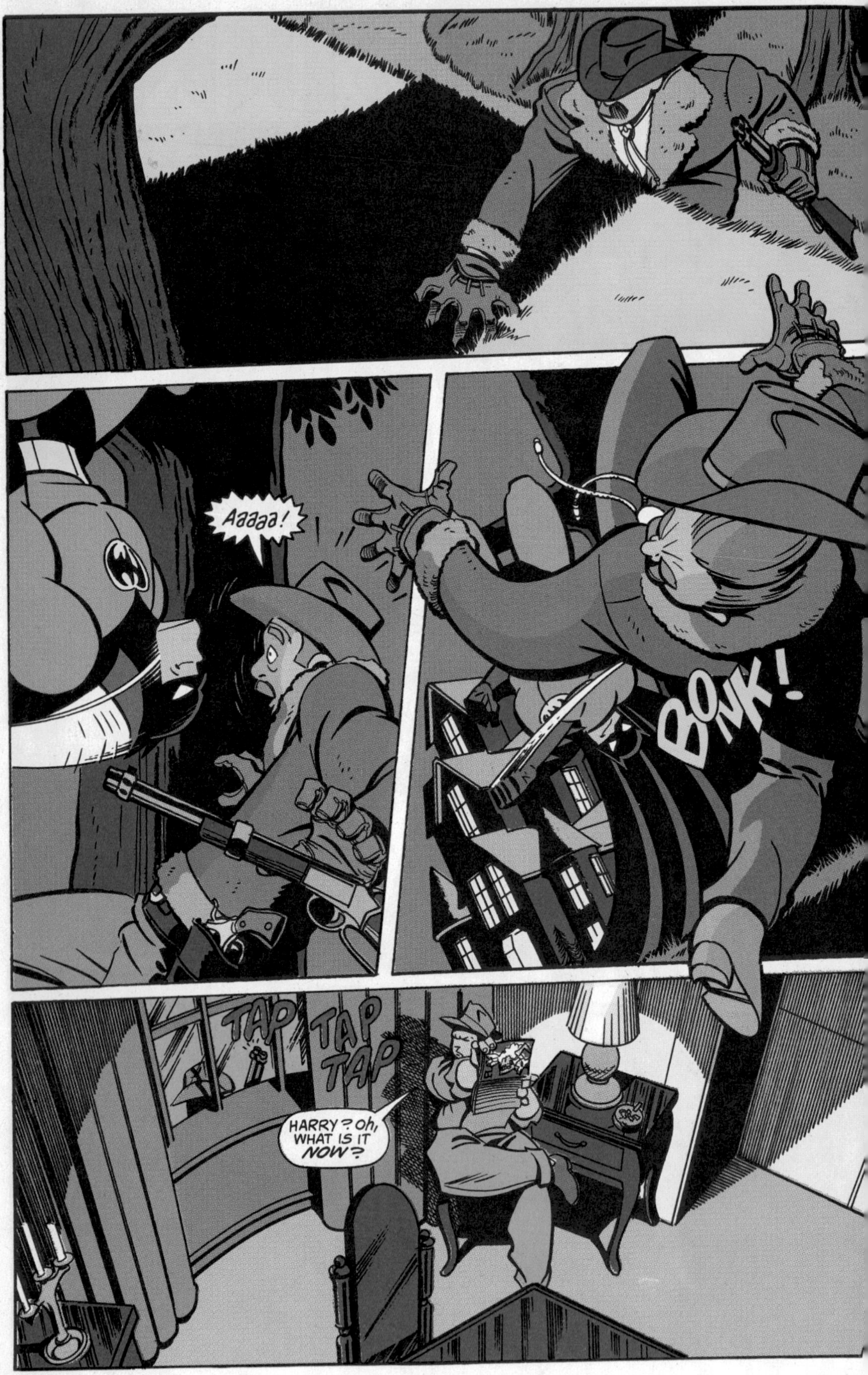
Aaaaa!
BONK!
TAP TAP TAP
HARRY? Oh, WHAT IS IT NOW?

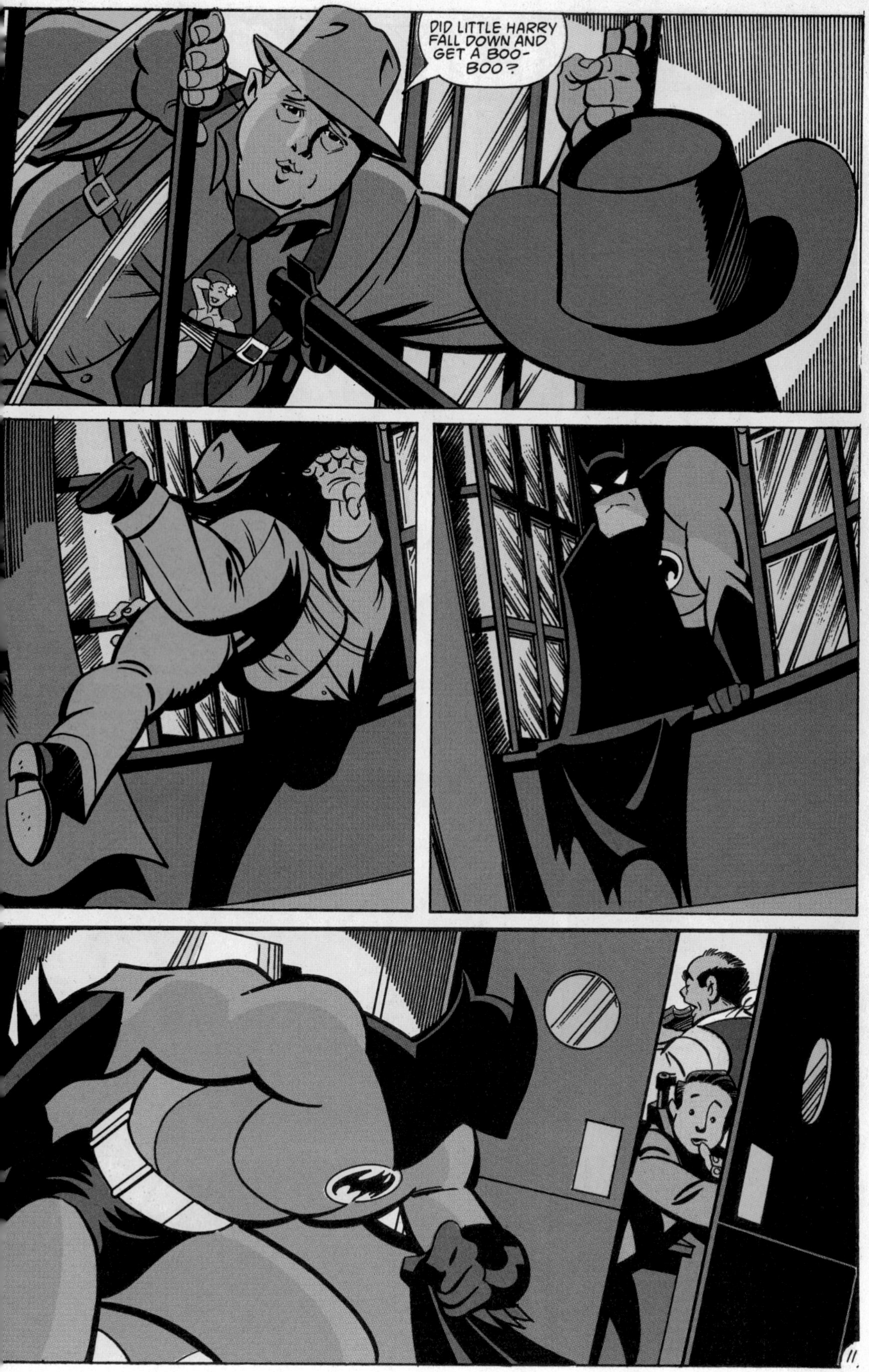
DID LITTLE HARRY FALL DOWN AND GET A BOO-BOO?
11.

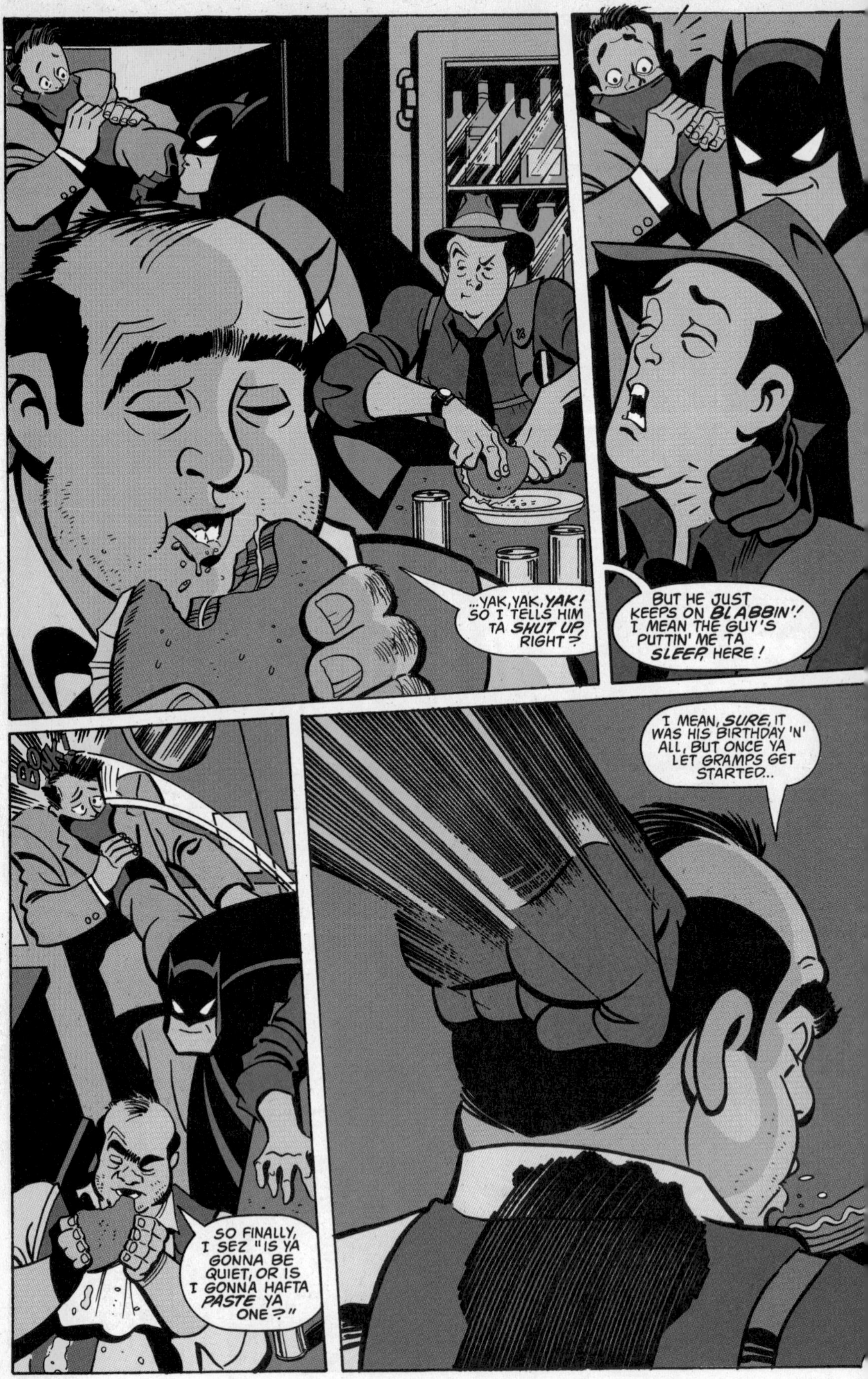
...YAK, YAK, YAK! SO I TELLS HIM TA SHUT UP, RIGHT?
BUT HE JUST KEEPS ON BLABBIN'! I MEAN THE GUY'S PUTTIN' ME TA SLEEP, HERE!
SO FINALLY, I SEZ "IS YA GONNA BE QUIET, OR IS I GONNA HAFTA PASTE YA ONE?"
I MEAN, SURE, IT WAS HIS BIRTHDAY 'N' ALL, BUT ONCE YA LET GRAMPS GET STARTED...

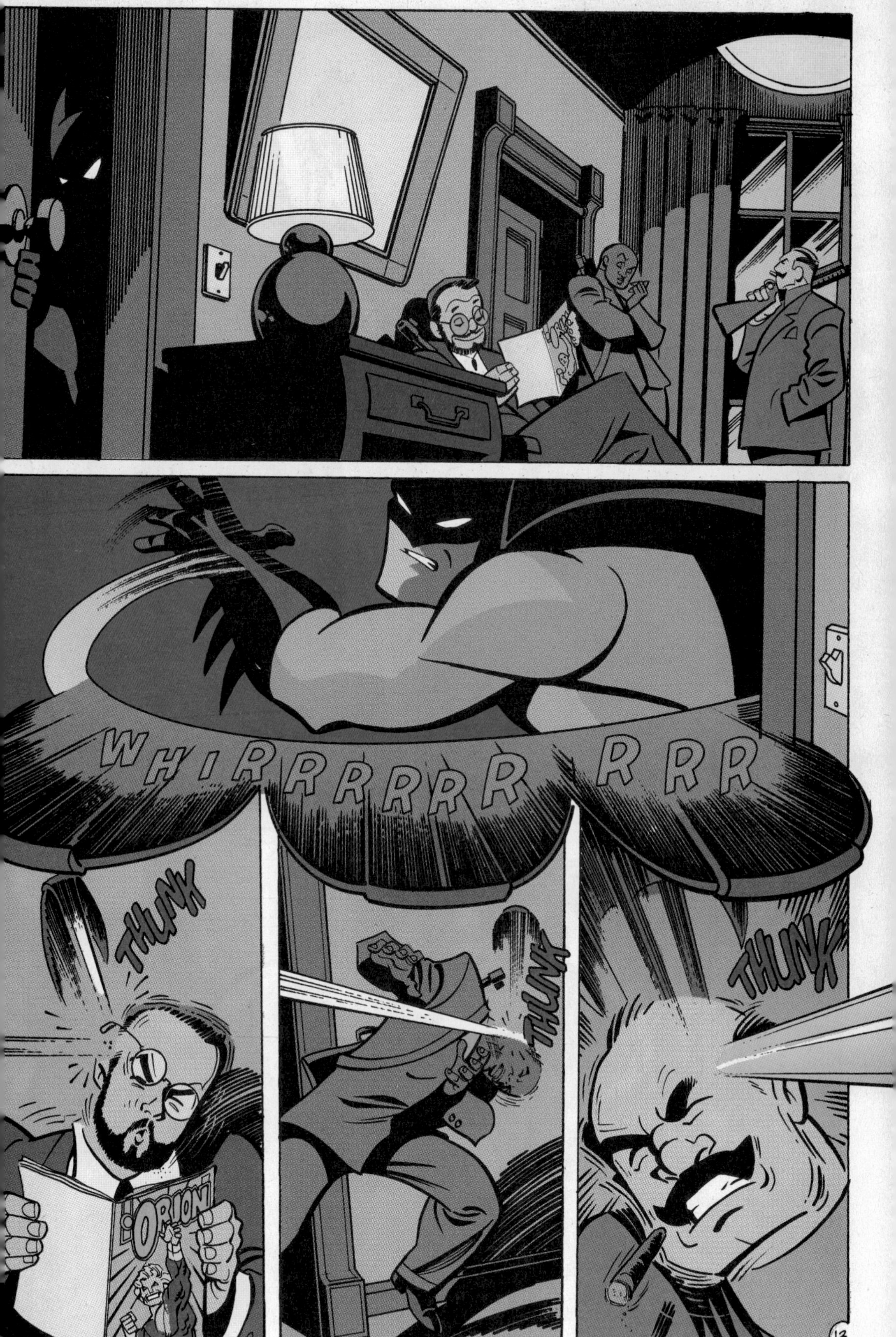
WHIRRRRRRR RRR
THUNK
THUNK
THUNK
ORION
13

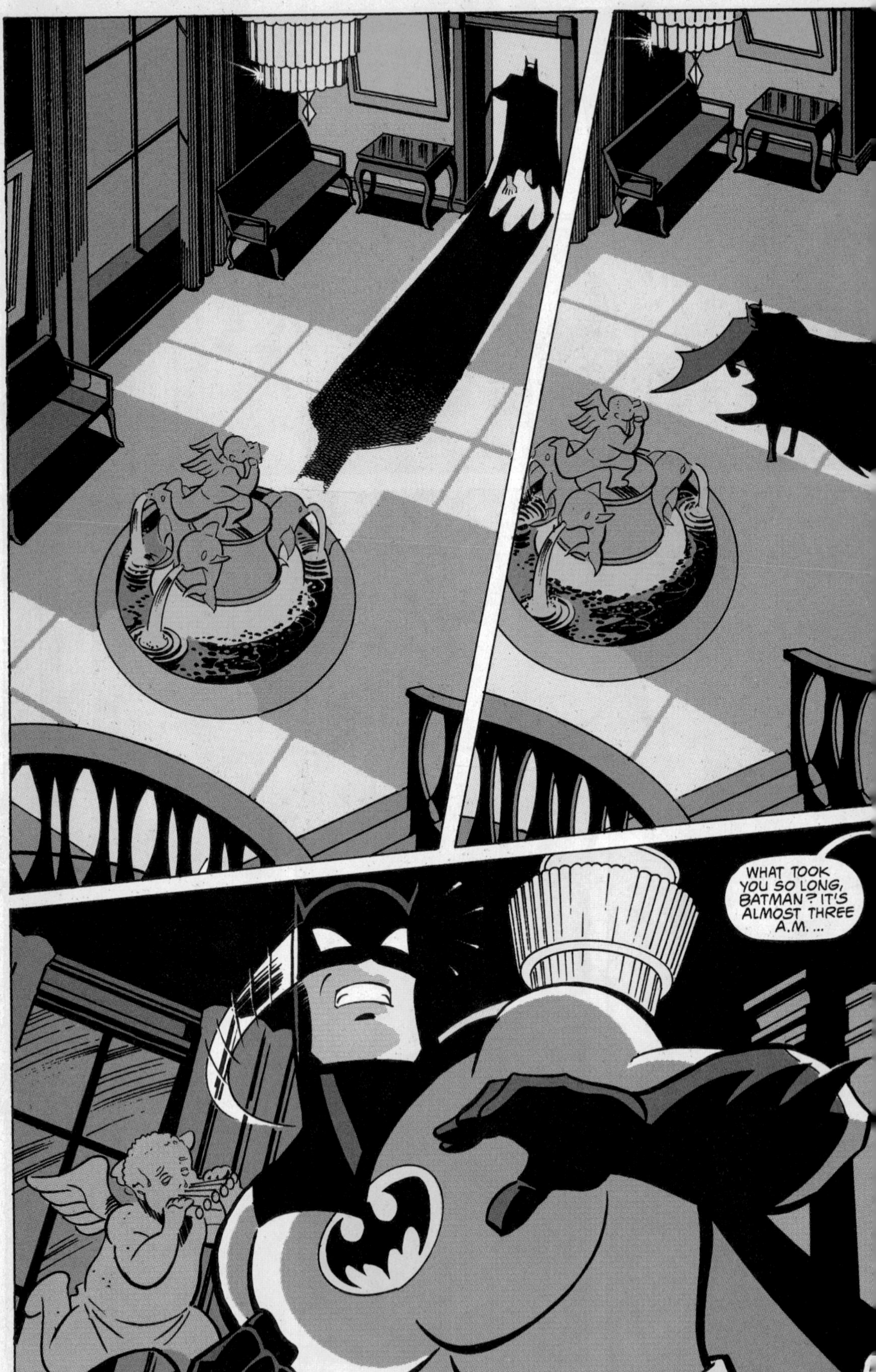
WHAT TOOK YOU SO LONG, BATMAN? IT'S ALMOST THREE A.M. ...

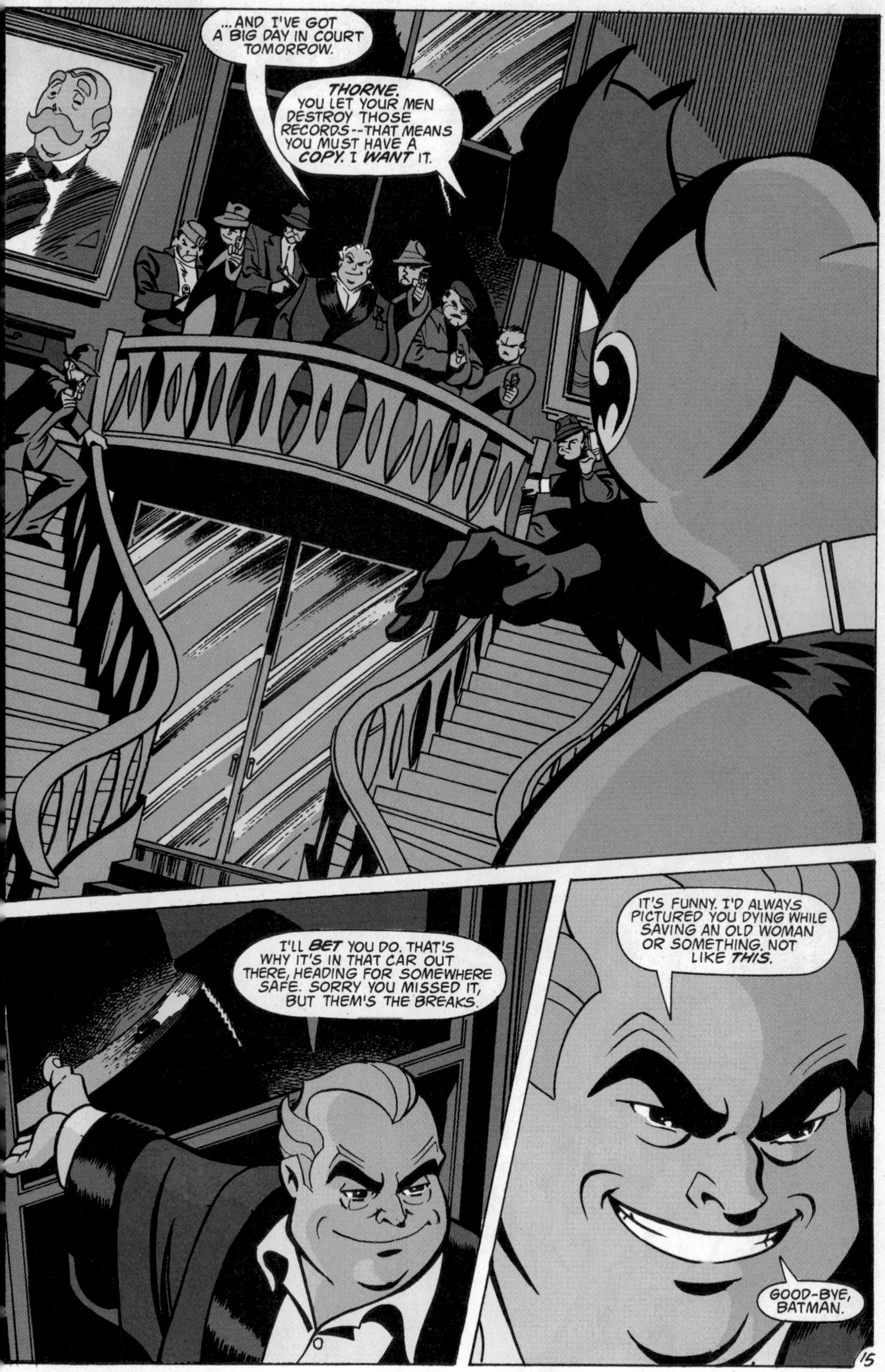
...AND I'VE GOT A BIG DAY IN COURT TOMORROW.
THORNE. YOU LET YOUR MEN DESTROY THOSE RECORDS--THAT MEANS YOU MUST HAVE A COPY. I WANT IT.
I'LL BET YOU DO. THAT'S WHY IT'S IN THAT CAR OUT THERE, HEADING FOR SOMEWHERE SAFE. SORRY YOU MISSED IT, BUT THEM'S THE BREAKS.
IT'S FUNNY. I'D ALWAYS PICTURED YOU DYING WHILE SAVING AN OLD WOMAN OR SOMETHING. NOT LIKE THIS.
GOOD-BYE, BATMAN.
15

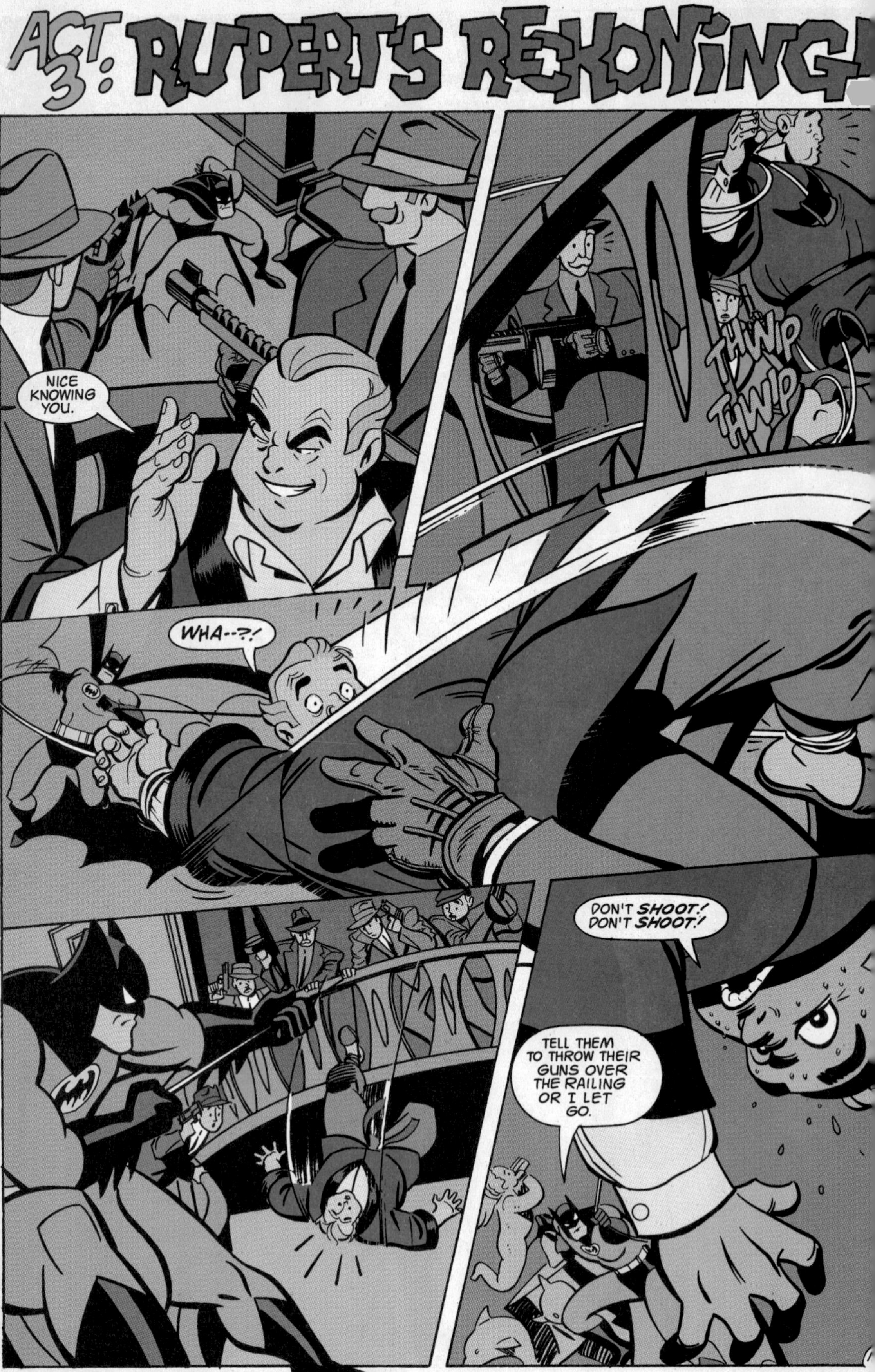
ACT 3: RUPERT'S RECKONING!
NICE KNOWING YOU.
THWIP THWIP
WHA--?!
DON'T SHOOT! DON'T SHOOT!
TELL THEM TO THROW THEIR GUNS OVER THE RAILING OR I LET GO.

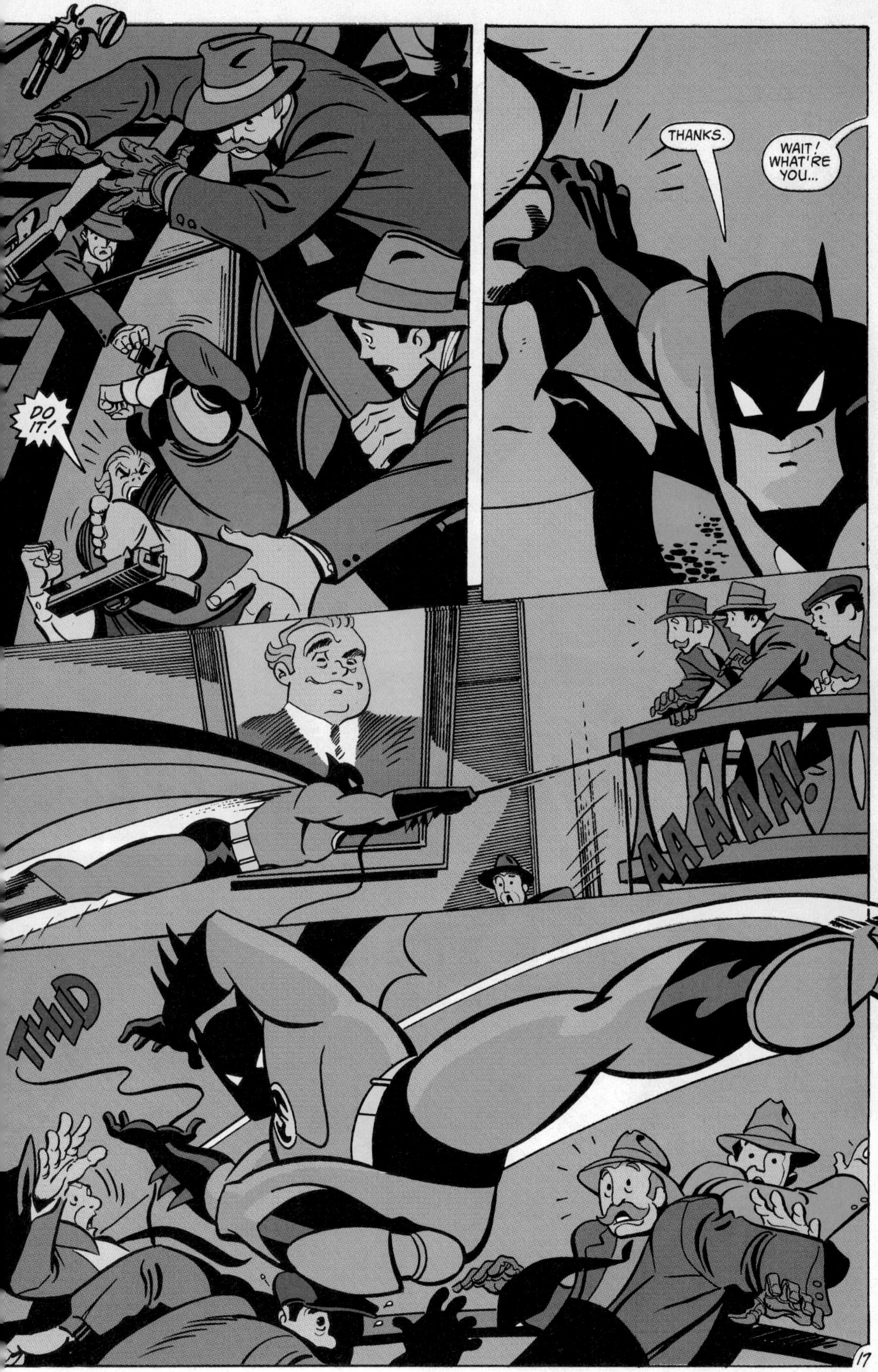
DO IT!
THANKS.
WAIT! WHAT'RE YOU...
AAAAAA!
THUD
17

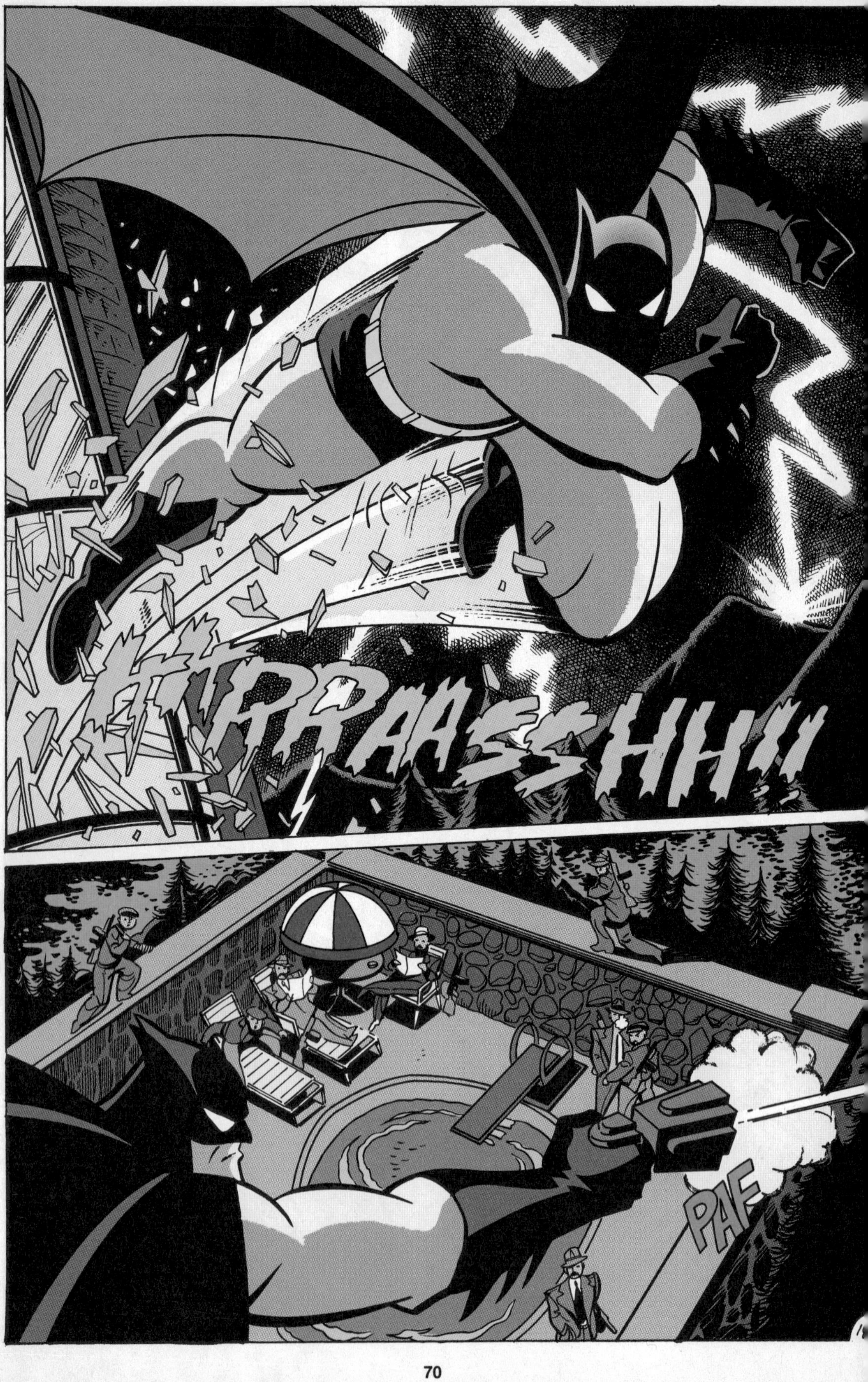
KRRAASSHH!!
PAF

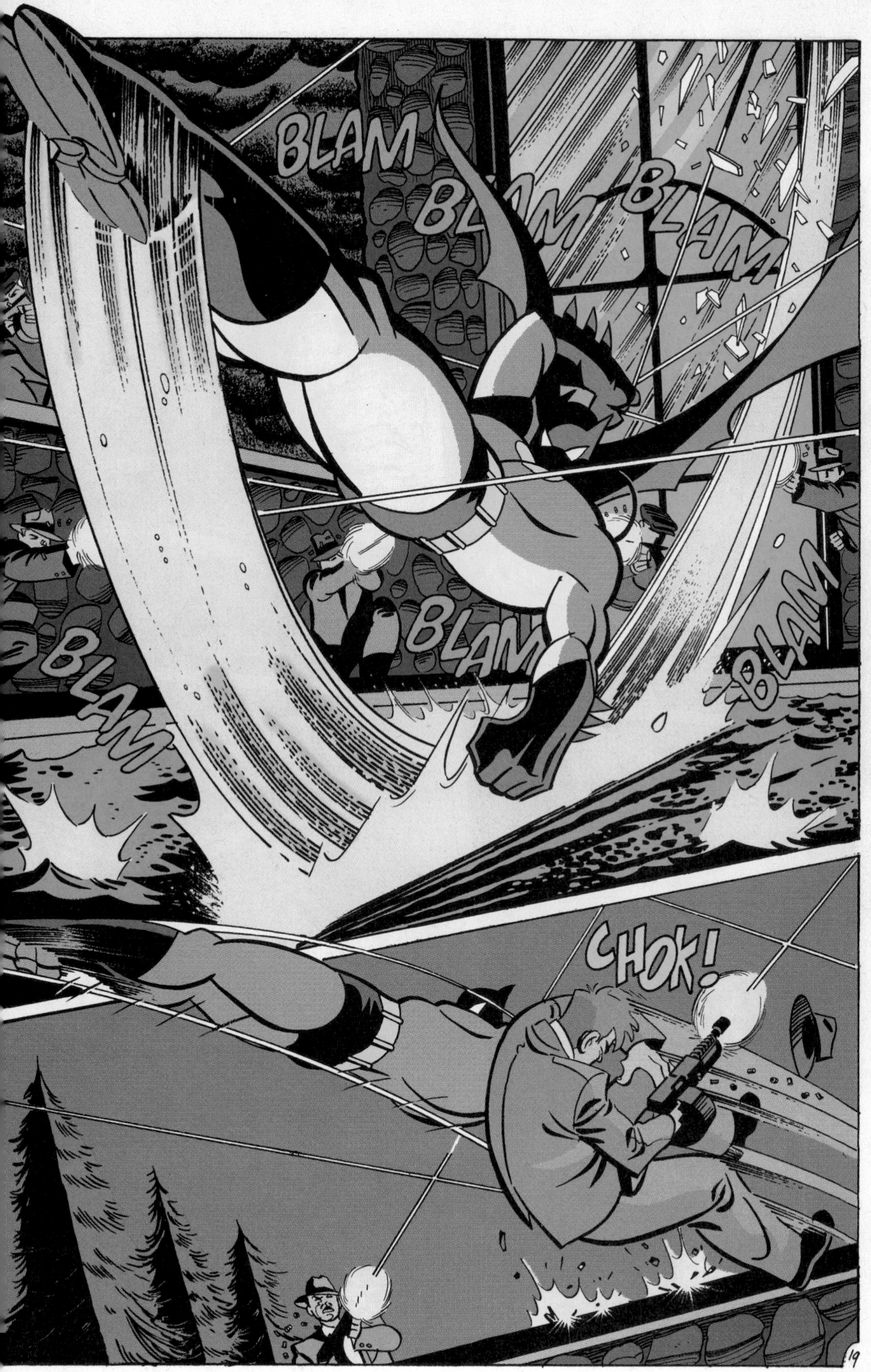
BLAM
BLAM BLAM BLAM
BLAM
BLAM
BLAM
CHOK!
19

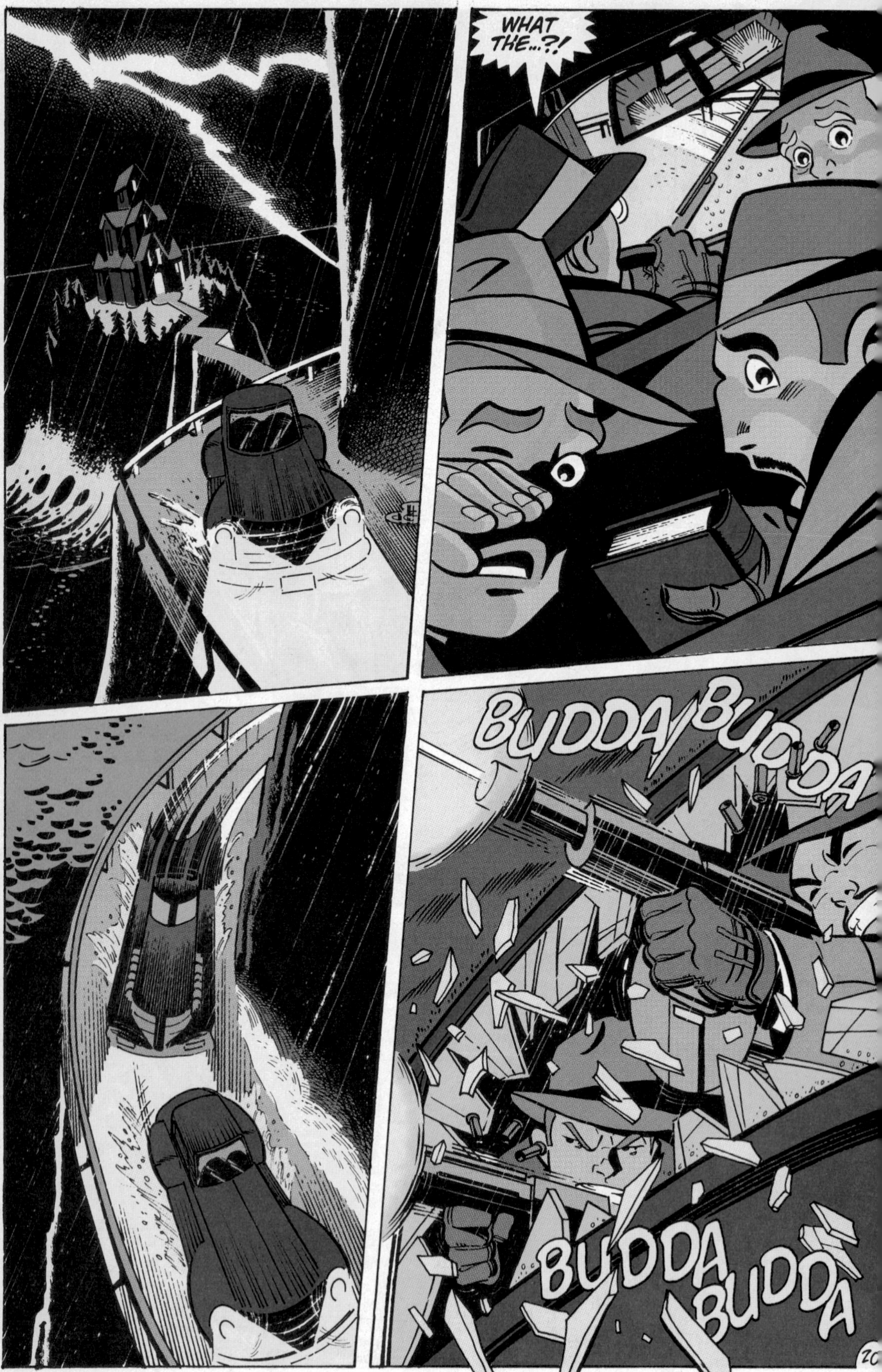
WHAT THE..?!
BUDDA BUDDA
BUDDA BUDDA

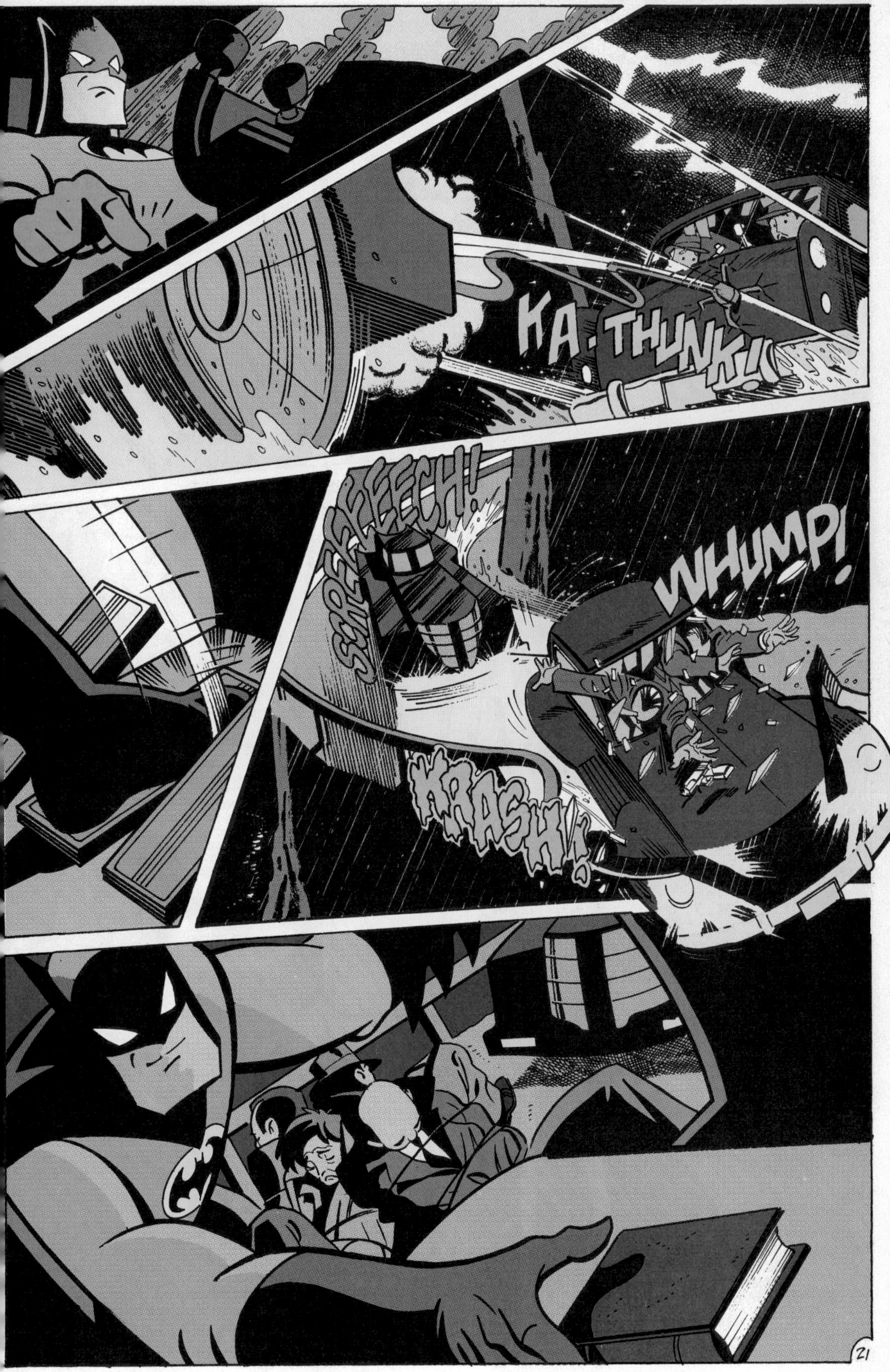
KA-THUNK!
SCREEEECH!
WHUMP!
KRASH!!
21

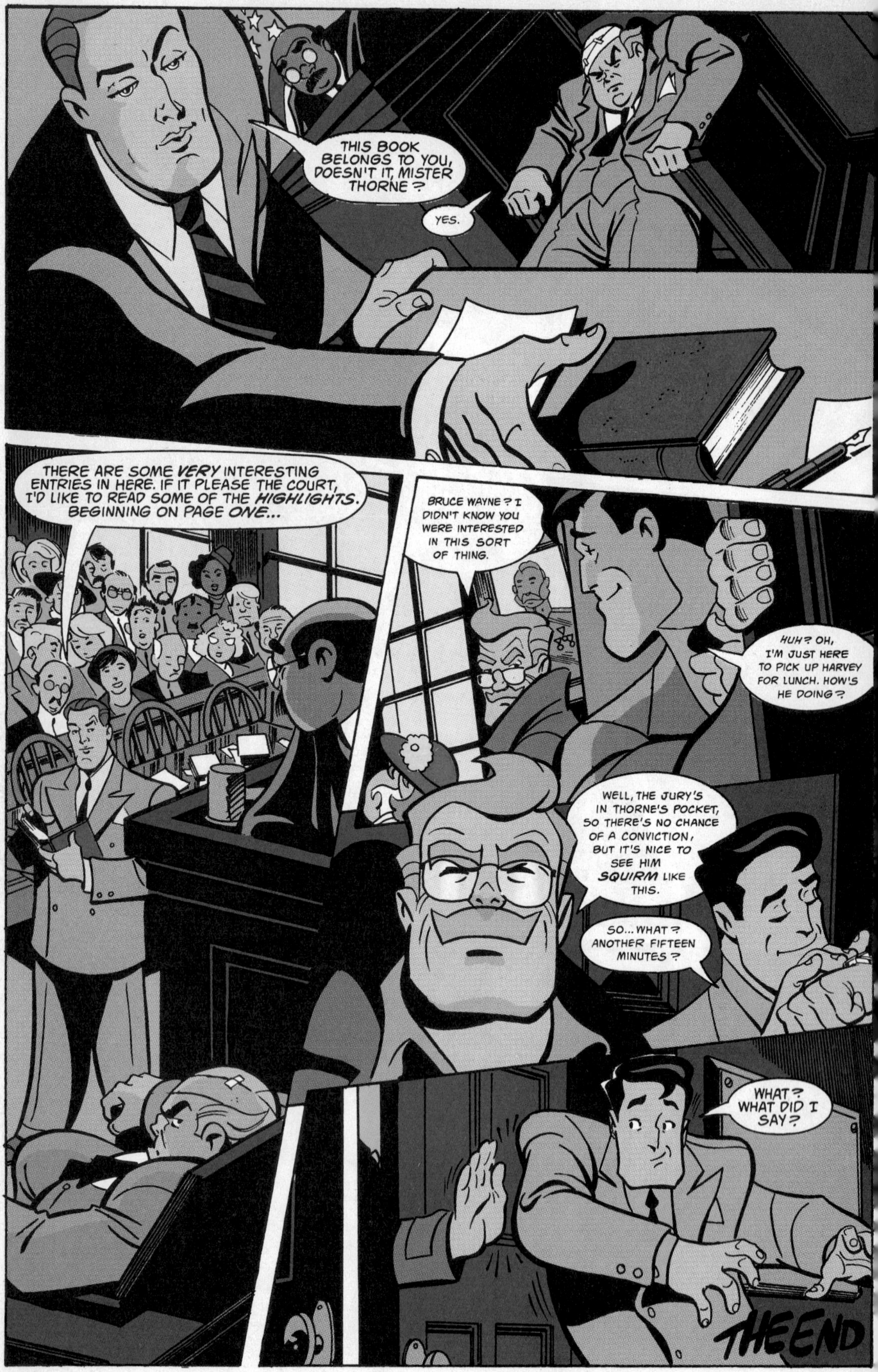
THIS BOOK BELONGS TO YOU, DOESN'T IT, MISTER THORNE?
YES.
THERE ARE SOME *VERY* INTERESTING ENTRIES IN HERE. IF IT PLEASE THE COURT, I'D LIKE TO READ SOME OF THE *HIGHLIGHTS*. BEGINNING ON PAGE *ONE*...
BRUCE WAYNE? I DIDN'T KNOW YOU WERE INTERESTED IN THIS SORT OF THING.
HUH? OH, I'M JUST HERE TO PICK UP HARVEY FOR LUNCH. HOW'S HE DOING?
WELL, THE JURY'S IN THORNE'S POCKET, SO THERE'S NO CHANCE OF A CONVICTION, BUT IT'S NICE TO SEE HIM **SQUIRM** LIKE THIS.
SO... WHAT? ANOTHER FIFTEEN MINUTES?
WHAT? WHAT DID I SAY?
THE END

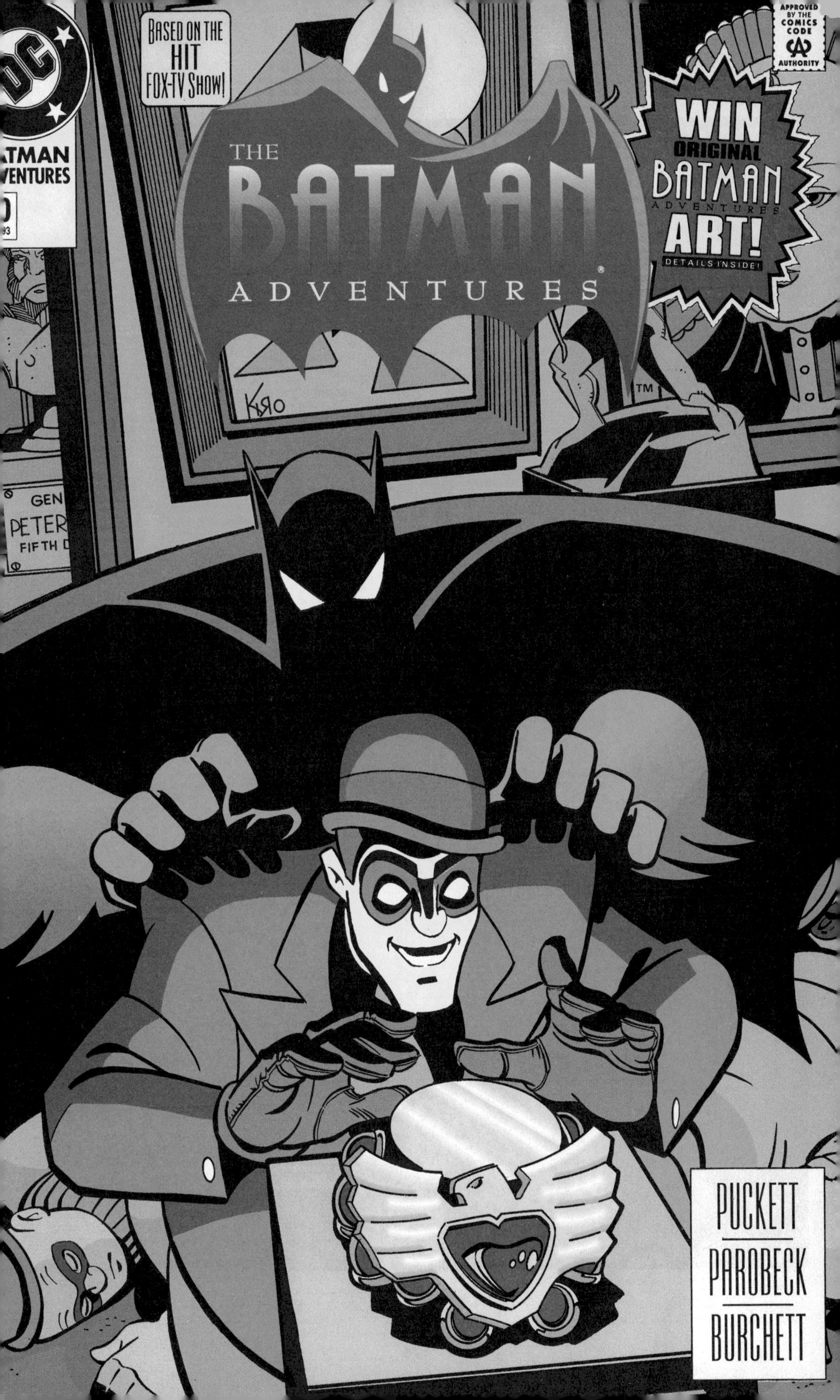
DC
BASED ON THE HIT FOX-TV SHOW!
THE BATMAN ADVENTURES
APPROVED BY THE COMICS CODE AUTHORITY
WIN ORIGINAL BATMAN ADVENTURES ART!
DETAILS INSIDE!
PUCKETT
PAROBECK
BURCHETT

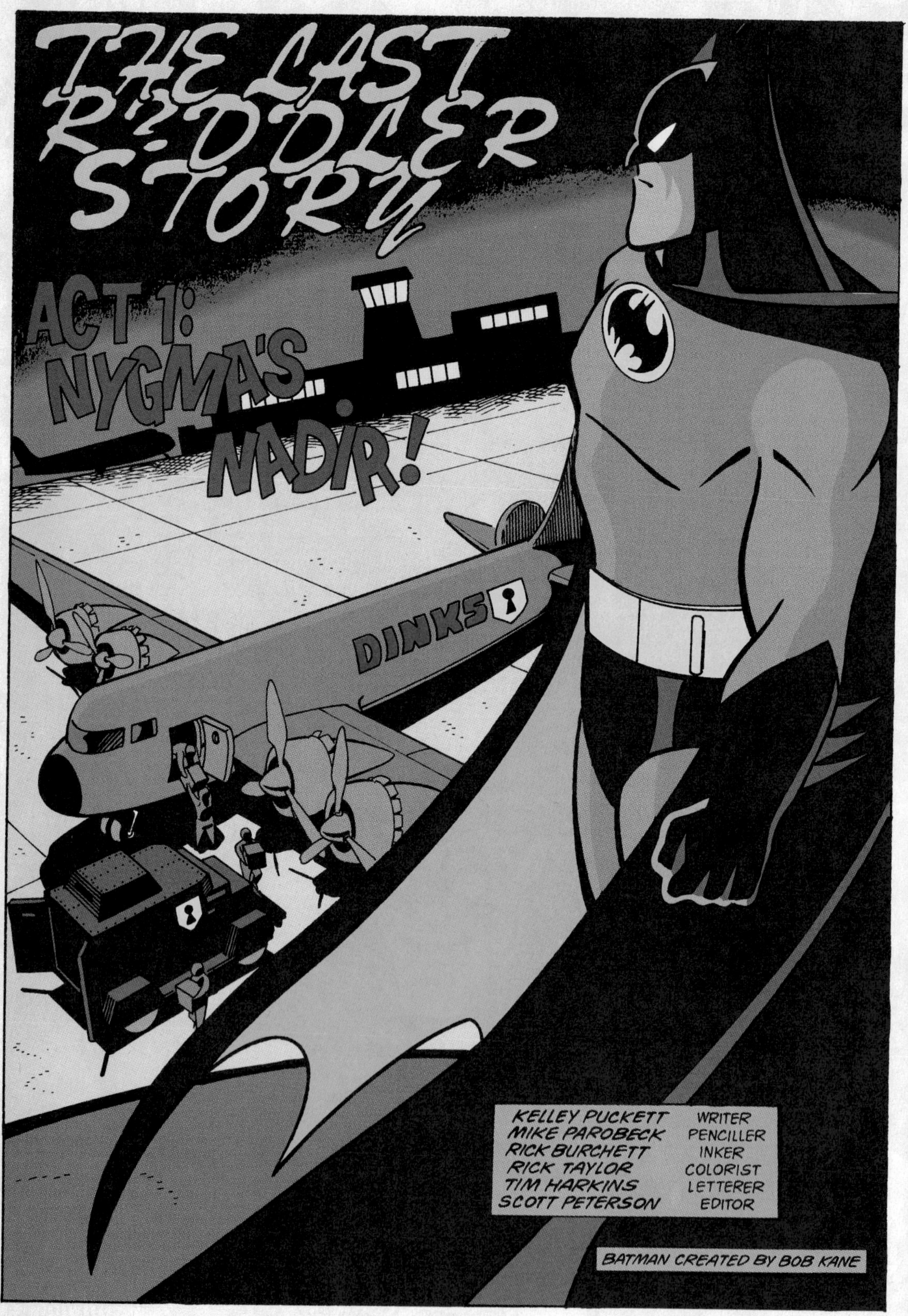
THE LAST RIDDLER STORY
ACT 1: NYGMA'S NADIR!
DINKS
KELLEY PUCKETT WRITER
MIKE PAROBECK PENCILLER
RICK BURCHETT INKER
RICK TAYLOR COLORIST
TIM HARKINS LETTERER
SCOTT PETERSON EDITOR
BATMAN CREATED BY BOB KANE

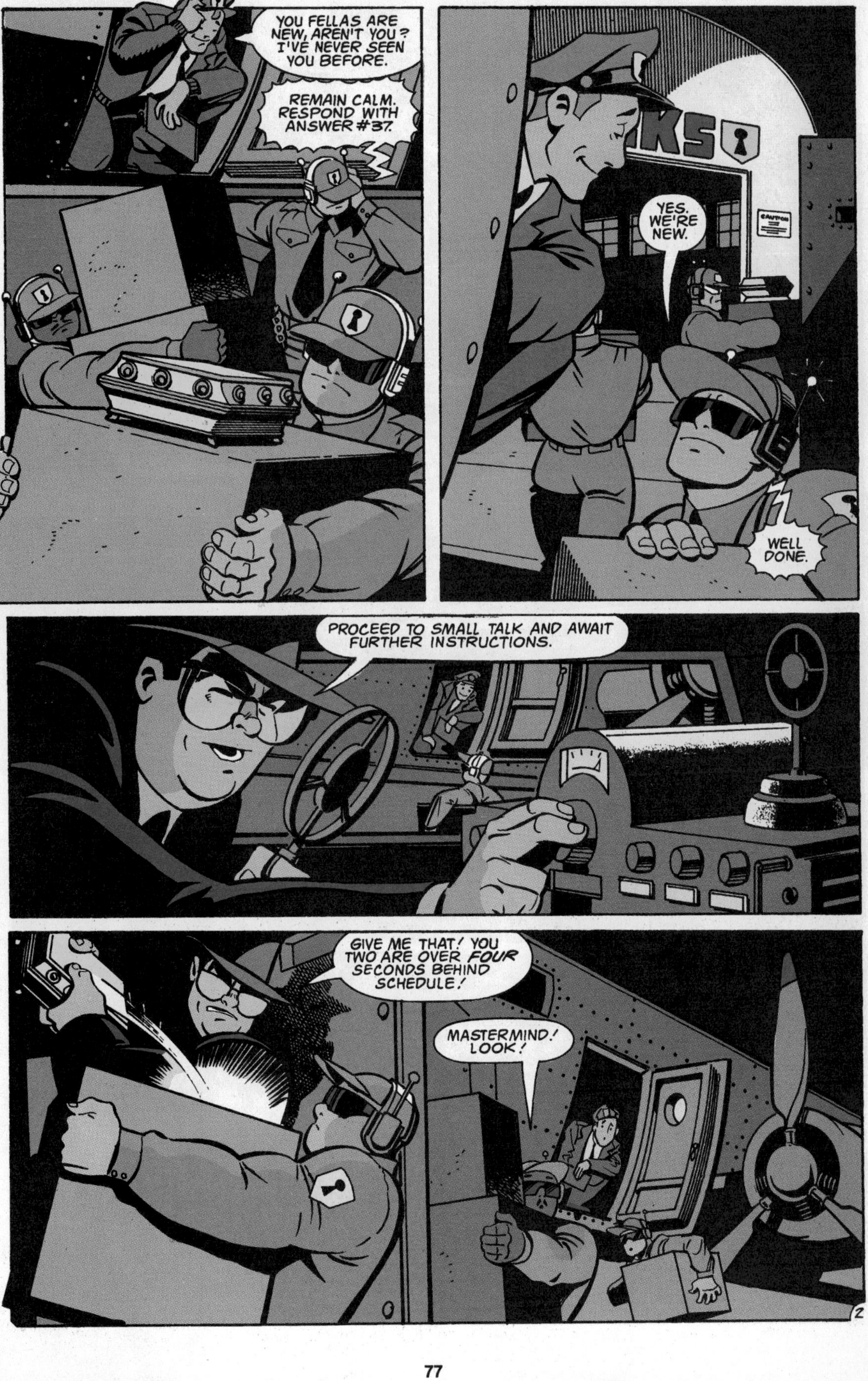
YOU FELLAS ARE NEW, AREN'T YOU? I'VE NEVER SEEN YOU BEFORE.
REMAIN CALM. RESPOND WITH ANSWER #37.
YES. WE'RE NEW.
WELL DONE.
PROCEED TO SMALL TALK AND AWAIT FURTHER INSTRUCTIONS.
GIVE ME THAT! YOU TWO ARE OVER FOUR SECONDS BEHIND SCHEDULE!
MASTERMIND! LOOK!
2

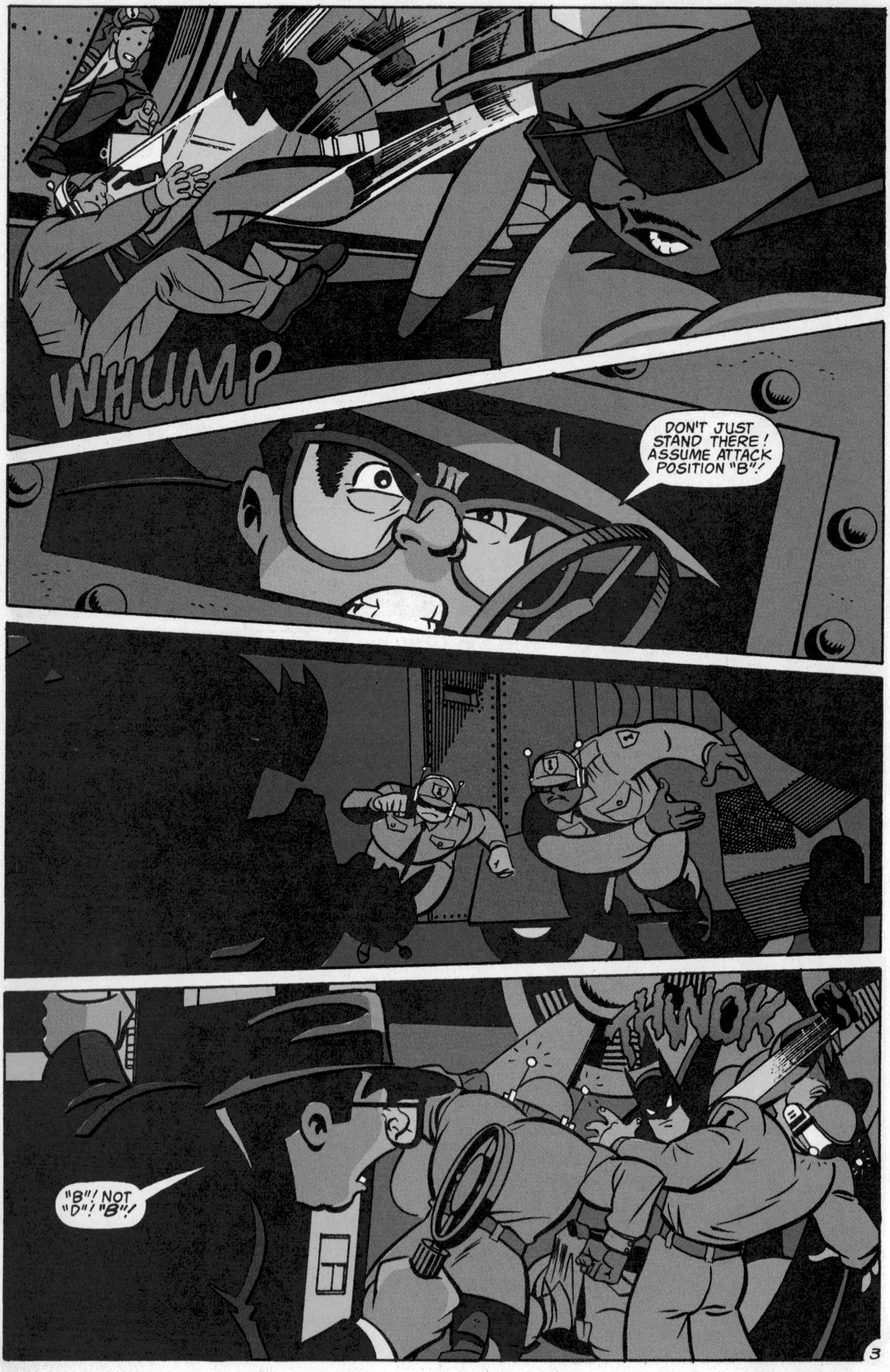
WHUMP
DON'T JUST STAND THERE! ASSUME ATTACK POSITION "B"!
THWOK
"B"! NOT "D"! "B"!
3

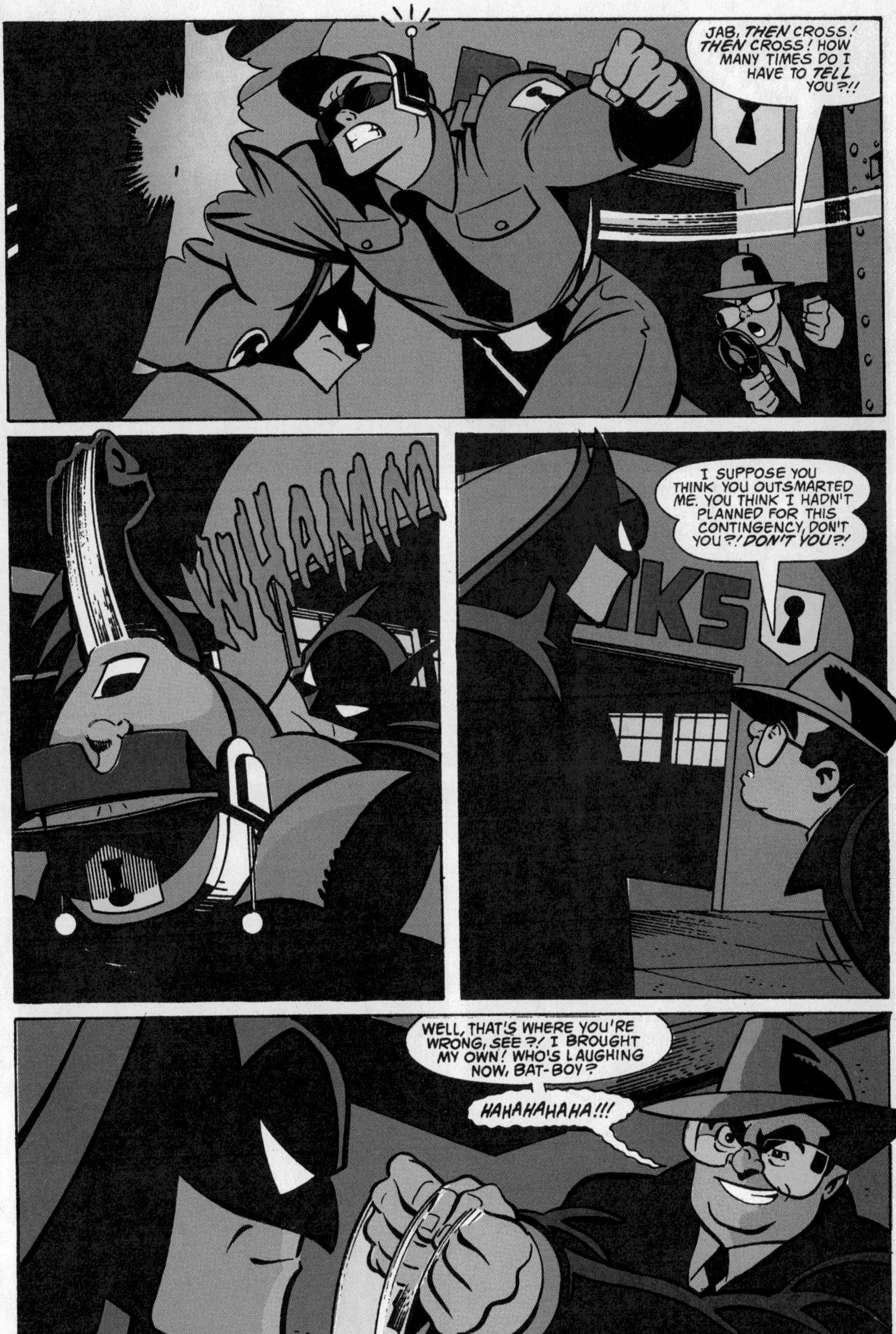
JAB, THEN CROSS! THEN CROSS! HOW MANY TIMES DO I HAVE TO TELL YOU?!!
WHAMM
I SUPPOSE YOU THINK YOU OUTSMARTED ME. YOU THINK I HADN'T PLANNED FOR THIS CONTINGENCY, DON'T YOU?! DON'T YOU?!
KS
WELL, THAT'S WHERE YOU'RE WRONG, SEE?! I BROUGHT MY OWN! WHO'S LAUGHING NOW, BAT-BOY?
HAHAHAHAHA!!!
4

RARE JEWELS BOUND FOR THE GOTHAM MUSEUM. I STOPPED BY TO CHAPERONE AND RAN INTO *HIM.*

MASTERMIND. HE FINALLY CAME OUT OF HIDING.

HA HA HA HA !!

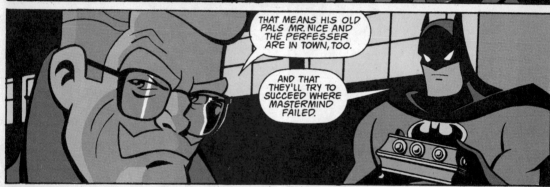

THAT MEANS HIS OLD PALS MR. NICE AND THE PERFESSER ARE IN TOWN, TOO.

AND THAT THEY'LL TRY TO SUCCEED WHERE MASTERMIND FAILED.

I'VE BEEN WAITING YEARS TO GET THOSE THREE BEHIND BARS...

I'LL SHADOW THE JEWELS FOR THE NEXT FEW NIGHTS. KEEP YOUR MEN AWAY OR THEY'LL BE SCARED OFF.

YOU GOT IT. THE TIMING COULD BE BETTER, THOUGH. OR HAVE YOU FORGOTTEN WHO GETS RELEASED TOMORROW ?

NO. I HAVEN'T FORGOTTEN.

5

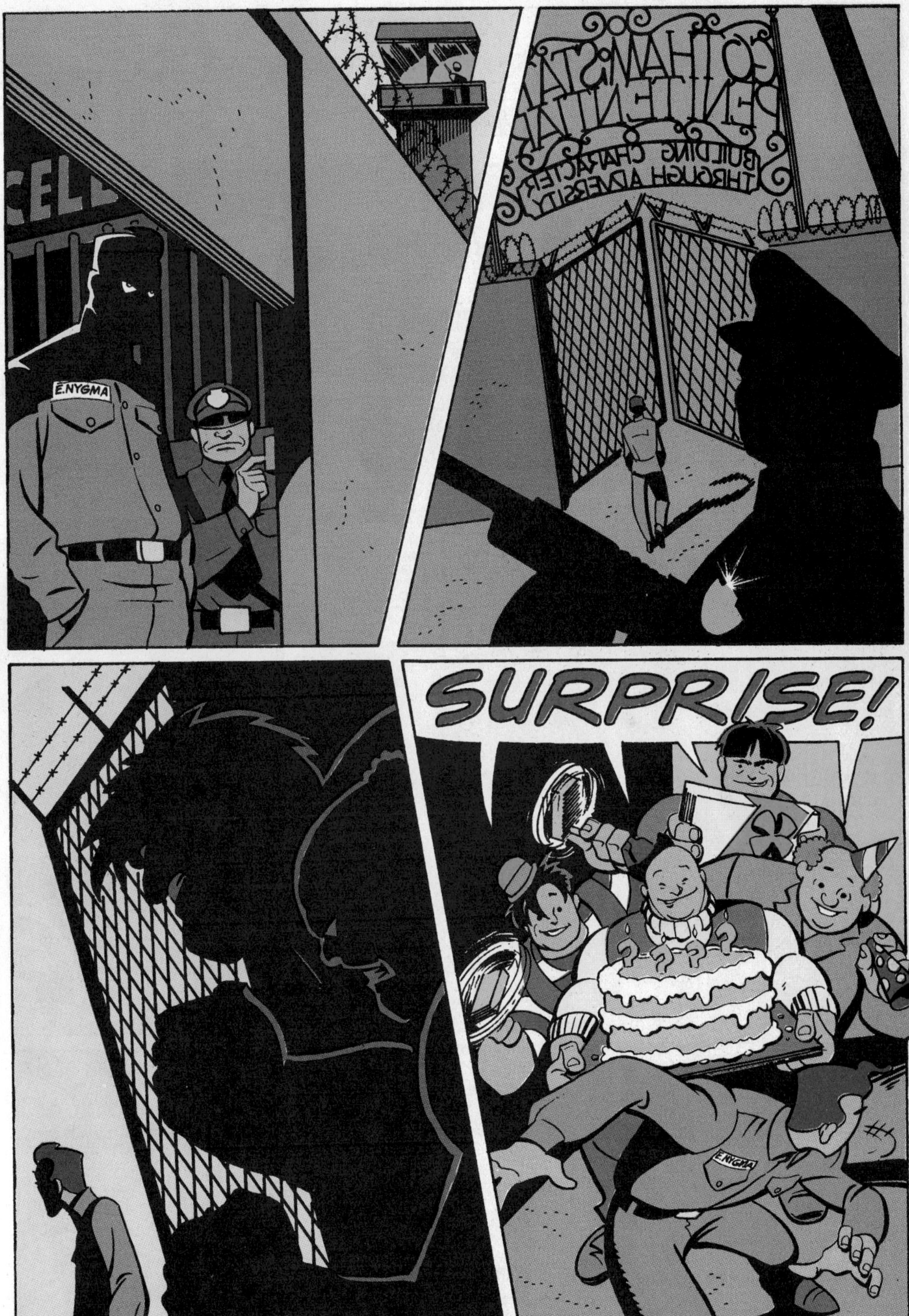
E.NYGMA
SURPRISE!
E.NYGMA

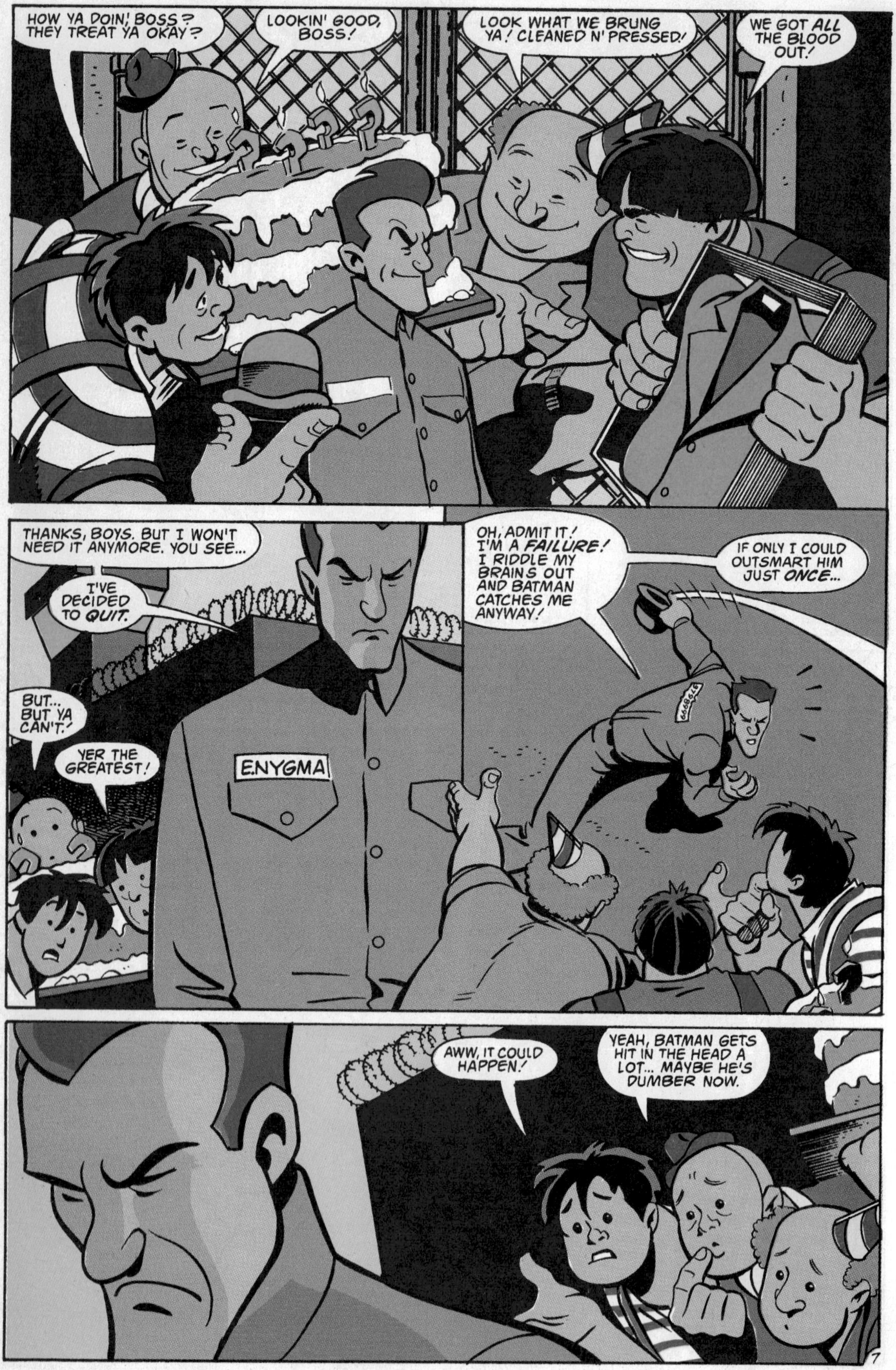
HOW YA DOIN', BOSS? THEY TREAT YA OKAY?
LOOKIN' GOOD, BOSS!
LOOK WHAT WE BRUNG YA! CLEANED N' PRESSED!
WE GOT ALL THE BLOOD OUT!
THANKS, BOYS. BUT I WON'T NEED IT ANYMORE. YOU SEE...
I'VE DECIDED TO QUIT.
BUT... BUT YA CAN'T!
YER THE GREATEST!
E.NYGMA
OH, ADMIT IT! I'M A FAILURE! I RIDDLE MY BRAINS OUT AND BATMAN CATCHES ME ANYWAY!
IF ONLY I COULD OUTSMART HIM JUST ONCE...
AWW, IT COULD HAPPEN!
YEAH, BATMAN GETS HIT IN THE HEAD A LOT... MAYBE HE'S DUMBER NOW.
7

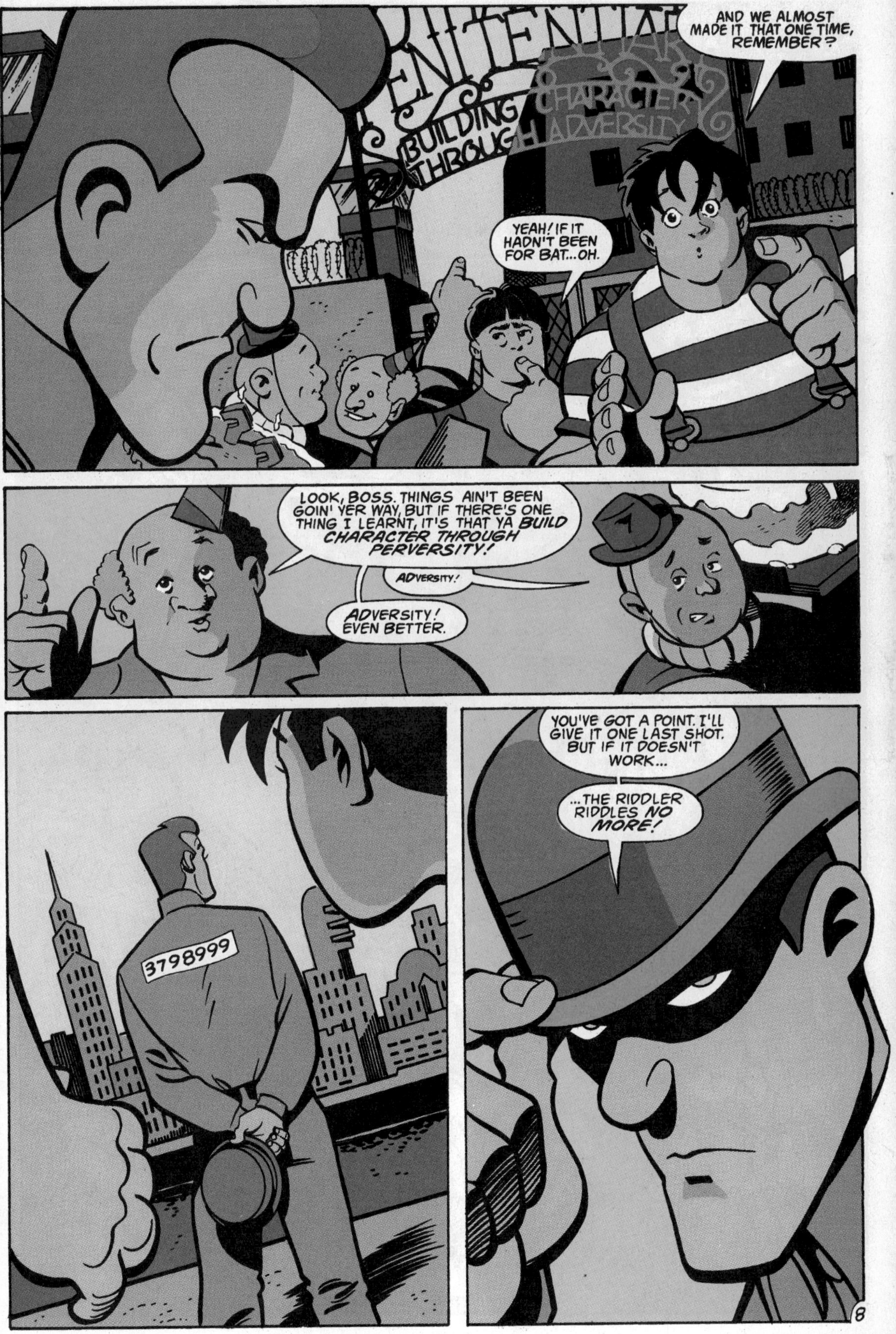
PENITENTIARY
BUILDING CHARACTER THROUGH ADVERSITY
AND WE ALMOST MADE IT THAT ONE TIME, REMEMBER?
YEAH! IF IT HADN'T BEEN FOR BAT...OH.
LOOK, BOSS. THINGS AIN'T BEEN GOIN' YER WAY, BUT IF THERE'S ONE THING I LEARNT, IT'S THAT YA BUILD CHARACTER THROUGH PERVERSITY!
ADVERSITY!
ADVERSITY! EVEN BETTER.
3798999
YOU'VE GOT A POINT. I'LL GIVE IT ONE LAST SHOT. BUT IF IT DOESN'T WORK...
...THE RIDDLER RIDDLES NO MORE!
8

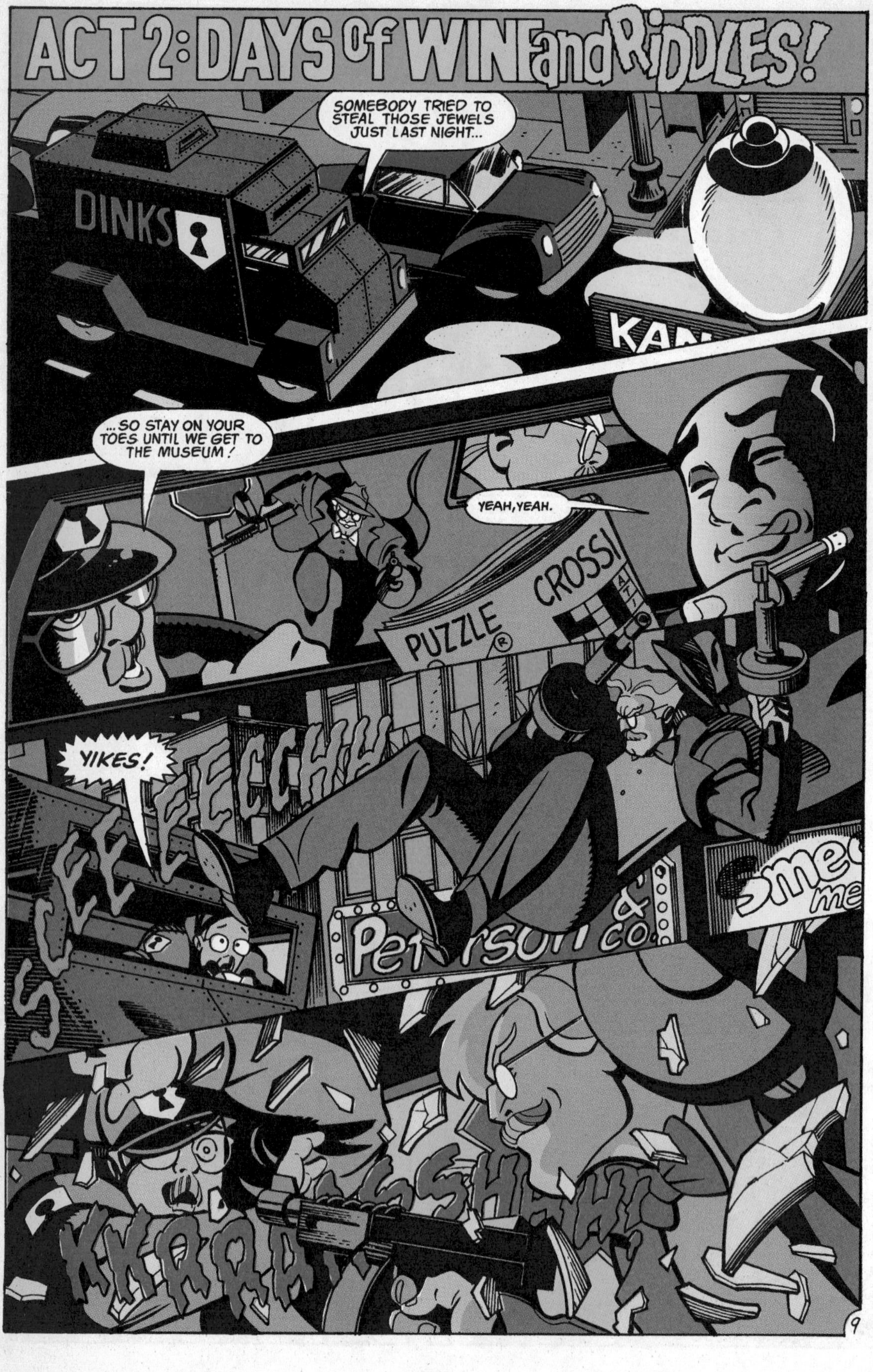
ACT 2: DAYS of WINE and RIDDLES!
SOMEBODY TRIED TO STEAL THOSE JEWELS JUST LAST NIGHT...
DINKS
KAN
...SO STAY ON YOUR TOES UNTIL WE GET TO THE MUSEUM!
YEAH, YEAH.
PUZZLE
CROSS
YIKES!
SKEEEECCHH
Petersun co.
KKRAASSHH
9

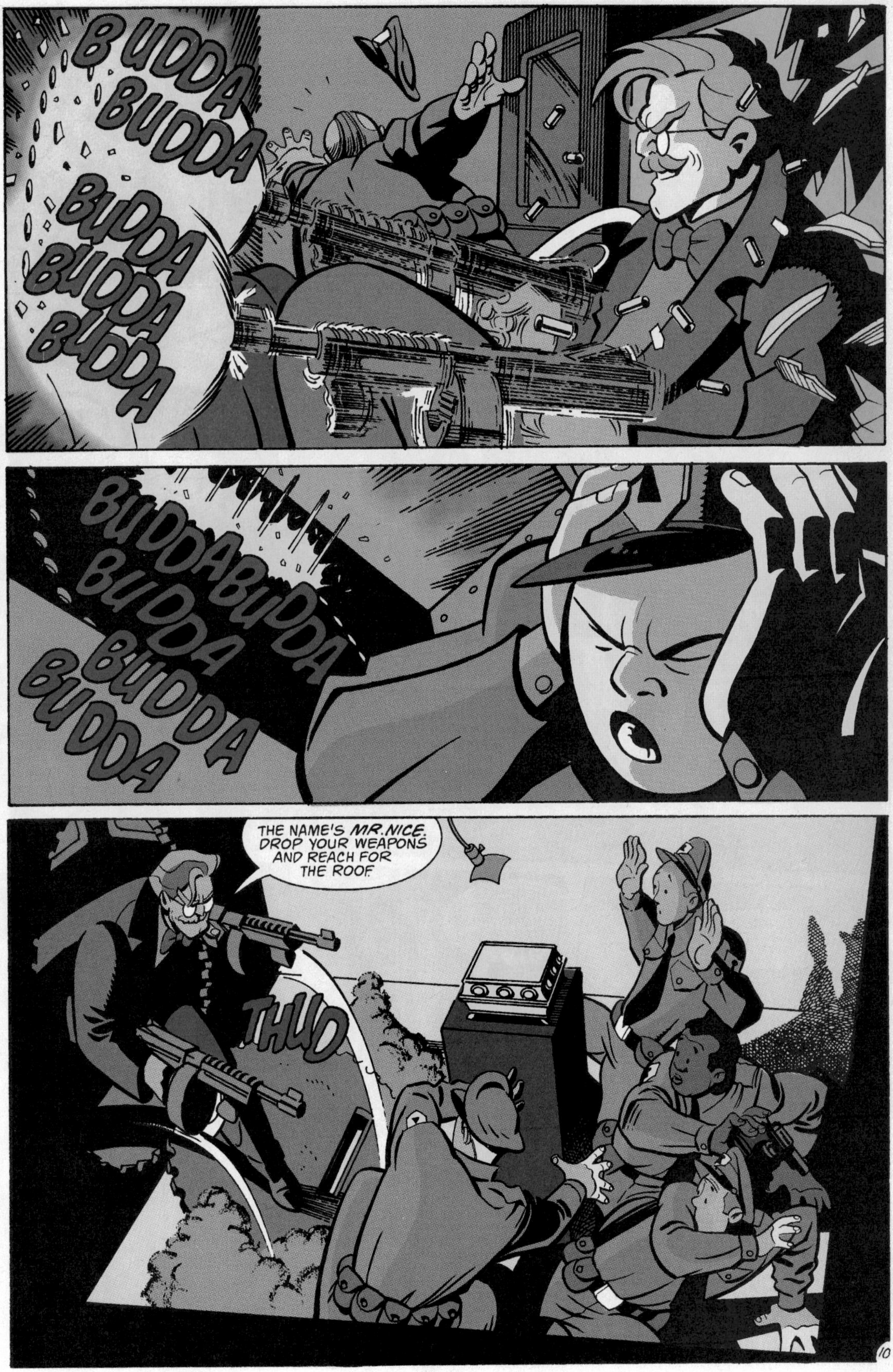
BUDDA BUDDA
BUDDA BUDDA BUDDA BUDDA
BUDDABUDDA BUDDA BUDDA BUDDA
THE NAME'S *MR. NICE.* DROP YOUR WEAPONS AND REACH FOR THE ROOF.
THUD
10

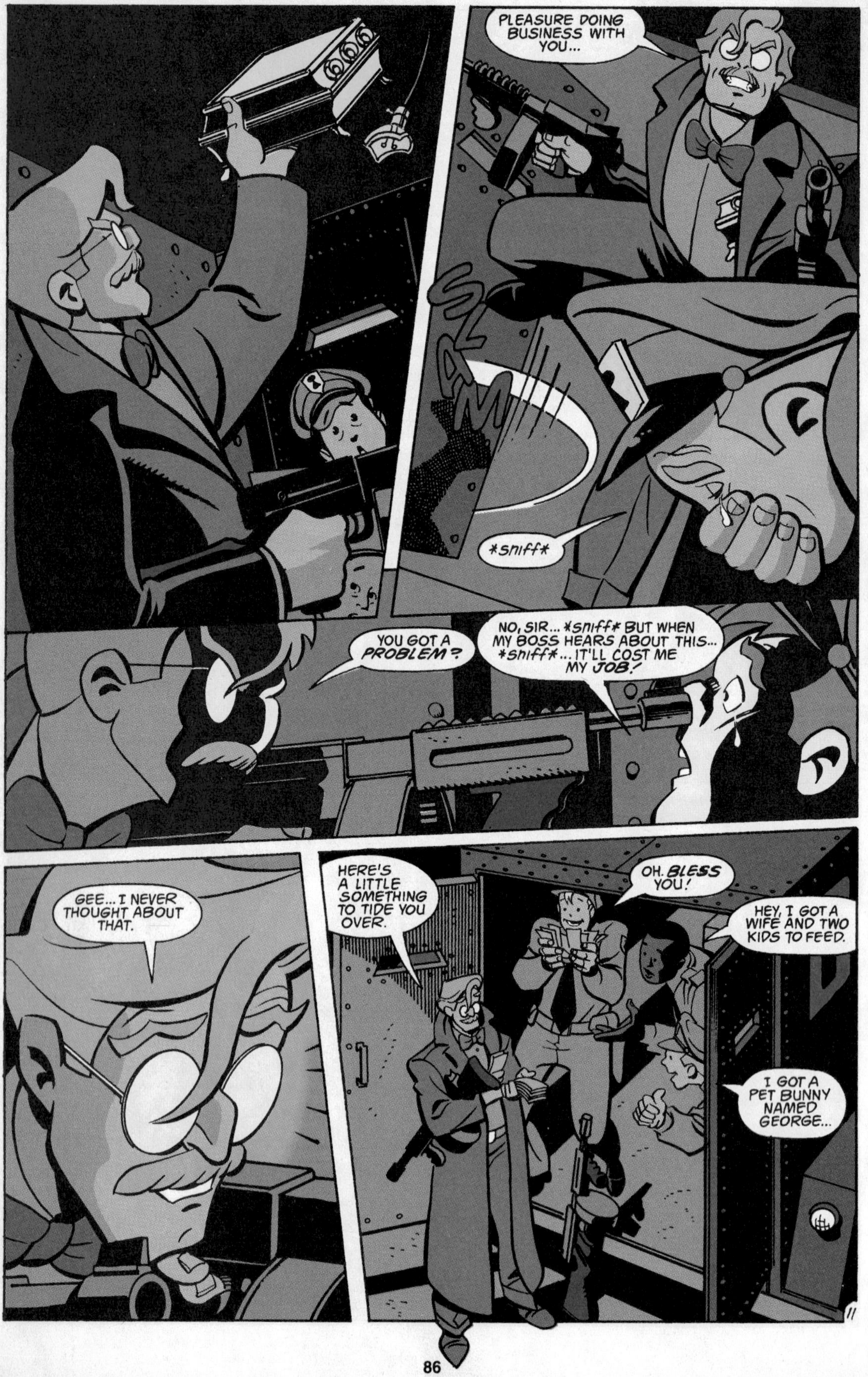
PLEASURE DOING BUSINESS WITH YOU...
SLAM
sniff
YOU GOT A PROBLEM?
NO, SIR... *sniff* BUT WHEN MY BOSS HEARS ABOUT THIS... *sniff*... IT'LL COST ME MY JOB!
GEE... I NEVER THOUGHT ABOUT THAT.
HERE'S A LITTLE SOMETHING TO TIDE YOU OVER.
OH. BLESS YOU!
HEY, I GOT A WIFE AND TWO KIDS TO FEED.
I GOT A PET BUNNY NAMED GEORGE...
11

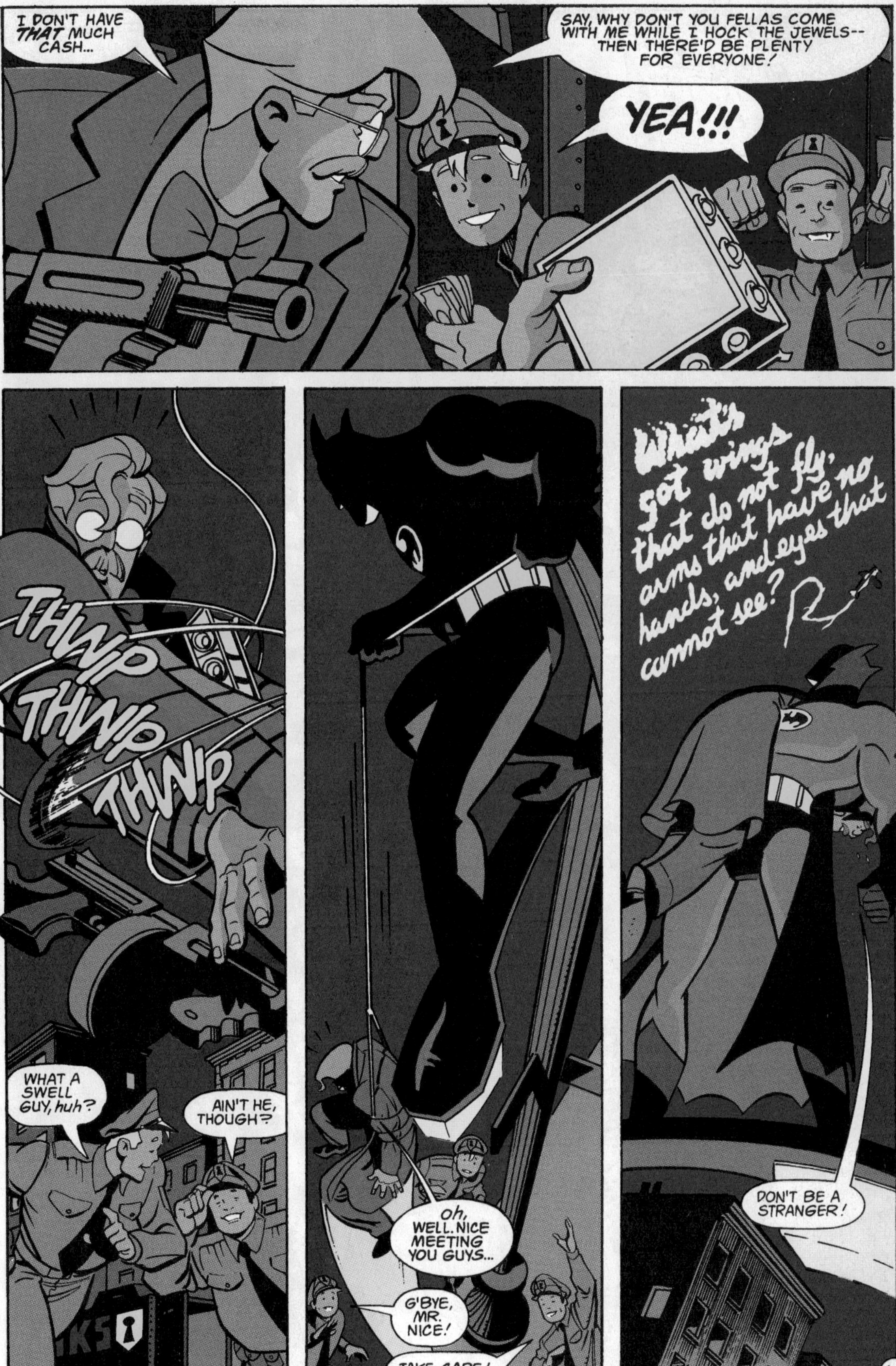
I DON'T HAVE THAT MUCH CASH...
SAY, WHY DON'T YOU FELLAS COME WITH ME WHILE I HOCK THE JEWELS-- THEN THERE'D BE PLENTY FOR EVERYONE!
YEA!!!
THWIP
THWIP
THWIP
WHAT A SWELL GUY, huh?
AIN'T HE, THOUGH?
Oh, WELL. NICE MEETING YOU GUYS...
G'BYE, MR. NICE!
TAKE CARE!
What's got wings that do not fly, arms that have no hands, and eyes that cannot see? R
DON'T BE A STRANGER!
12

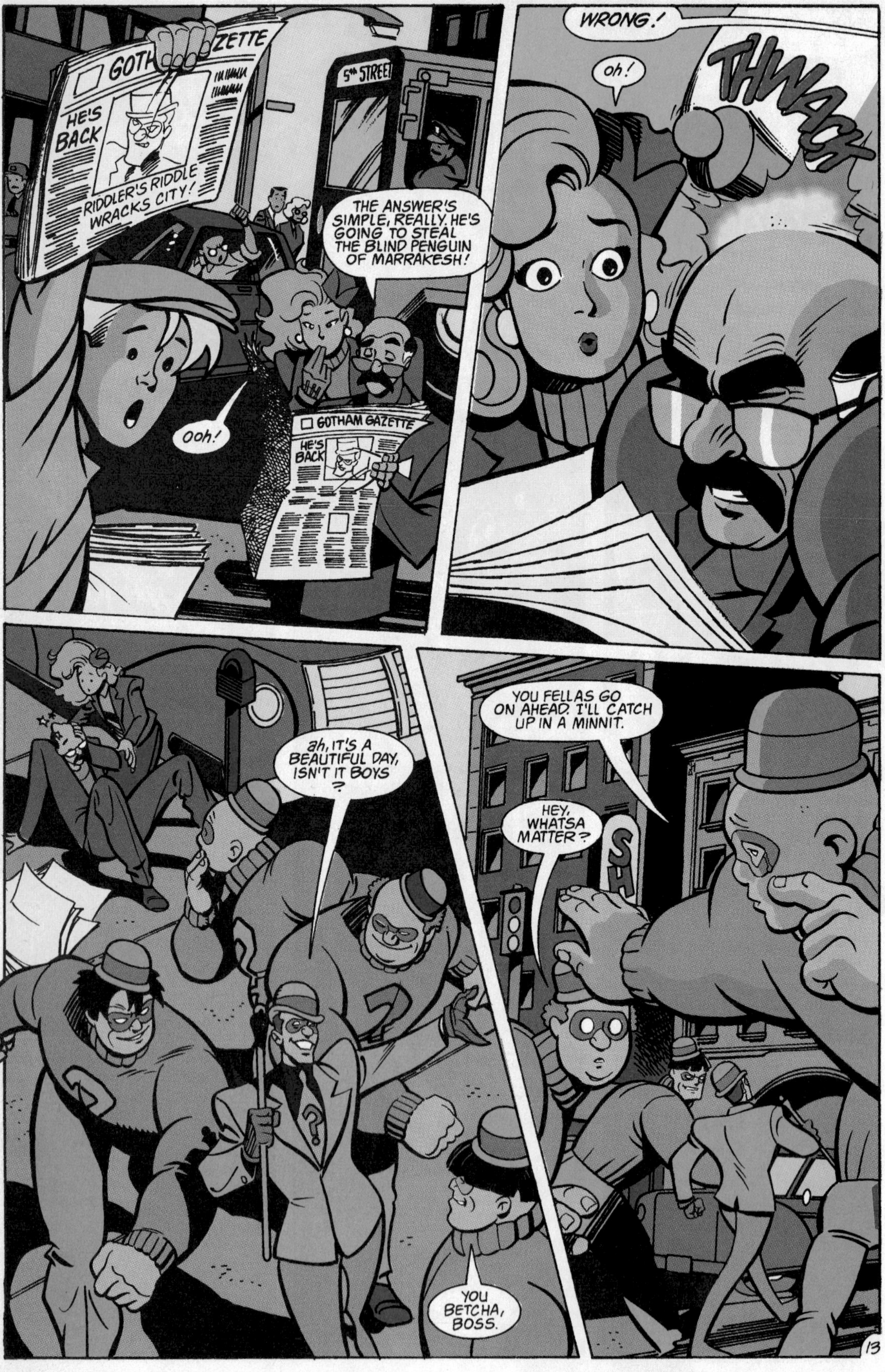
GOTHAM GAZETTE
HE'S BACK
RIDDLER'S RIDDLE WRACKS CITY!
5th STREET
THE ANSWER'S SIMPLE, REALLY. HE'S GOING TO STEAL THE BLIND PENGUIN OF MARRAKESH!
Ooh!
GOTHAM GAZETTE
HE'S BACK
WRONG!
oh!
THWACK
ah, IT'S A BEAUTIFUL DAY, ISN'T IT BOYS?
YOU BETCHA, BOSS.
YOU FELLAS GO ON AHEAD. I'LL CATCH UP IN A MINNIT.
HEY, WHATSA MATTER?
13

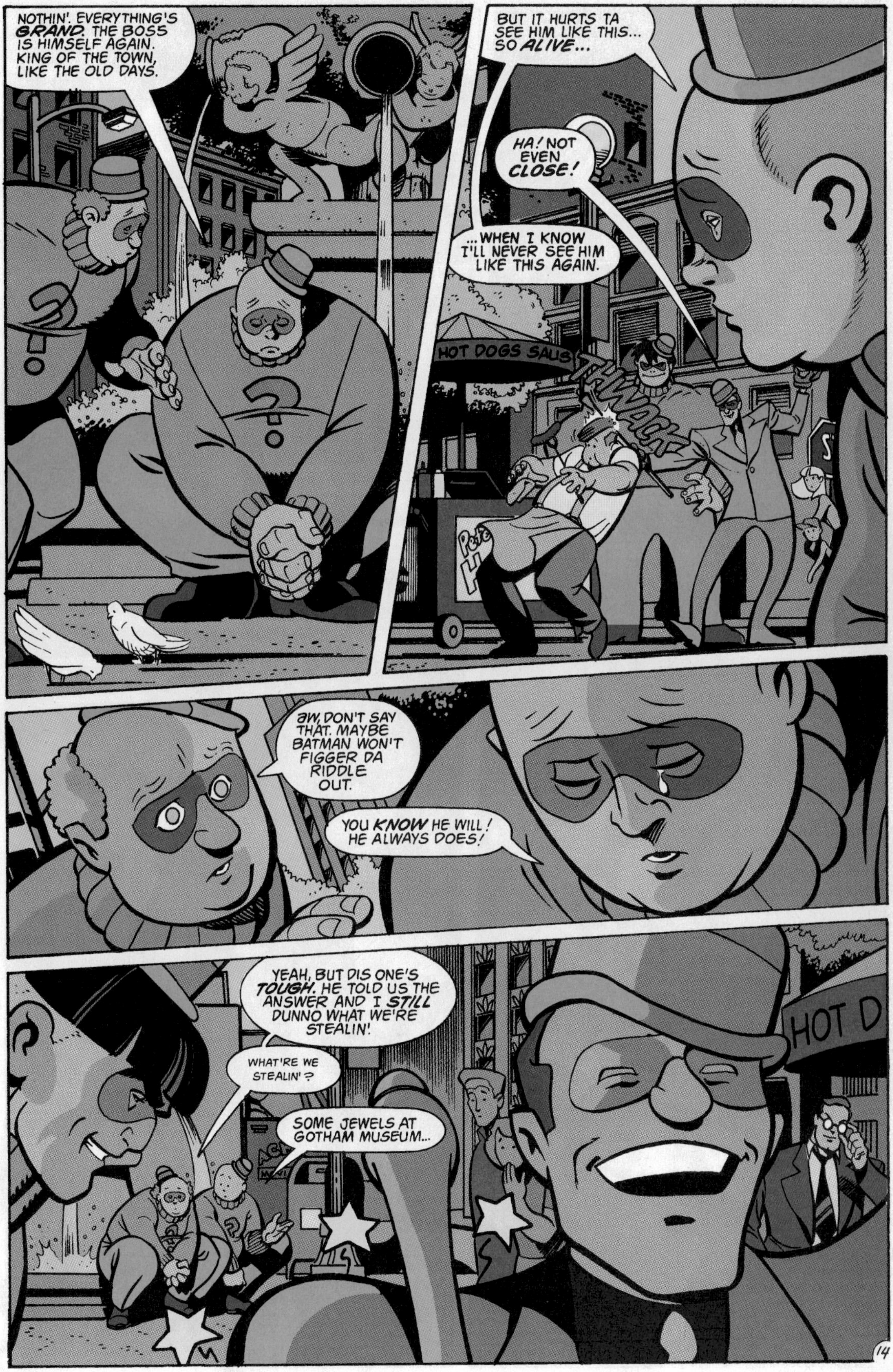
NOTHIN'. EVERYTHING'S GRAND. THE BOSS IS HIMSELF AGAIN. KING OF THE TOWN, LIKE THE OLD DAYS.
BUT IT HURTS TA SEE HIM LIKE THIS... SO ALIVE...
HA! NOT EVEN CLOSE!
...WHEN I KNOW I'LL NEVER SEE HIM LIKE THIS AGAIN.
HOT DOGS SAUS
THWACK
AW, DON'T SAY THAT. MAYBE BATMAN WON'T FIGGER DA RIDDLE OUT.
YOU KNOW HE WILL! HE ALWAYS DOES!
YEAH, BUT DIS ONE'S TOUGH. HE TOLD US THE ANSWER AND I STILL DUNNO WHAT WE'RE STEALIN'!
WHAT'RE WE STEALIN'?
SOME JEWELS AT GOTHAM MUSEUM...
HOT D
14

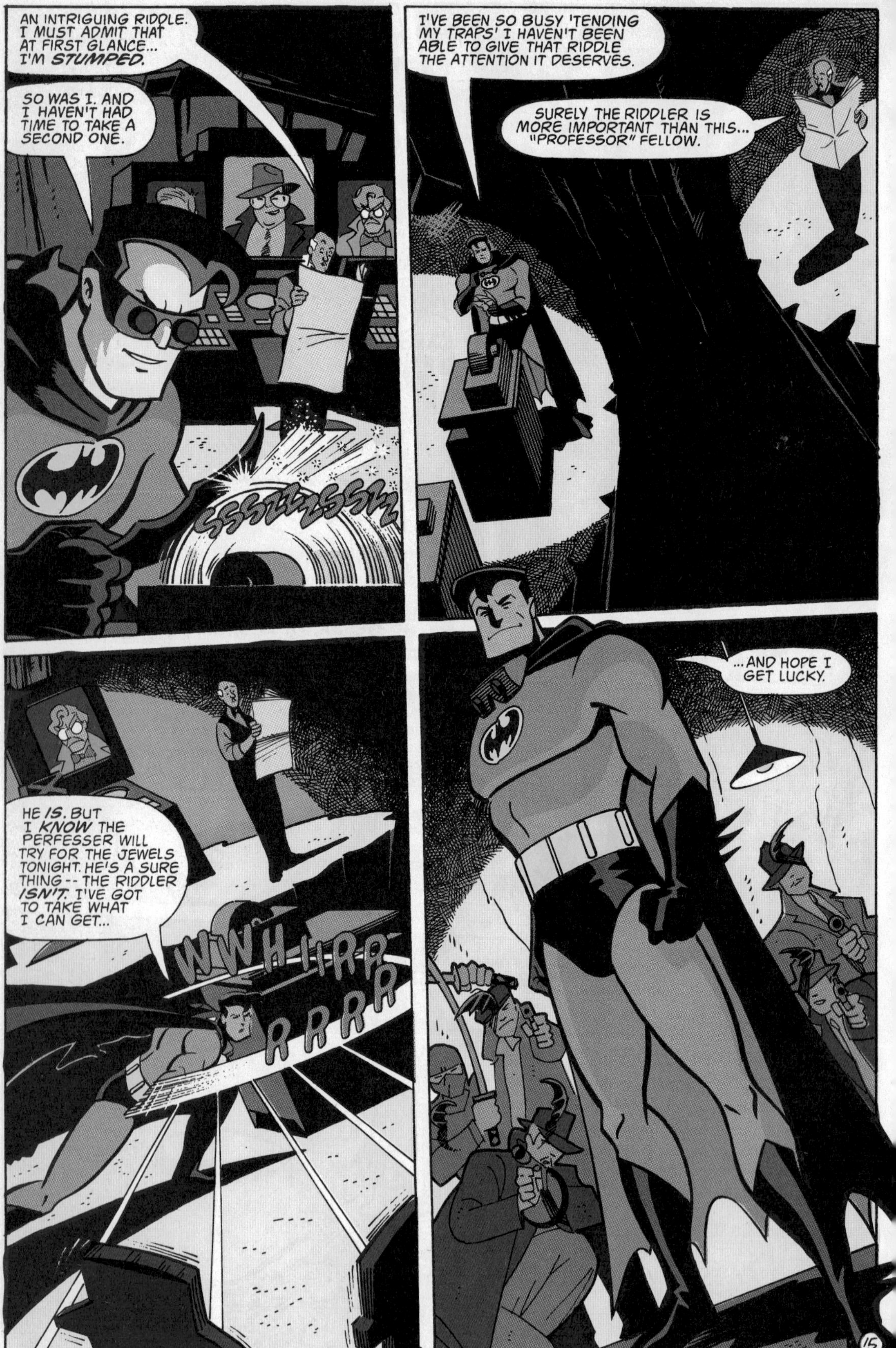
AN INTRIGUING RIDDLE. I MUST ADMIT THAT AT FIRST GLANCE... I'M STUMPED.
SO WAS I. AND I HAVEN'T HAD TIME TO TAKE A SECOND ONE.
SSSZZZSSSZZ
I'VE BEEN SO BUSY 'TENDING MY TRAPS' I HAVEN'T BEEN ABLE TO GIVE THAT RIDDLE THE ATTENTION IT DESERVES.
SURELY THE RIDDLER IS MORE IMPORTANT THAN THIS... "PROFESSOR" FELLOW.
HE IS. BUT I KNOW THE PERFESSER WILL TRY FOR THE JEWELS TONIGHT. HE'S A SURE THING -- THE RIDDLER ISN'T. I'VE GOT TO TAKE WHAT I CAN GET...
WWHIIRRRRRR
...AND HOPE I GET LUCKY.
15

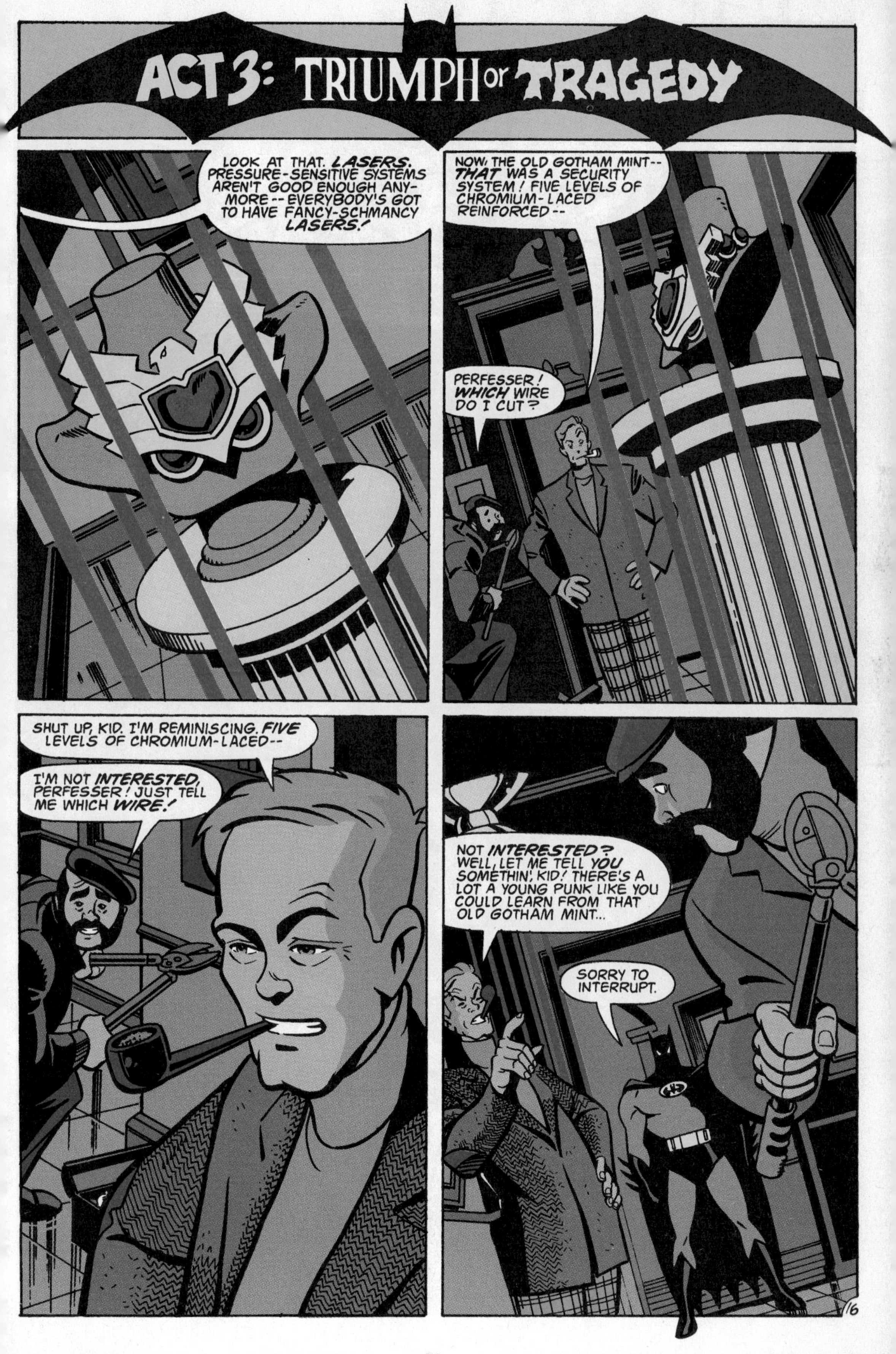
ACT 3: TRIUMPH or TRAGEDY
LOOK AT THAT. LASERS. PRESSURE-SENSITIVE SYSTEMS AREN'T GOOD ENOUGH ANY-MORE -- EVERYBODY'S GOT TO HAVE FANCY-SCHMANCY LASERS!
NOW, THE OLD GOTHAM MINT-- THAT WAS A SECURITY SYSTEM! FIVE LEVELS OF CHROMIUM-LACED REINFORCED --
PERFESSER! WHICH WIRE DO I CUT?
SHUT UP, KID. I'M REMINISCING. FIVE LEVELS OF CHROMIUM-LACED--
I'M NOT INTERESTED, PERFESSER! JUST TELL ME WHICH WIRE!
NOT INTERESTED? WELL, LET ME TELL YOU SOMETHIN', KID! THERE'S A LOT A YOUNG PUNK LIKE YOU COULD LEARN FROM THAT OLD GOTHAM MINT...
SORRY TO INTERRUPT.
16

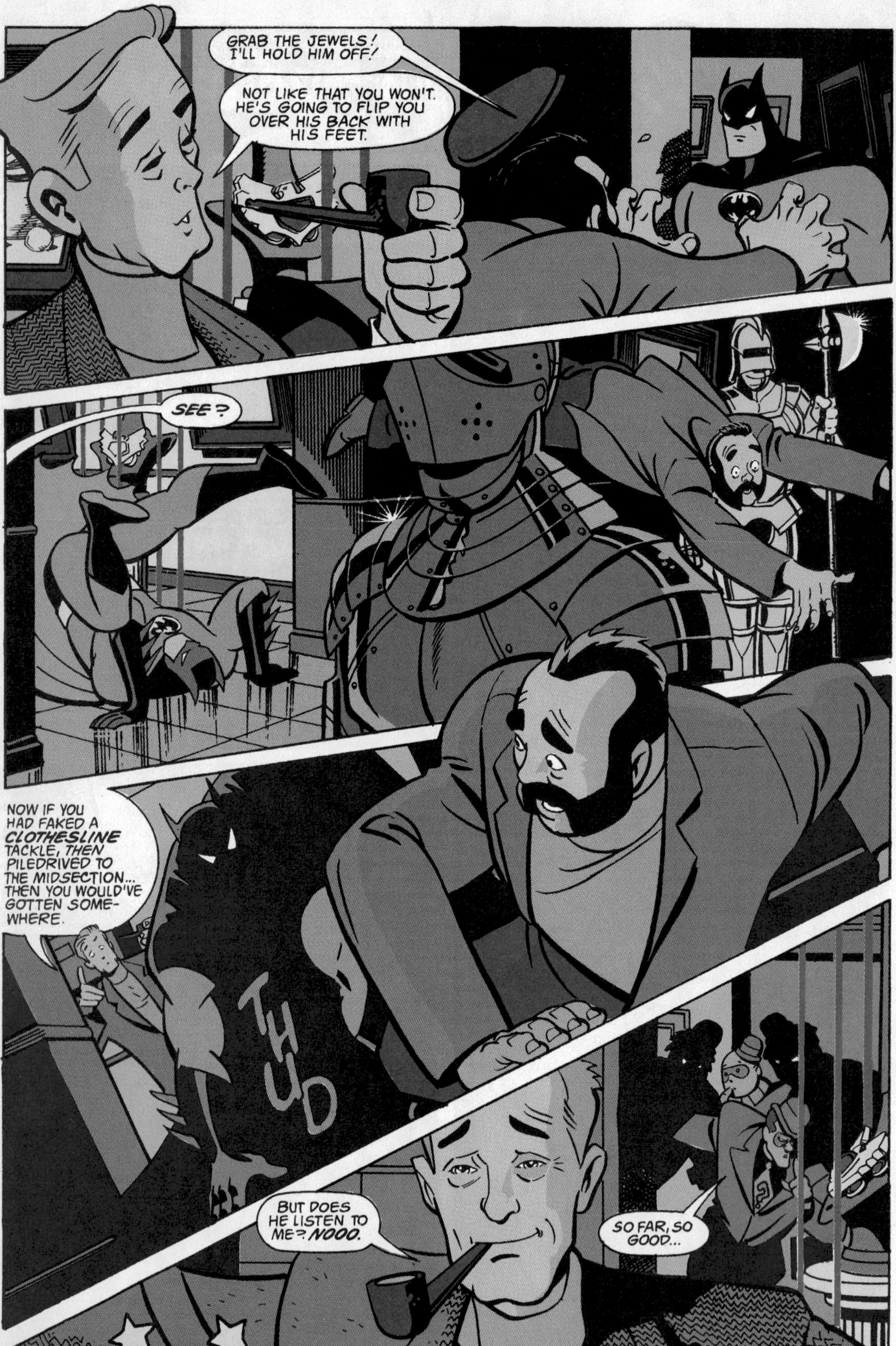
GRAB THE JEWELS! I'LL HOLD HIM OFF!
NOT LIKE THAT YOU WON'T. HE'S GOING TO FLIP YOU OVER HIS BACK WITH HIS FEET.
SEE?
NOW IF YOU HAD FAKED A CLOTHESLINE TACKLE, THEN PILEDRIVED TO THE MIDSECTION... THEN YOU WOULD'VE GOTTEN SOME-WHERE.
THUD
BUT DOES HE LISTEN TO ME? NOOO.
SO FAR, SO GOOD...
17

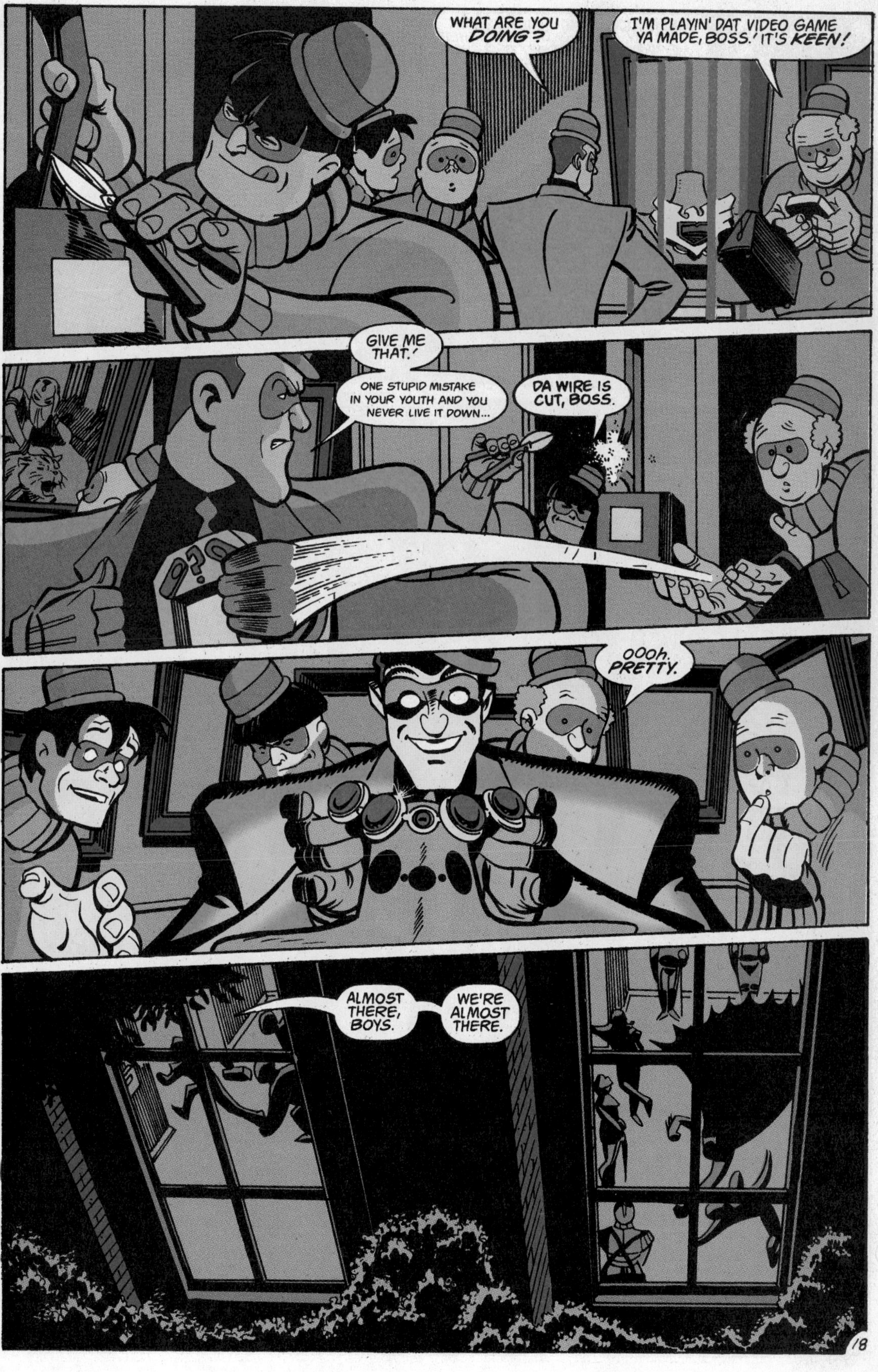
WHAT ARE YOU DOING?
I'M PLAYIN' DAT VIDEO GAME YA MADE, BOSS.' IT'S KEEN!
GIVE ME THAT.'
ONE STUPID MISTAKE IN YOUR YOUTH AND YOU NEVER LIVE IT DOWN...
DA WIRE IS CUT, BOSS.
oooh. PRETTY.
ALMOST THERE, BOYS.
WE'RE ALMOST THERE.
18

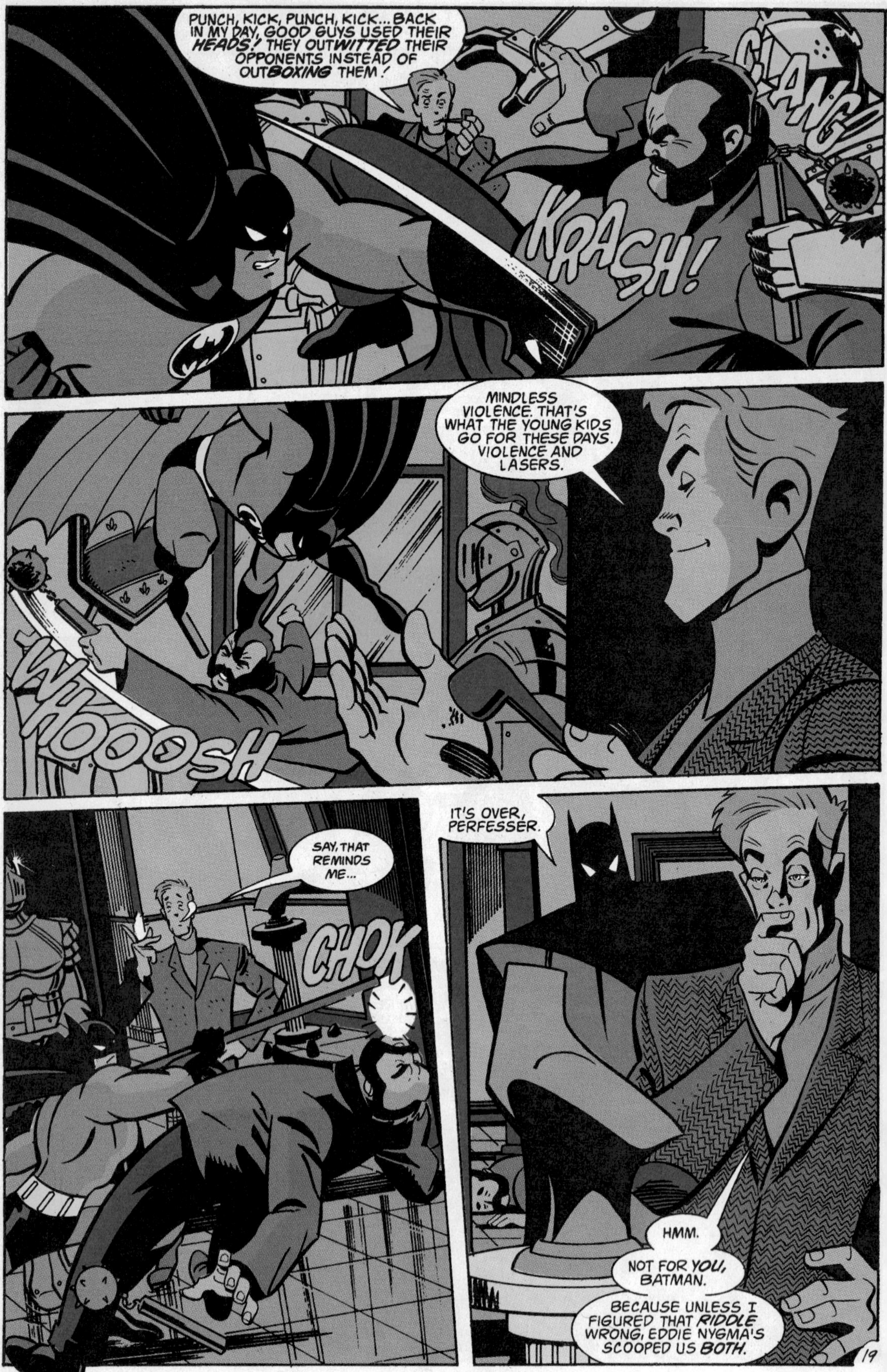
PUNCH, KICK, PUNCH, KICK... BACK IN MY DAY, GOOD GUYS USED THEIR HEADS! THEY OUTWITTED THEIR OPPONENTS INSTEAD OF OUTBOXING THEM!
CLANG!
KRASH!
MINDLESS VIOLENCE. THAT'S WHAT THE YOUNG KIDS GO FOR THESE DAYS. VIOLENCE AND LASERS.
WHOOOSH
SAY, THAT REMINDS ME...
CHOK
IT'S OVER, PERFESSER.
HMM.
NOT FOR YOU, BATMAN.
BECAUSE UNLESS I FIGURED THAT RIDDLE WRONG, EDDIE NYGMA'S SCOOPED US BOTH.
19

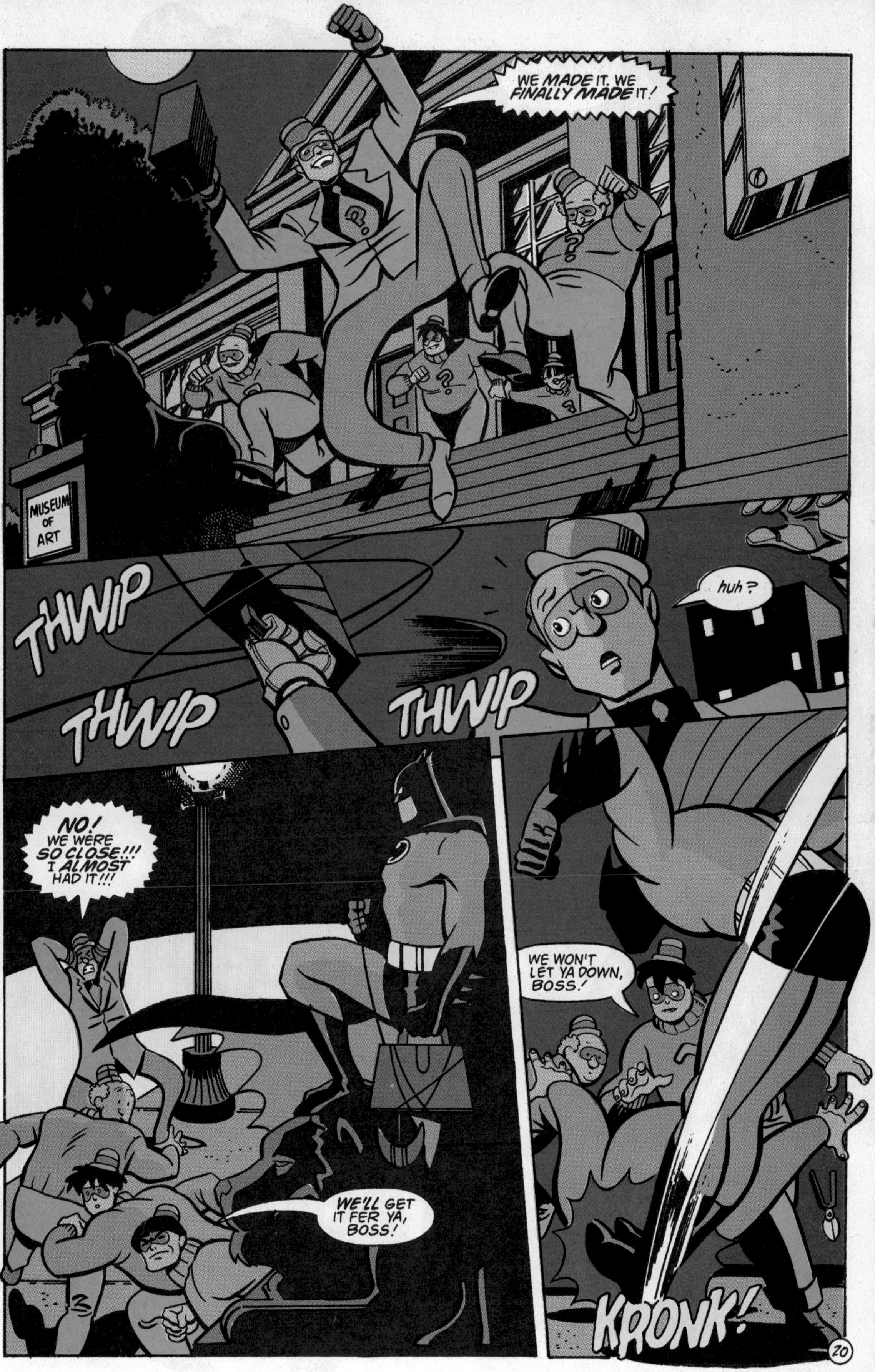
WE MADE IT. WE FINALLY MADE IT!
MUSEUM OF ART
THWIP
THWIP
THWIP
huh?
NO! WE WERE SO CLOSE!!! I ALMOST HAD IT!!!
WE'LL GET IT FER YA, BOSS!
WE WON'T LET YA DOWN, BOSS!
KRONK!
20

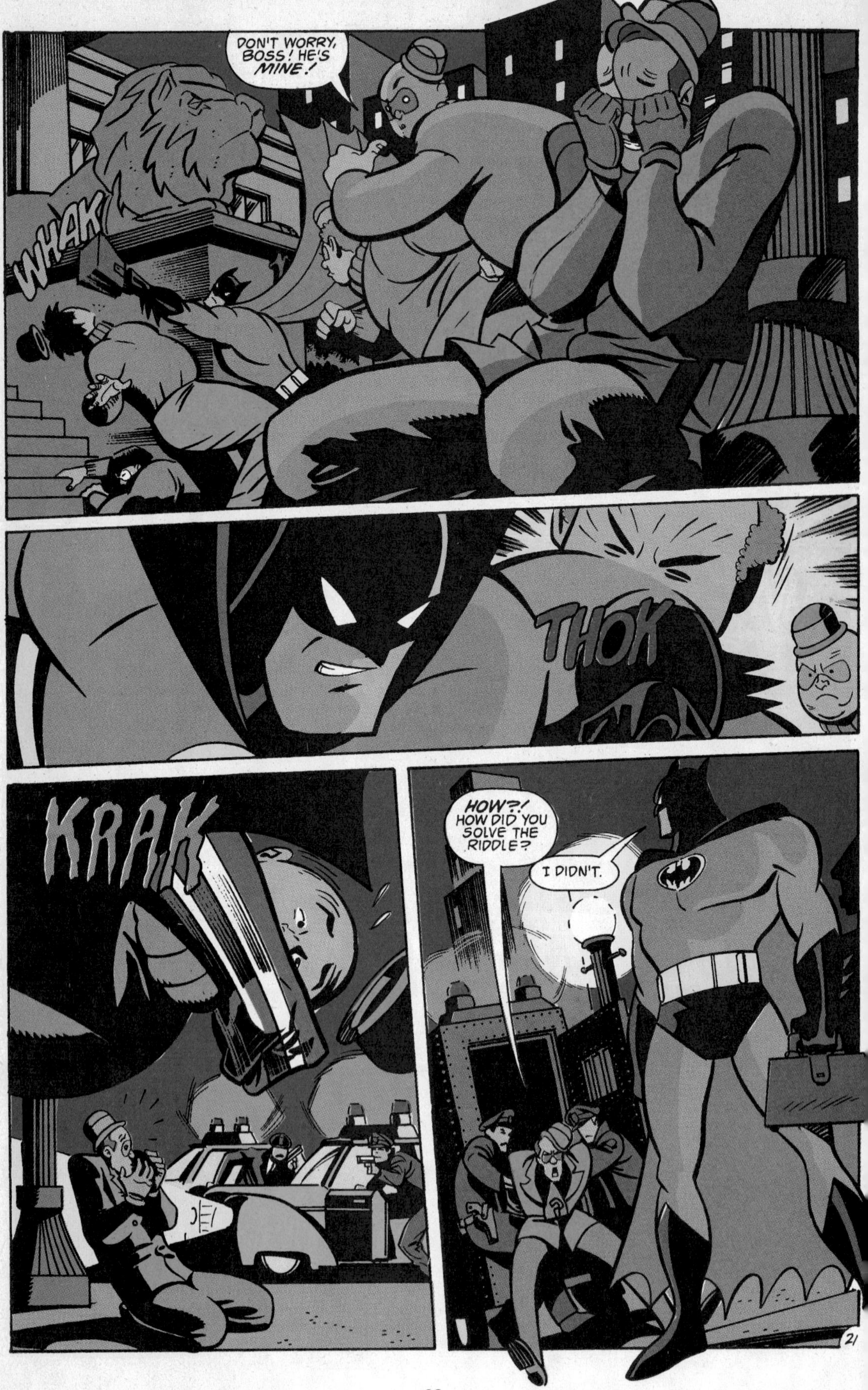
DON'T WORRY, BOSS! HE'S MINE!
WHAK
THOK
KRAK
HOW?! HOW DID YOU SOLVE THE RIDDLE?
I DIDN'T.
21

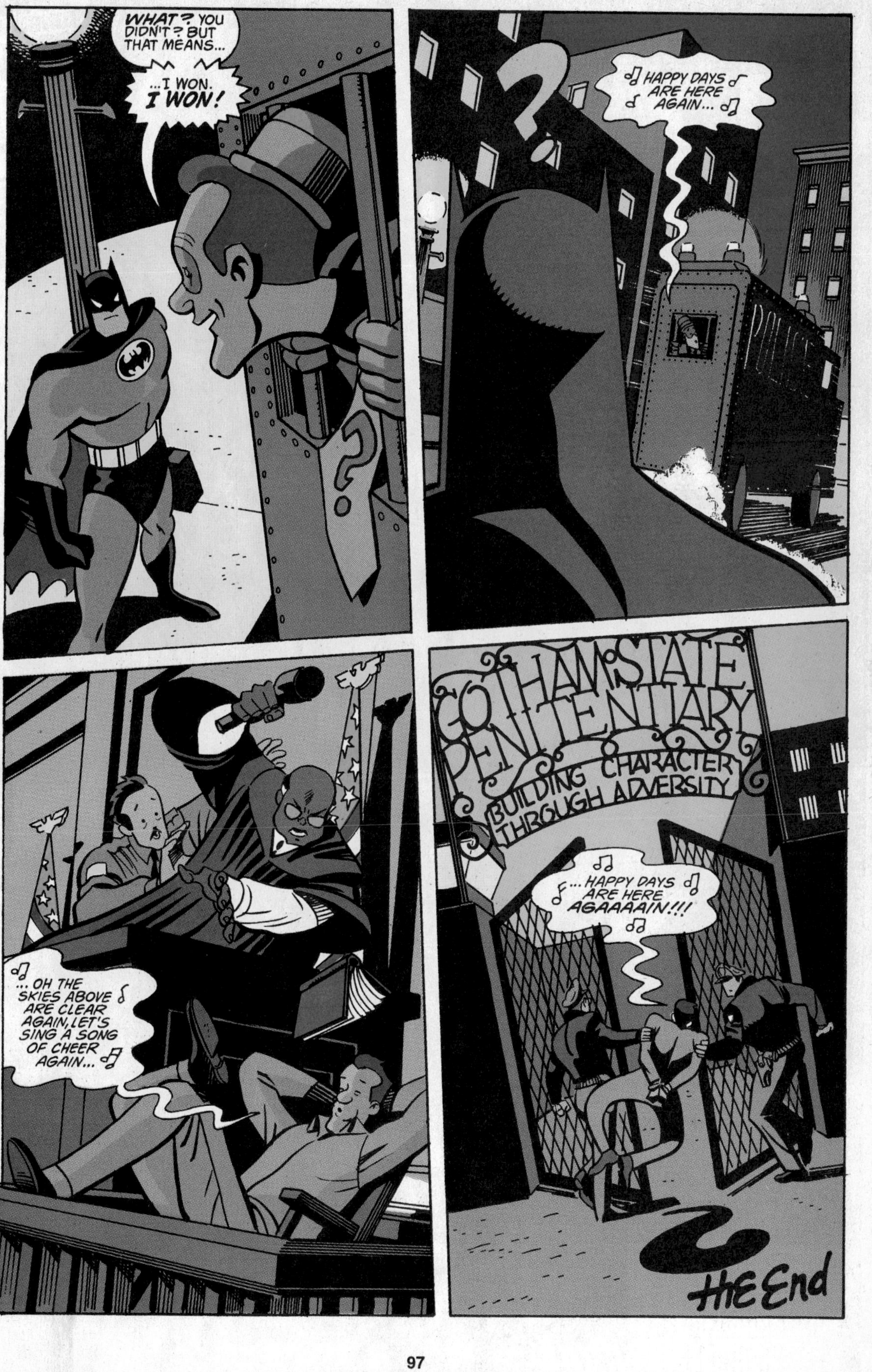
WHAT? YOU DIDN'T? BUT THAT MEANS...
...I WON. I WON!
HAPPY DAYS ARE HERE AGAIN...
...OH THE SKIES ABOVE ARE CLEAR AGAIN, LET'S SING A SONG OF CHEER AGAIN...
GOTHAM STATE PENITENTIARY
BUILDING CHARACTER THROUGH ADVERSITY
...HAPPY DAYS ARE HERE AGAAAAIN!!!
THE END

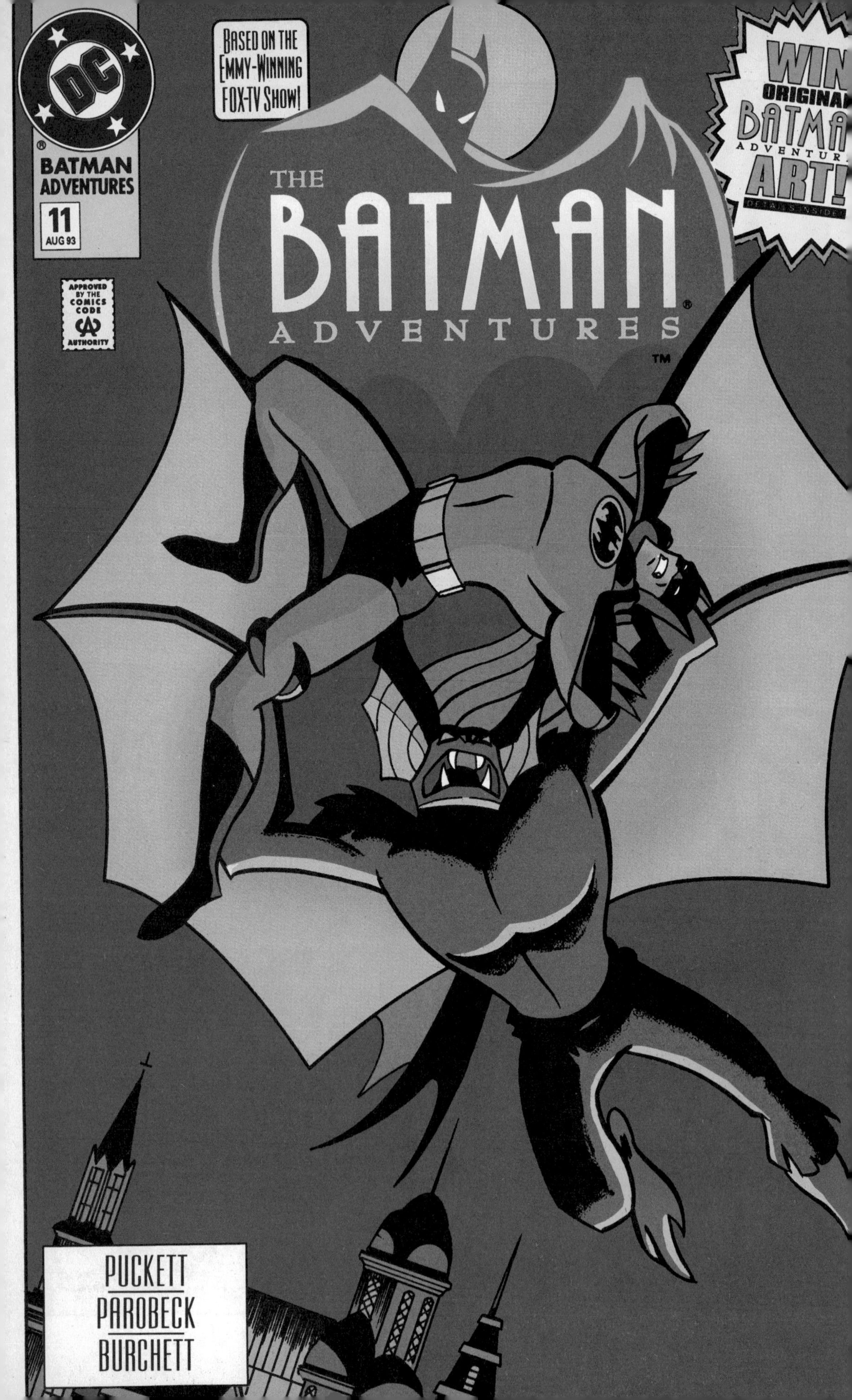
BATMAN ADVENTURES
11
AUG 93
APPROVED BY THE COMICS CODE AUTHORITY
BASED ON THE EMMY-WINNING FOX-TV SHOW!
THE BATMAN ADVENTURES
WIN
ART!
PUCKETT
PAROBECK
BURCHETT

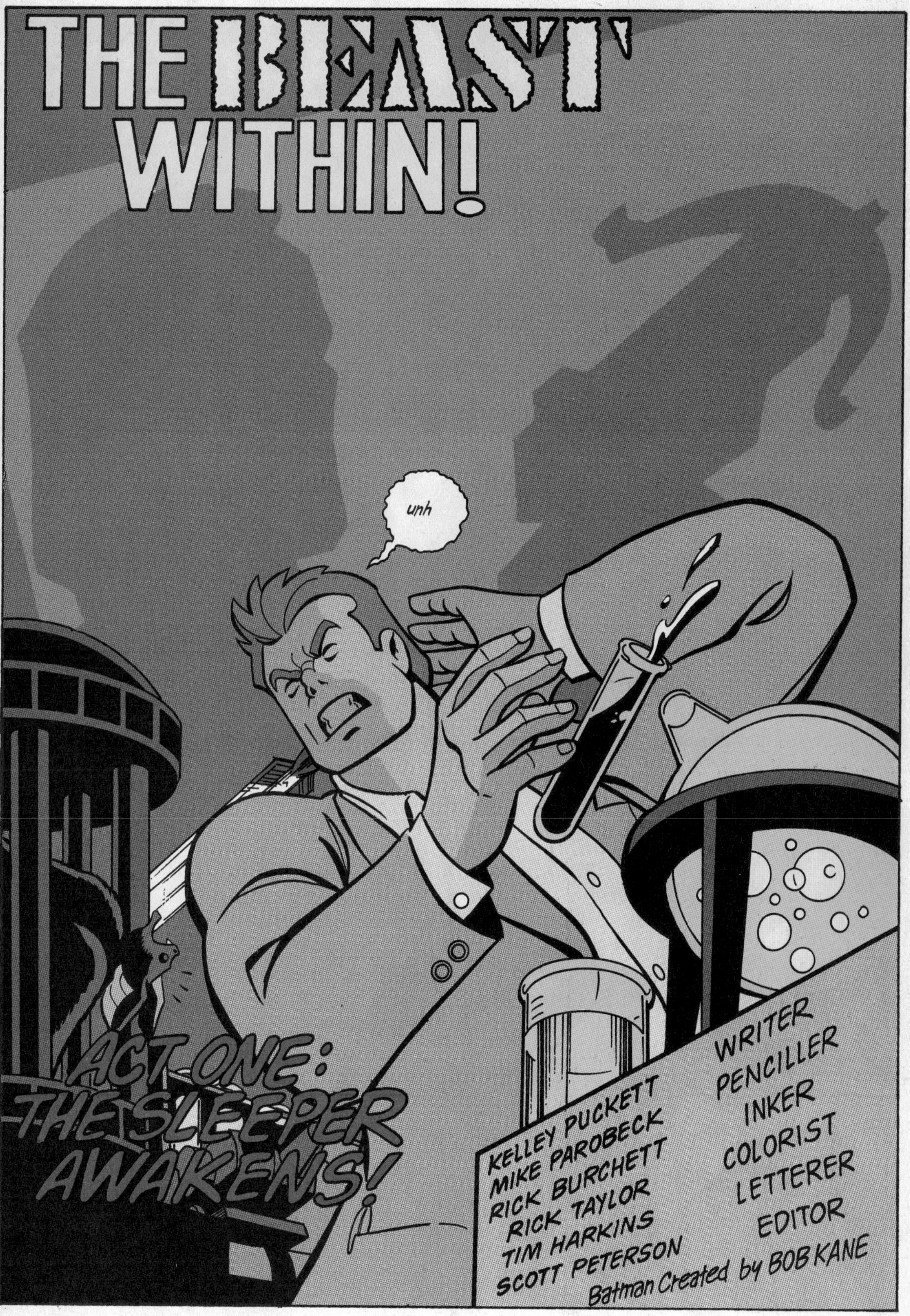
THE BEAST WITHIN!
unh
ACT ONE: THE SLEEPER AWAKENS!
KELLEY PUCKETT WRITER
MIKE PAROBECK PENCILLER
RICK BURCHETT INKER
RICK TAYLOR COLORIST
TIM HARKINS LETTERER
SCOTT PETERSON EDITOR
Batman Created by BOB KANE

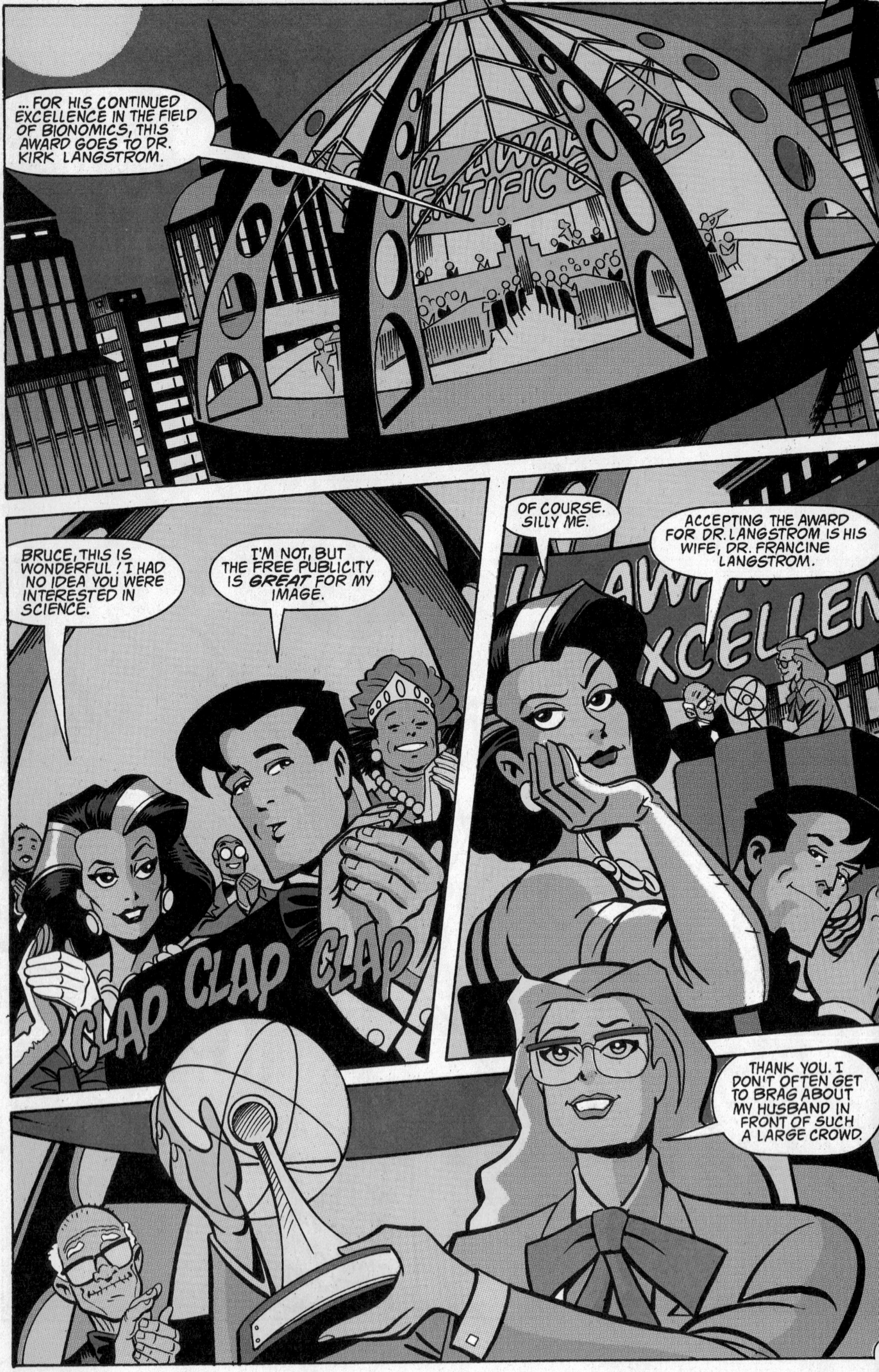
...FOR HIS CONTINUED EXCELLENCE IN THE FIELD OF BIONOMICS, THIS AWARD GOES TO DR. KIRK LANGSTROM.
BRUCE, THIS IS WONDERFUL! I HAD NO IDEA YOU WERE INTERESTED IN SCIENCE.
I'M NOT, BUT THE FREE PUBLICITY IS GREAT FOR MY IMAGE.
CLAP CLAP CLAP
OF COURSE. SILLY ME.
ACCEPTING THE AWARD FOR DR. LANGSTROM IS HIS WIFE, DR. FRANCINE LANGSTROM.
EXCELLEN
THANK YOU. I DON'T OFTEN GET TO BRAG ABOUT MY HUSBAND IN FRONT OF SUCH A LARGE CROWD.

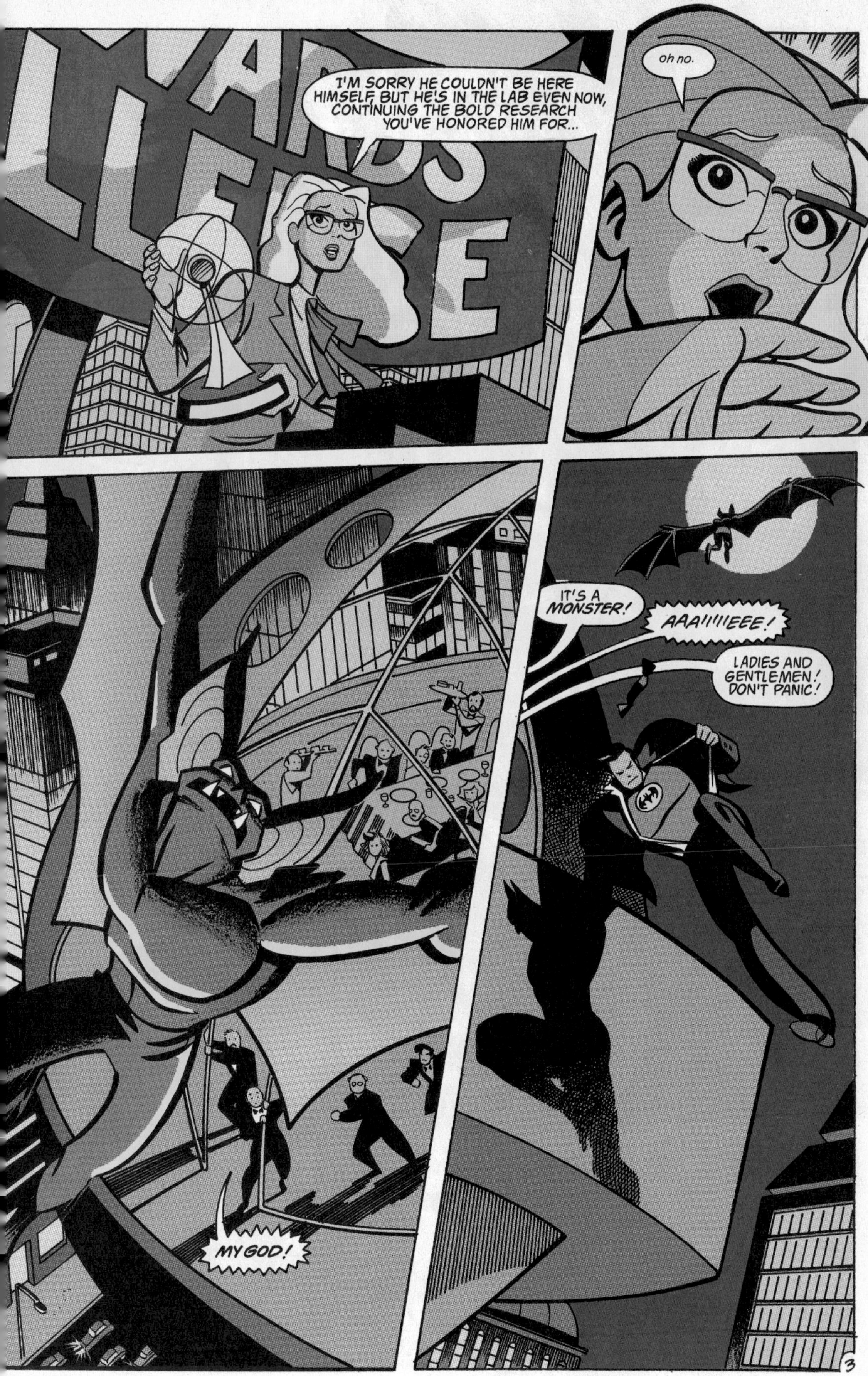
I'M SORRY HE COULDN'T BE HERE HIMSELF, BUT HE'S IN THE LAB EVEN NOW, CONTINUING THE BOLD RESEARCH YOU'VE HONORED HIM FOR...
oh no.
IT'S A MONSTER!
AAA!!!!EEE!
LADIES AND GENTLEMEN! DON'T PANIC!
MY GOD!
3

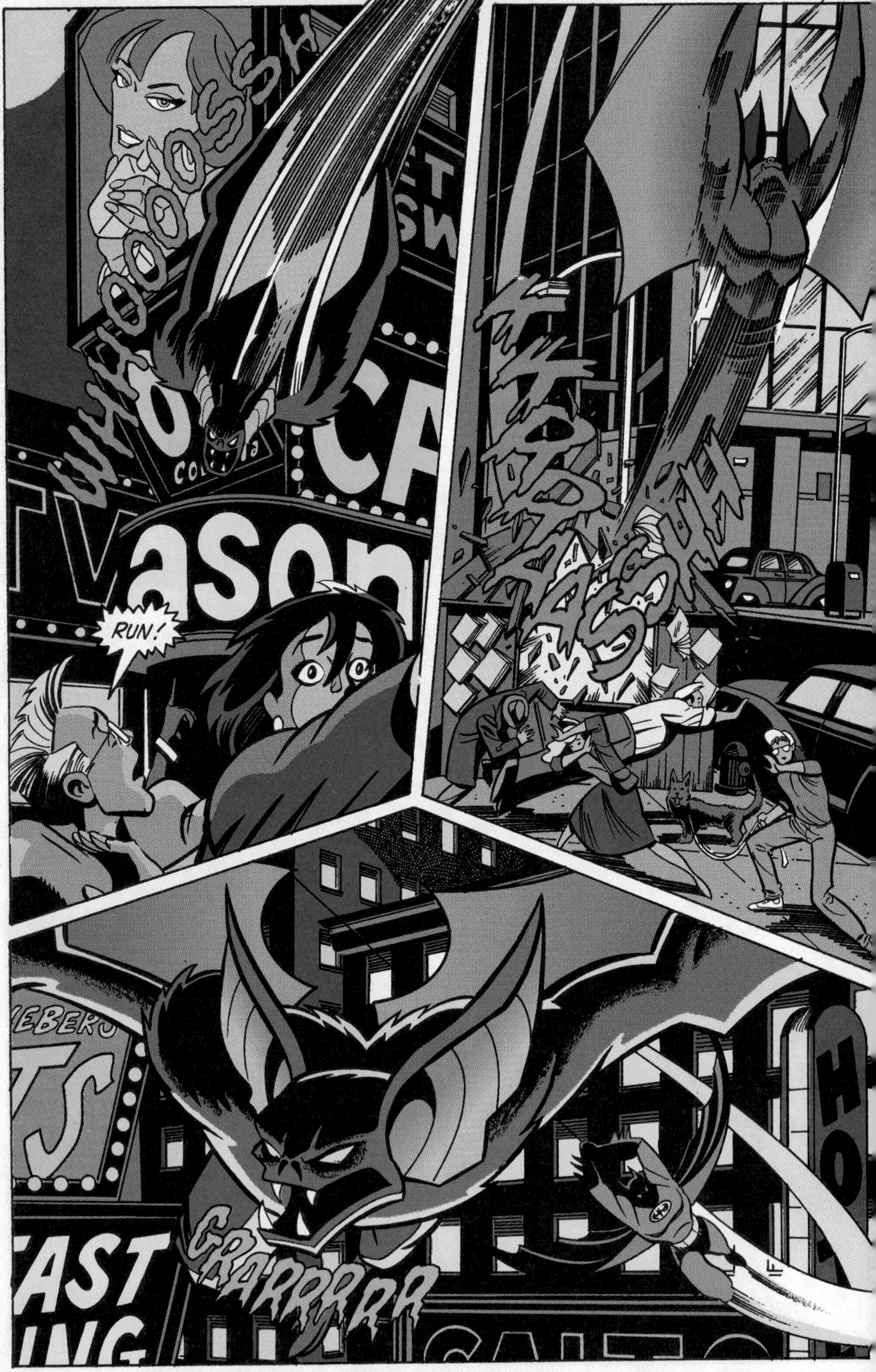
WHOOOOOOSH
RUN!
GRARRRRR

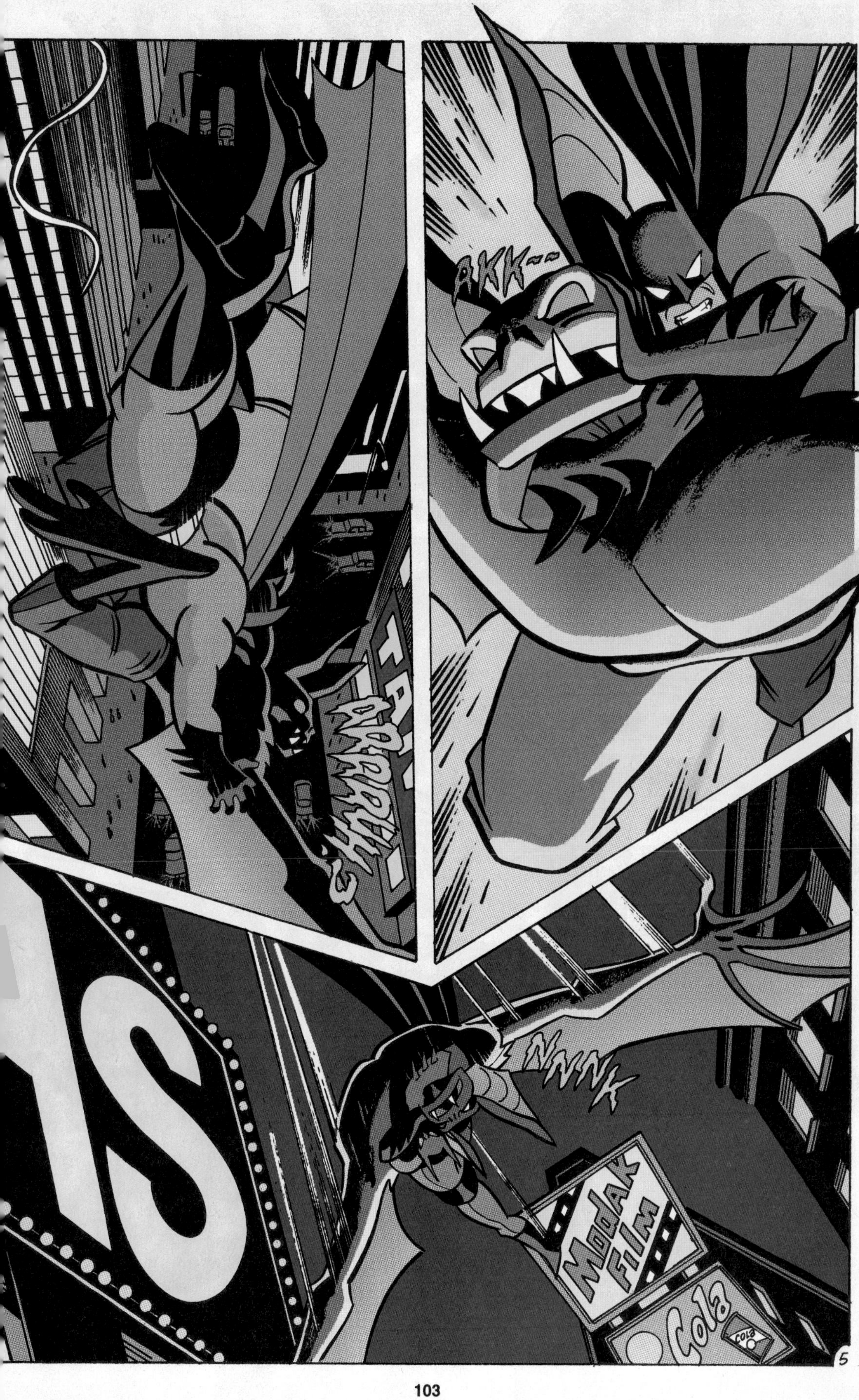
AKK--
NNNK
Modak Film
Cola
5

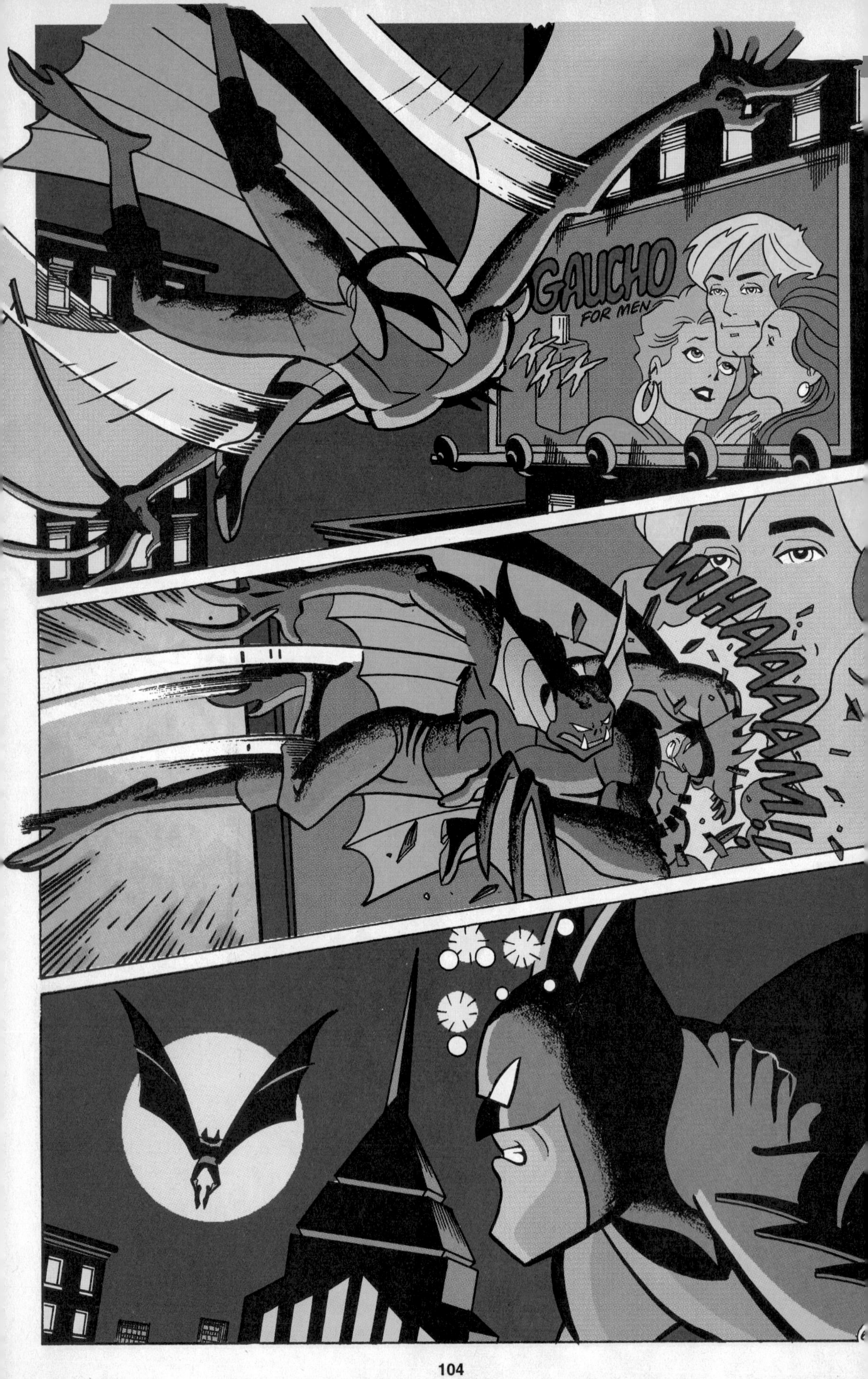
GAUCHO
FOR MEN
WHHAAAAAM!!

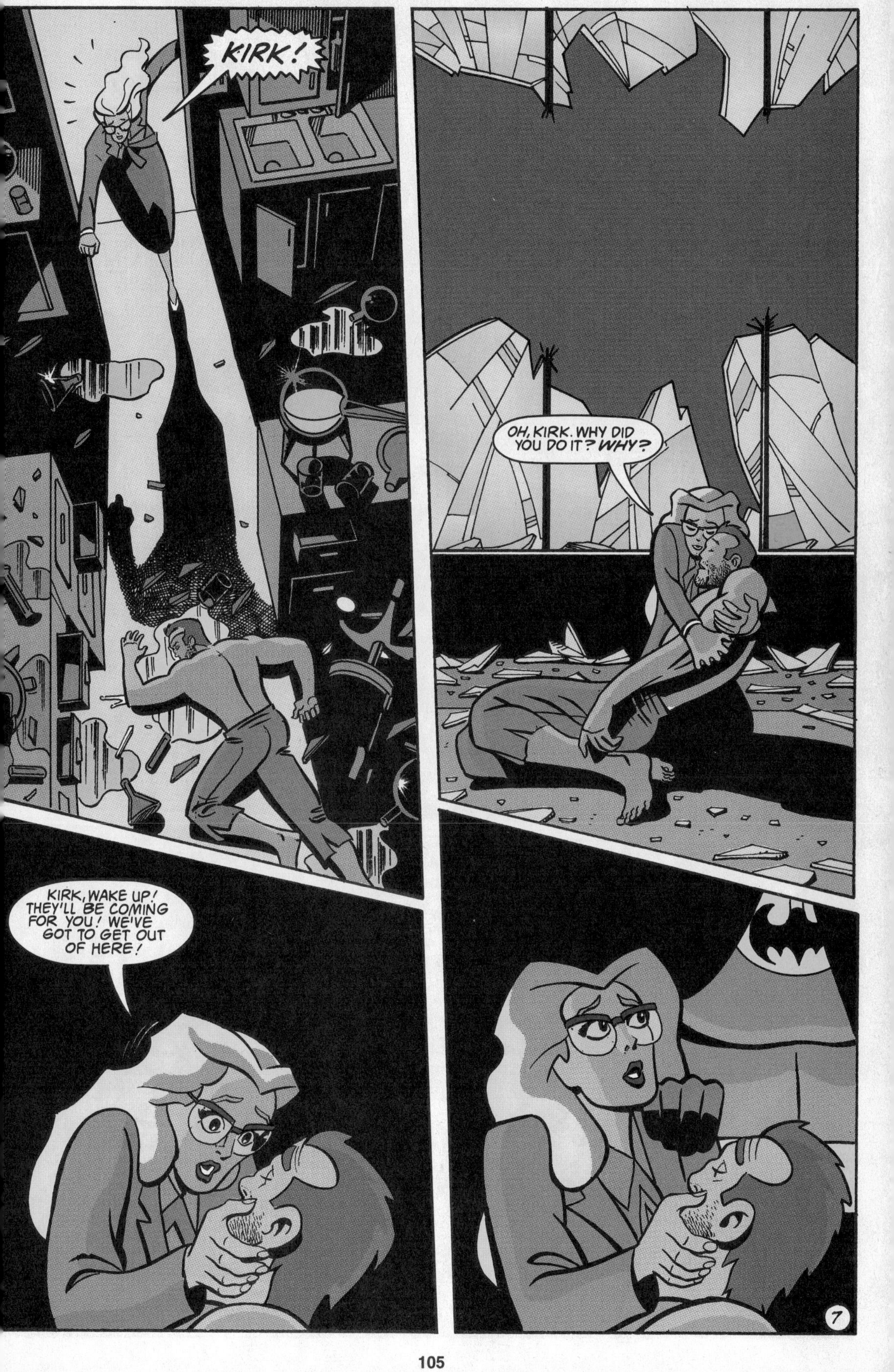
KIRK!
OH, KIRK. WHY DID YOU DO IT? WHY?
KIRK, WAKE UP! THEY'LL BE COMING FOR YOU! WE'VE GOT TO GET OUT OF HERE!
7

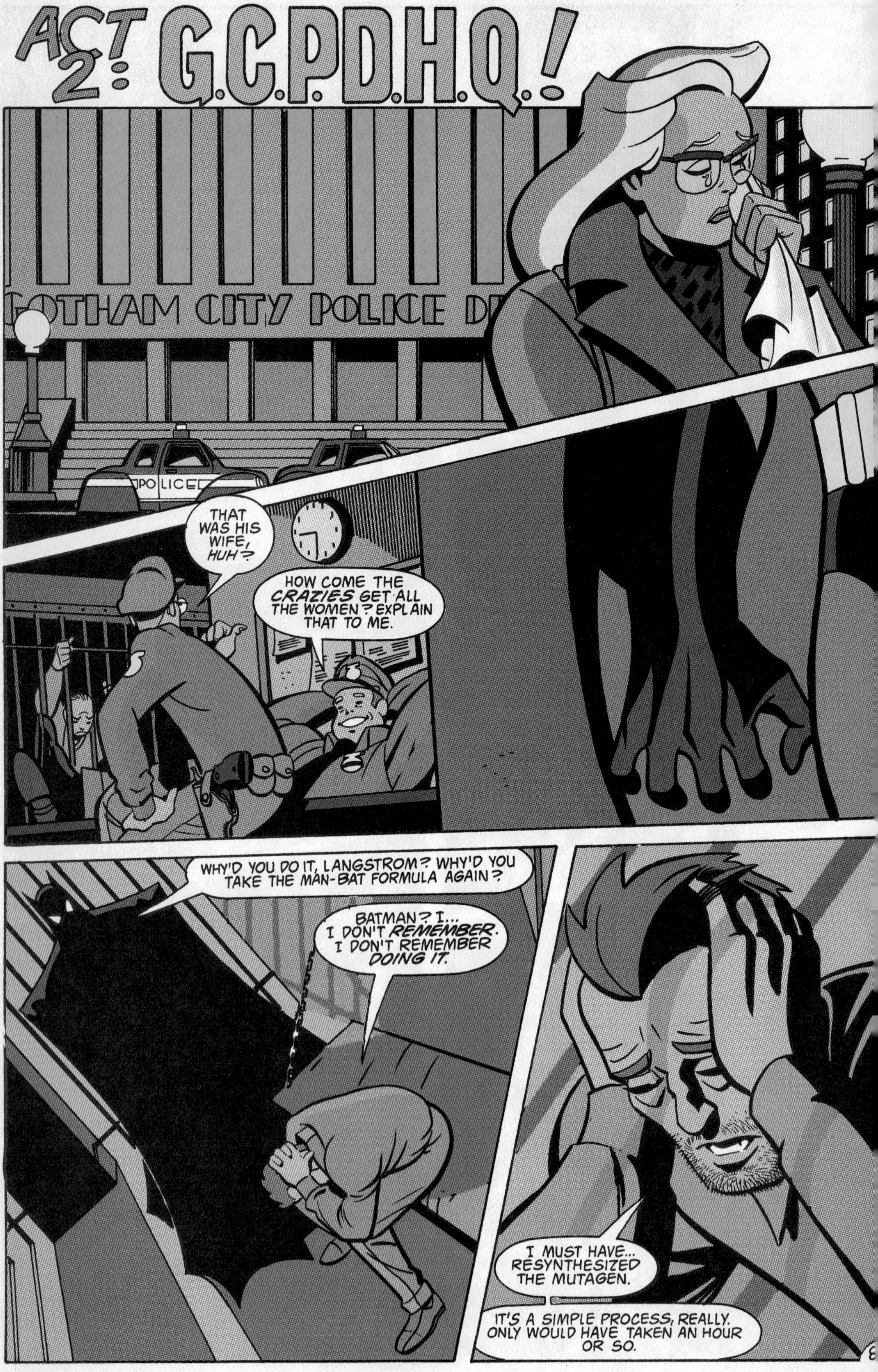
ACT 2: G.C.P.D.H.Q.!
GOTHAM CITY POLICE DE
POLICE
THAT WAS HIS WIFE, *HUH?*
HOW COME THE *CRAZIES* GET ALL THE WOMEN? EXPLAIN THAT TO ME.
WHY'D YOU DO IT, LANGSTROM? WHY'D YOU TAKE THE MAN-BAT FORMULA AGAIN?
BATMAN? I... I DON'T *REMEMBER*. I DON'T REMEMBER *DOING IT.*
I MUST HAVE... RESYNTHESIZED THE MUTAGEN.
IT'S A SIMPLE PROCESS, REALLY. ONLY WOULD HAVE TAKEN AN HOUR OR SO.
8

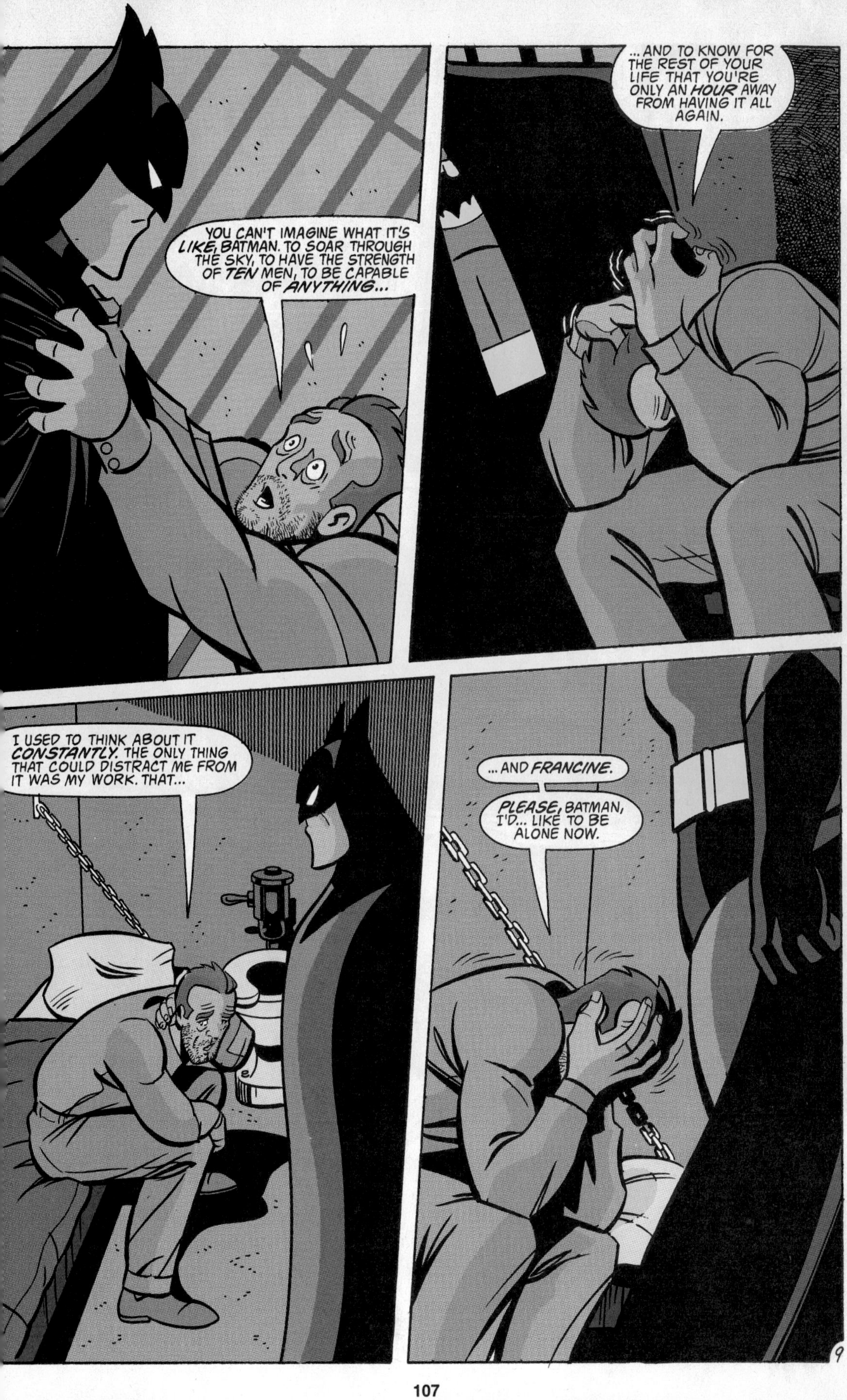

YOU CAN'T IMAGINE WHAT IT'S LIKE, BATMAN. TO SOAR THROUGH THE SKY, TO HAVE THE STRENGTH OF TEN MEN, TO BE CAPABLE OF ANYTHING...
... AND TO KNOW FOR THE REST OF YOUR LIFE THAT YOU'RE ONLY AN HOUR AWAY FROM HAVING IT ALL AGAIN.
I USED TO THINK ABOUT IT CONSTANTLY. THE ONLY THING THAT COULD DISTRACT ME FROM IT WAS MY WORK. THAT...
... AND FRANCINE.
PLEASE, BATMAN, I'D... LIKE TO BE ALONE NOW.
9

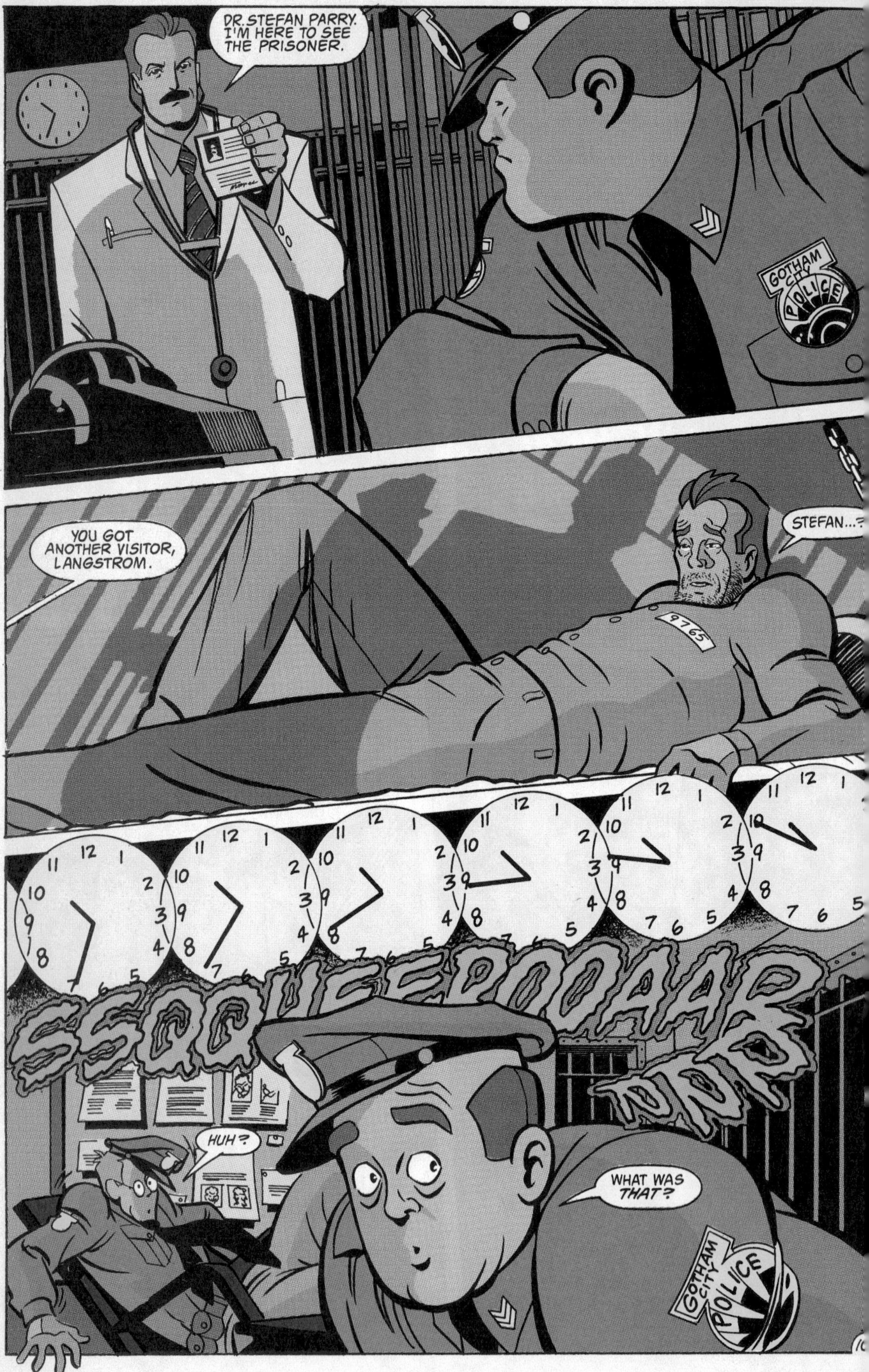
DR. STEFAN PARRY. I'M HERE TO SEE THE PRISONER.
YOU GOT ANOTHER VISITOR, LANGSTROM.
STEFAN...?
9765
HUH?
WHAT WAS THAT?
GOTHAM CITY POLICE

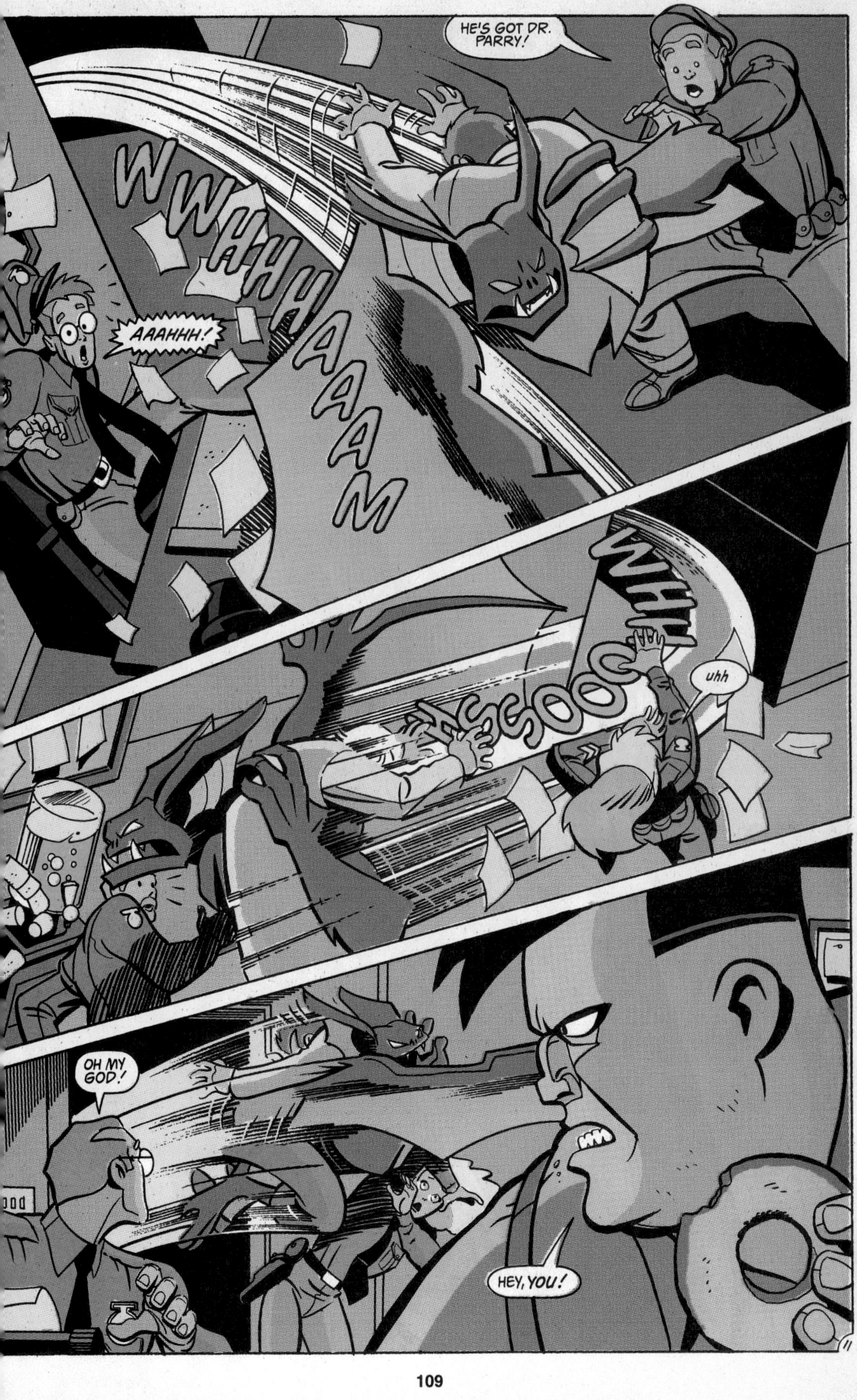
HE'S GOT DR. PARRY!
WWHHHAAAAM
AAAHHH!
WHOOSSH
uhh
OH MY GOD!
HEY, YOU!
11

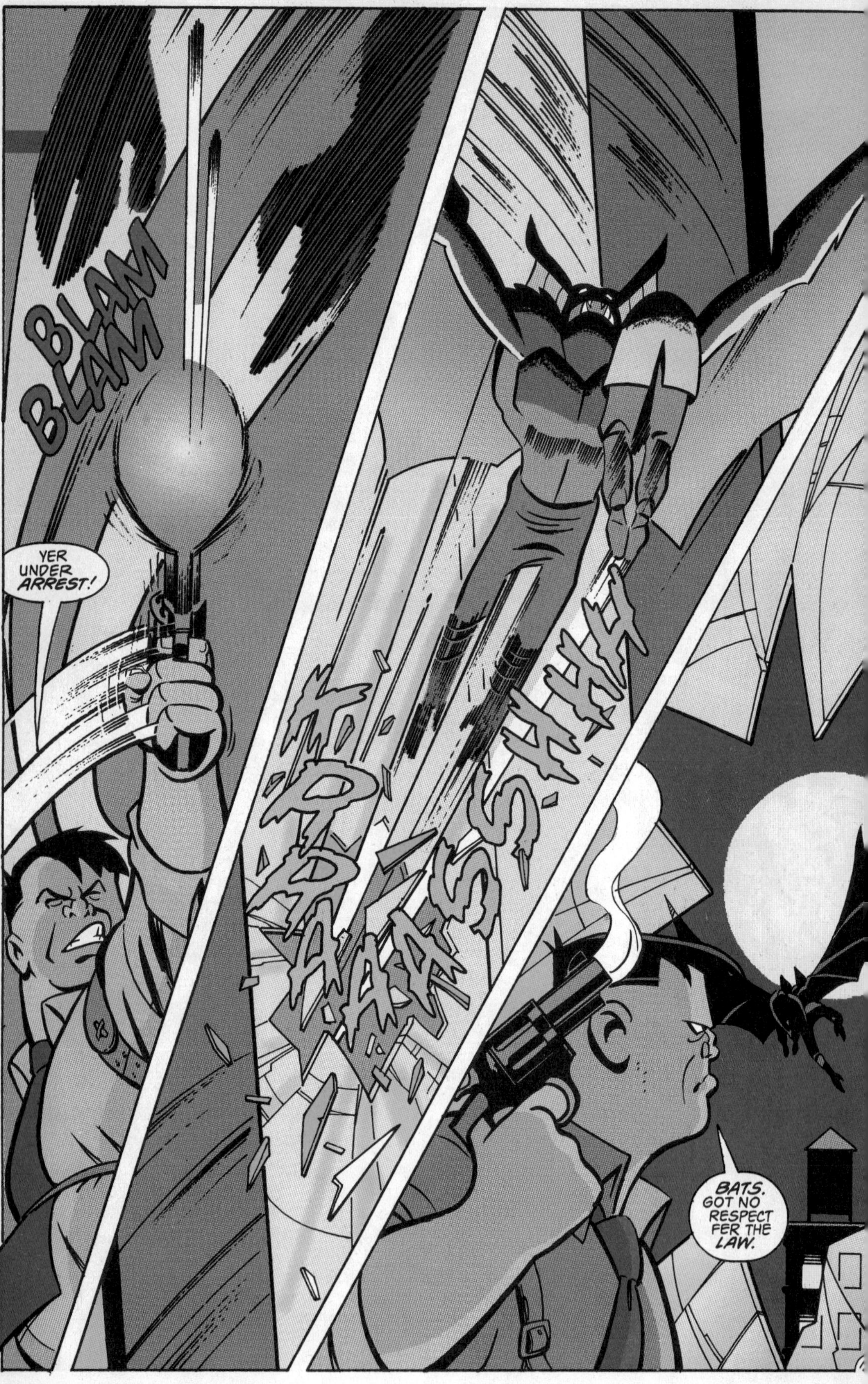
BLAM
BLAM
YER UNDER ARREST!
KRRAAASSHHH
BATS. GOT NO RESPECT FER THE LAW.

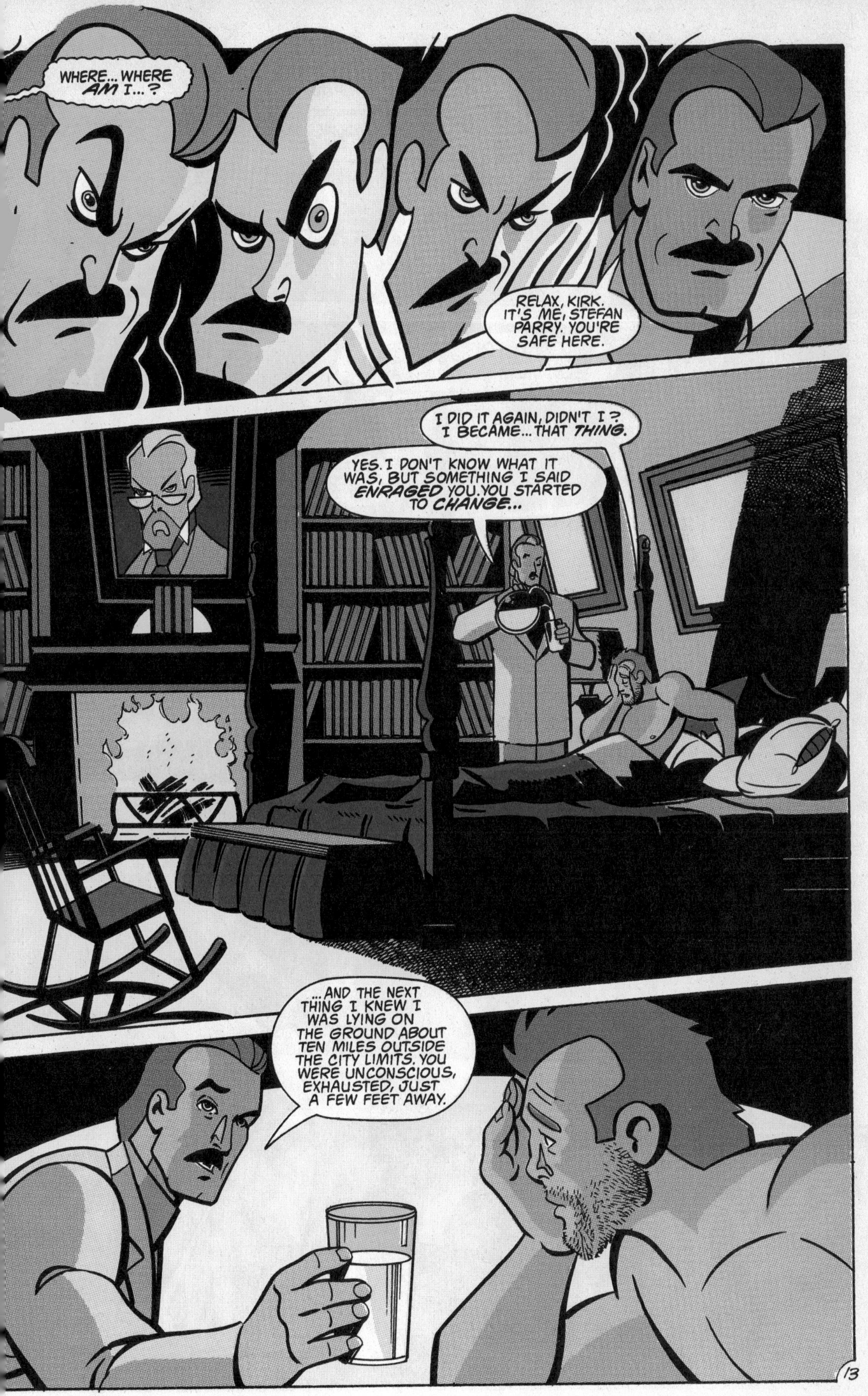
WHERE... WHERE AM I...?
RELAX, KIRK. IT'S ME, STEFAN PARRY. YOU'RE SAFE HERE.
I DID IT AGAIN, DIDN'T I? I BECAME... THAT THING.
YES. I DON'T KNOW WHAT IT WAS, BUT SOMETHING I SAID ENRAGED YOU. YOU STARTED TO CHANGE...
...AND THE NEXT THING I KNEW I WAS LYING ON THE GROUND ABOUT TEN MILES OUTSIDE THE CITY LIMITS. YOU WERE UNCONSCIOUS, EXHAUSTED, JUST A FEW FEET AWAY.
13

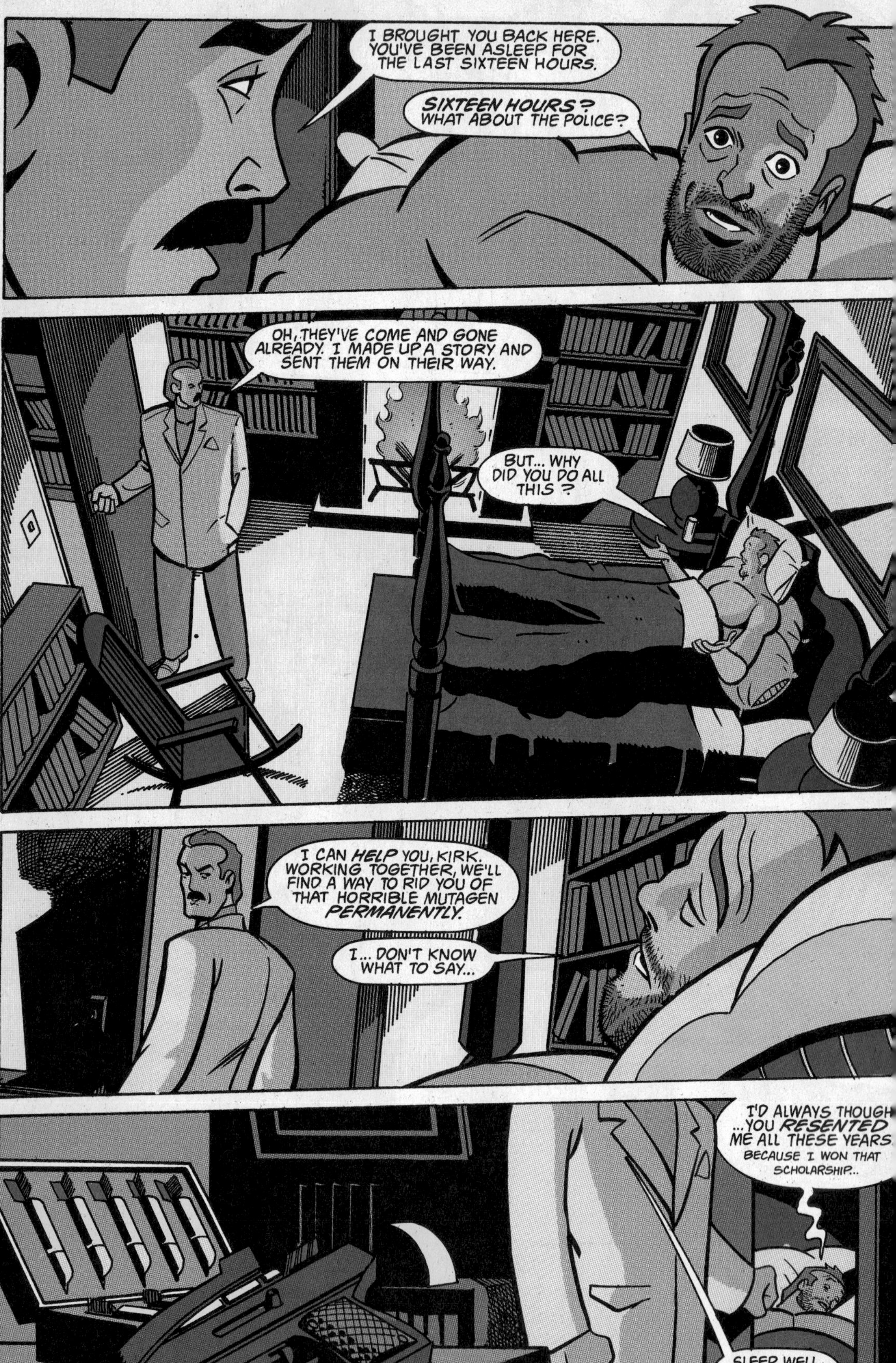
I BROUGHT YOU BACK HERE. YOU'VE BEEN ASLEEP FOR THE LAST SIXTEEN HOURS.
SIXTEEN HOURS? WHAT ABOUT THE POLICE?
OH, THEY'VE COME AND GONE ALREADY. I MADE UP A STORY AND SENT THEM ON THEIR WAY.
BUT... WHY DID YOU DO ALL THIS?
I CAN HELP YOU, KIRK. WORKING TOGETHER, WE'LL FIND A WAY TO RID YOU OF THAT HORRIBLE MUTAGEN PERMANENTLY.
I... DON'T KNOW WHAT TO SAY...
I'D ALWAYS THOUGH ...YOU RESENTED ME ALL THESE YEARS BECAUSE I WON THAT SCHOLARSHIP...
SLEEP WELL, LANGSTROM.

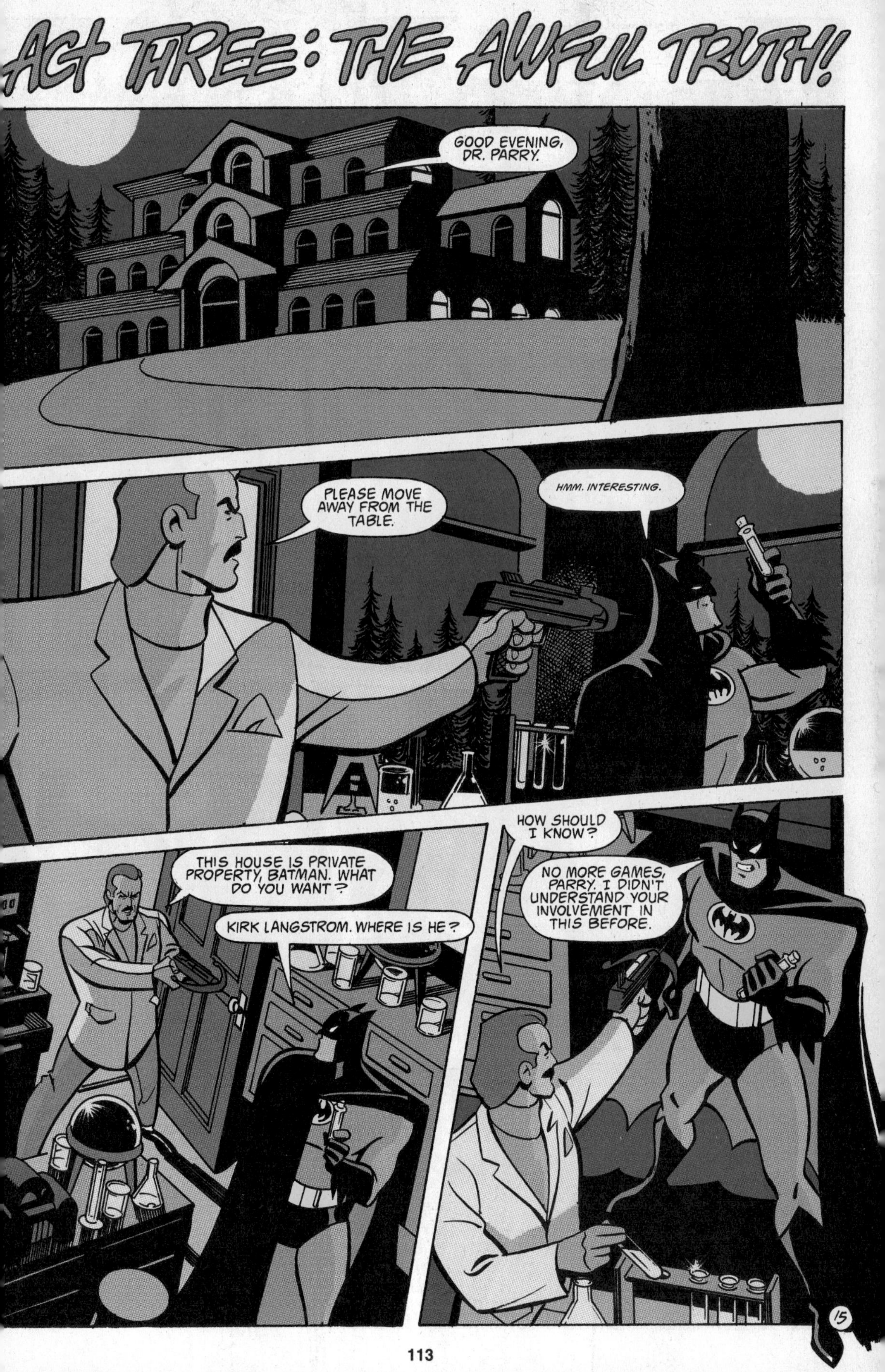
ACT THREE: THE AWFUL TRUTH!
GOOD EVENING, DR. PARRY.
PLEASE MOVE AWAY FROM THE TABLE.
HMM. INTERESTING.
THIS HOUSE IS PRIVATE PROPERTY, BATMAN. WHAT DO YOU WANT?
KIRK LANGSTROM. WHERE IS HE?
HOW SHOULD I KNOW?
NO MORE GAMES, PARRY. I DIDN'T UNDERSTAND YOUR INVOLVEMENT IN THIS BEFORE.
15

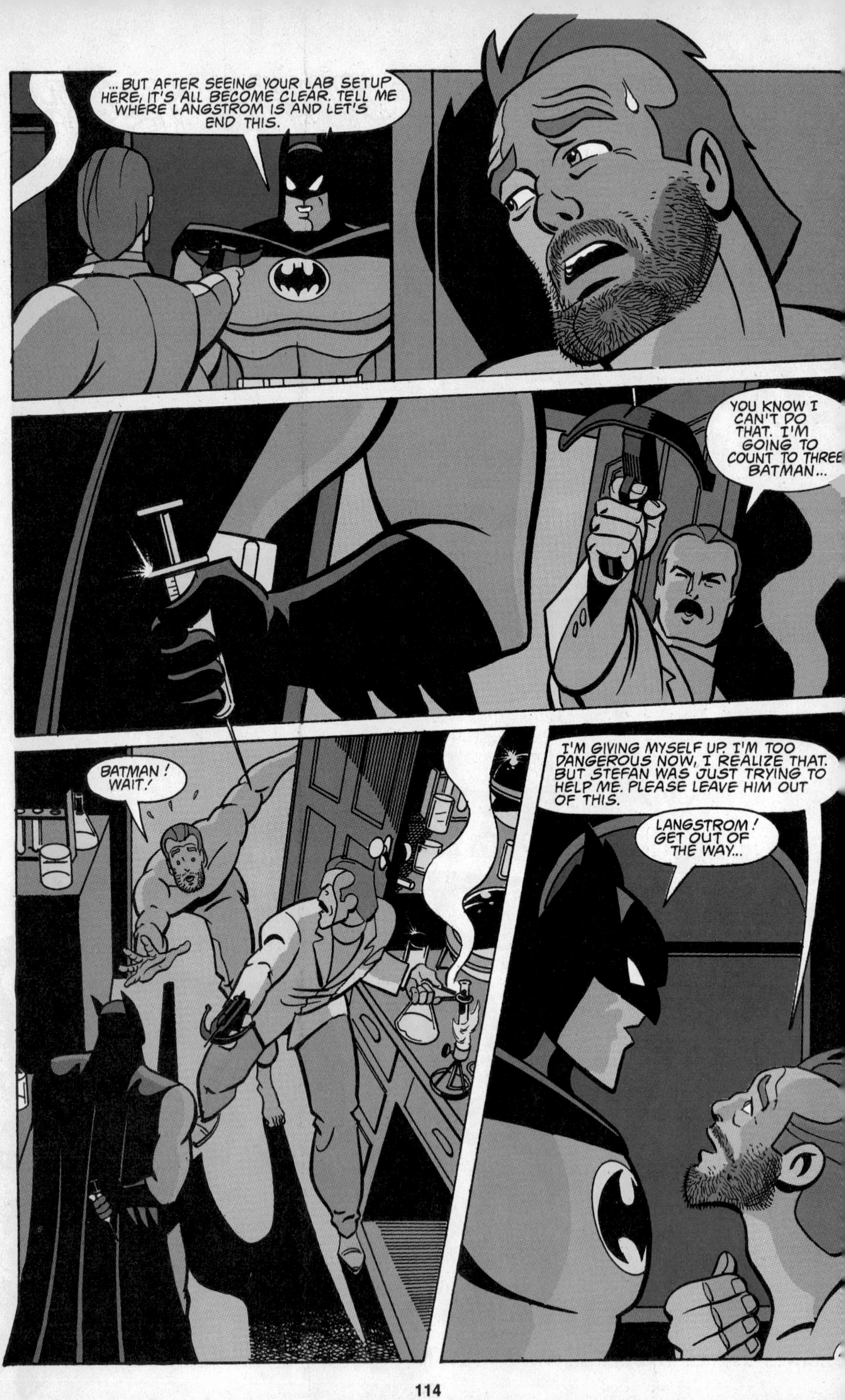

... BUT AFTER SEEING YOUR LAB SETUP HERE, IT'S ALL BECOME CLEAR. TELL ME WHERE LANGSTROM IS AND LET'S END THIS.
YOU KNOW I CAN'T DO THAT. I'M GOING TO COUNT TO THREE BATMAN...
BATMAN! WAIT!
I'M GIVING MYSELF UP. I'M TOO DANGEROUS NOW, I REALIZE THAT. BUT STEFAN WAS JUST TRYING TO HELP ME. PLEASE LEAVE HIM OUT OF THIS.
LANGSTROM! GET OUT OF THE WAY...

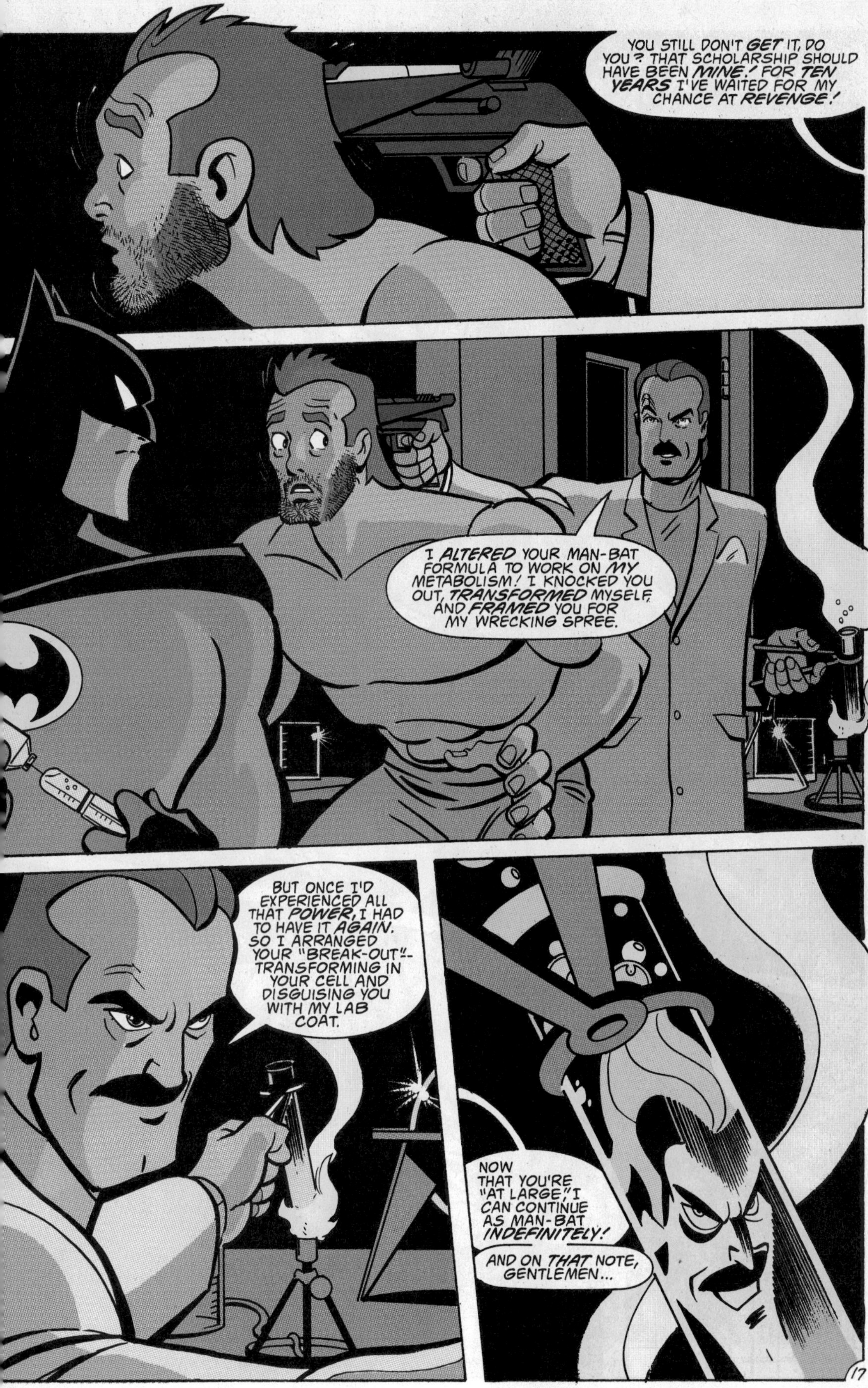
YOU STILL DON'T GET IT, DO YOU? THAT SCHOLARSHIP SHOULD HAVE BEEN MINE! FOR TEN YEARS I'VE WAITED FOR MY CHANCE AT REVENGE!
I ALTERED YOUR MAN-BAT FORMULA TO WORK ON MY METABOLISM! I KNOCKED YOU OUT, TRANSFORMED MYSELF, AND FRAMED YOU FOR MY WRECKING SPREE.
BUT ONCE I'D EXPERIENCED ALL THAT POWER, I HAD TO HAVE IT AGAIN. SO I ARRANGED YOUR "BREAK-OUT"-- TRANSFORMING IN YOUR CELL AND DISGUISING YOU WITH MY LAB COAT.
NOW THAT YOU'RE "AT LARGE," I CAN CONTINUE AS MAN-BAT INDEFINITELY!
AND ON THAT NOTE, GENTLEMEN...
17

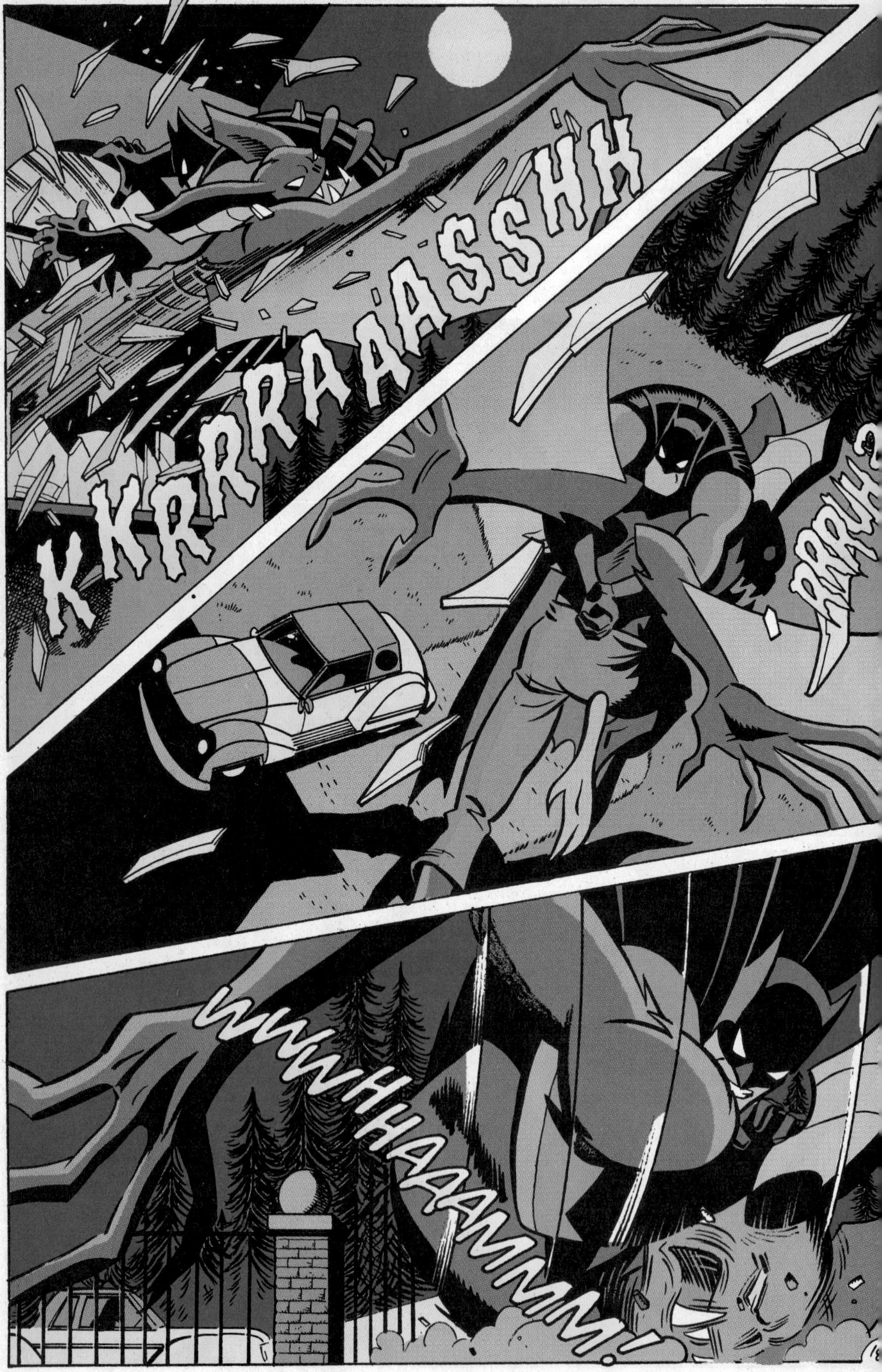
KKRRRAAASSHH
RRRUH?
WWWHHAAAMMMM!

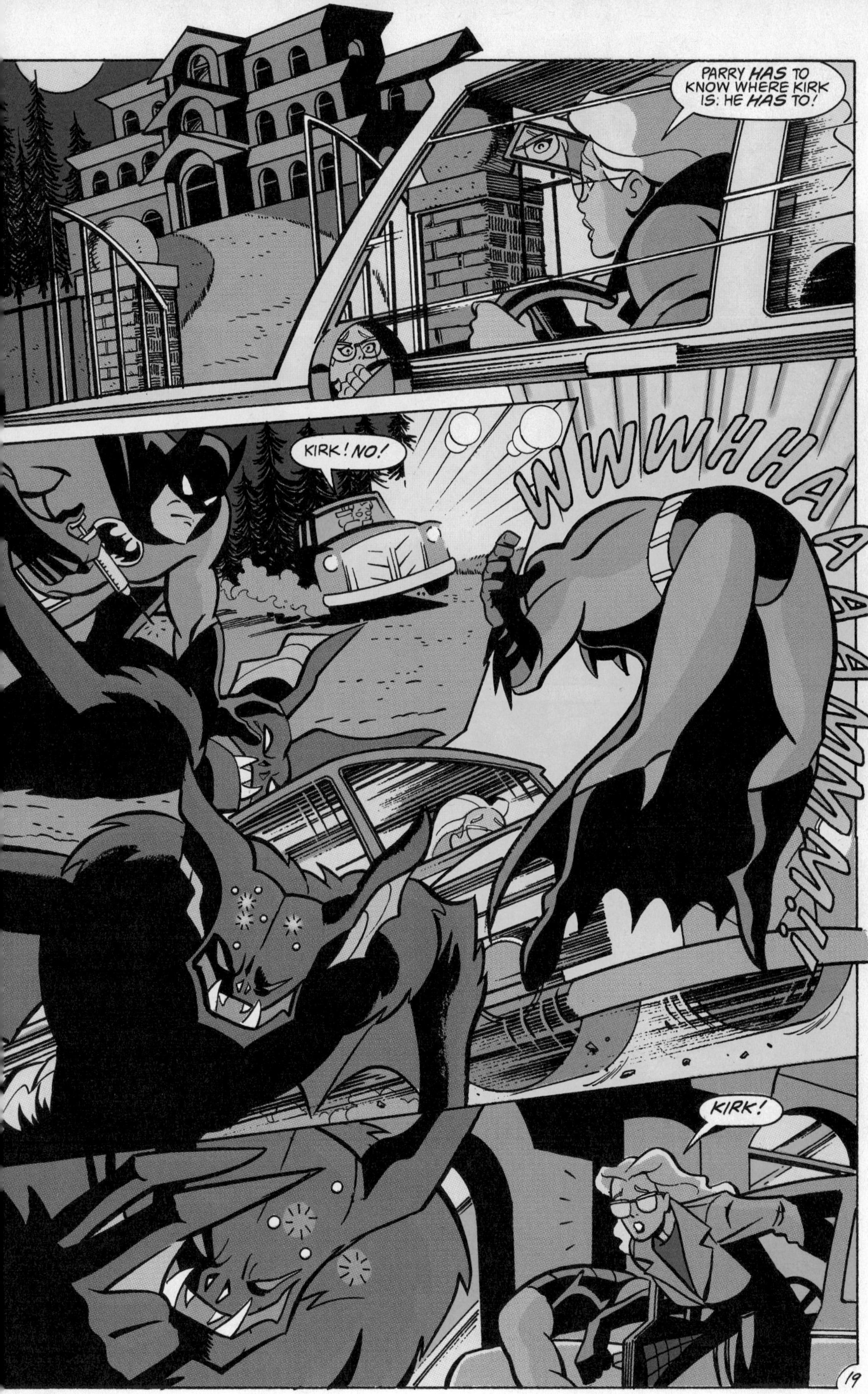
PARRY HAS TO KNOW WHERE KIRK IS: HE HAS TO!
KIRK! NO!
WWWHHAAAAAMMMM!!
KIRK!
19

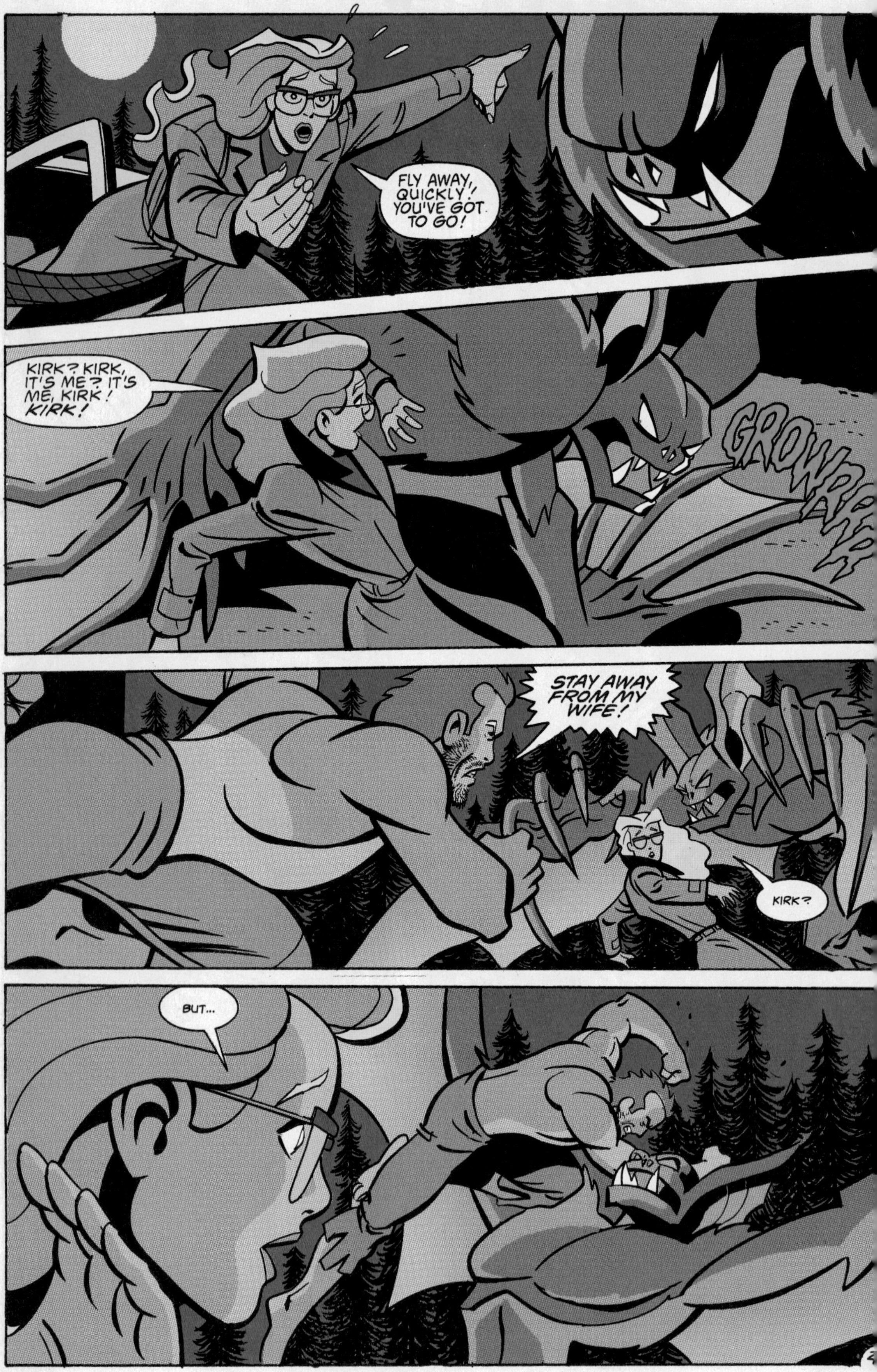
FLY AWAY, QUICKLY! YOU'VE GOT TO GO!
KIRK? KIRK, IT'S ME? IT'S ME, KIRK! KIRK!
GROWRRRR
STAY AWAY FROM MY WIFE!
KIRK?
BUT...

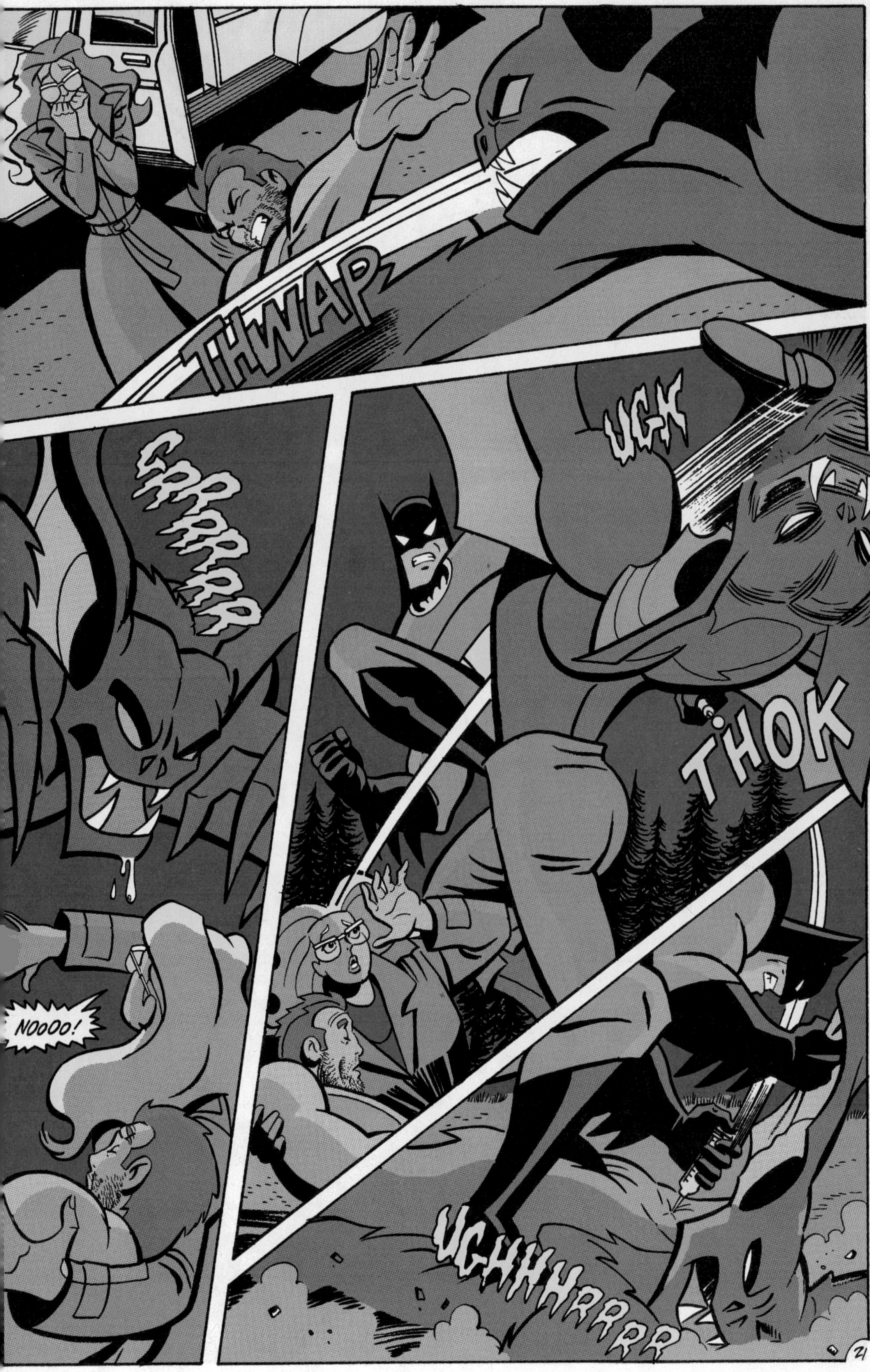
THWAP
GRRRRRR
UGK
THOK
NOOOO!
UGHHHRRRRR
21

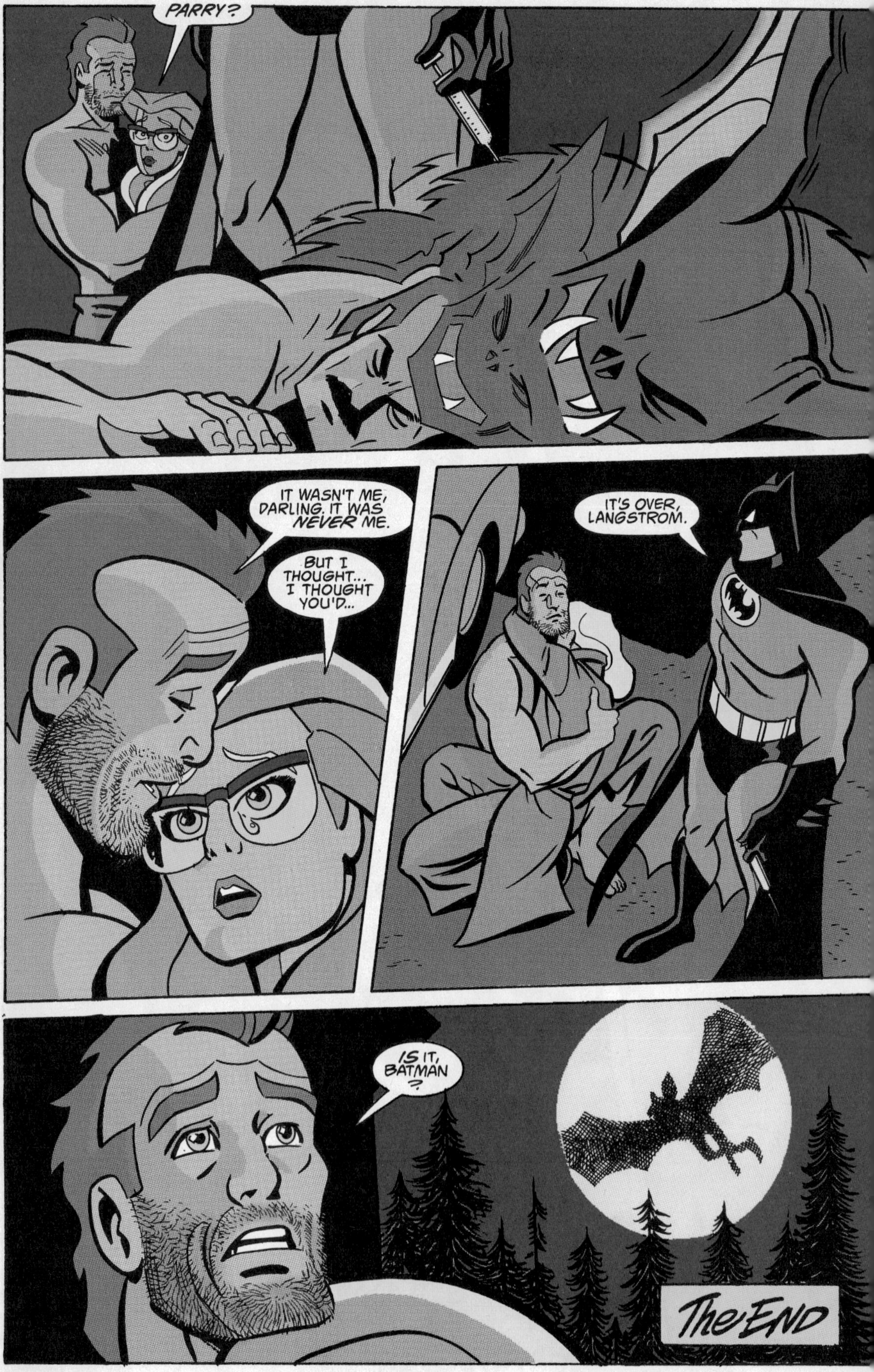
PARRY?
IT WASN'T ME, DARLING. IT WAS NEVER ME.
BUT I THOUGHT... I THOUGHT YOU'D...
IT'S OVER, LANGSTROM.
IS IT, BATMAN?
The End

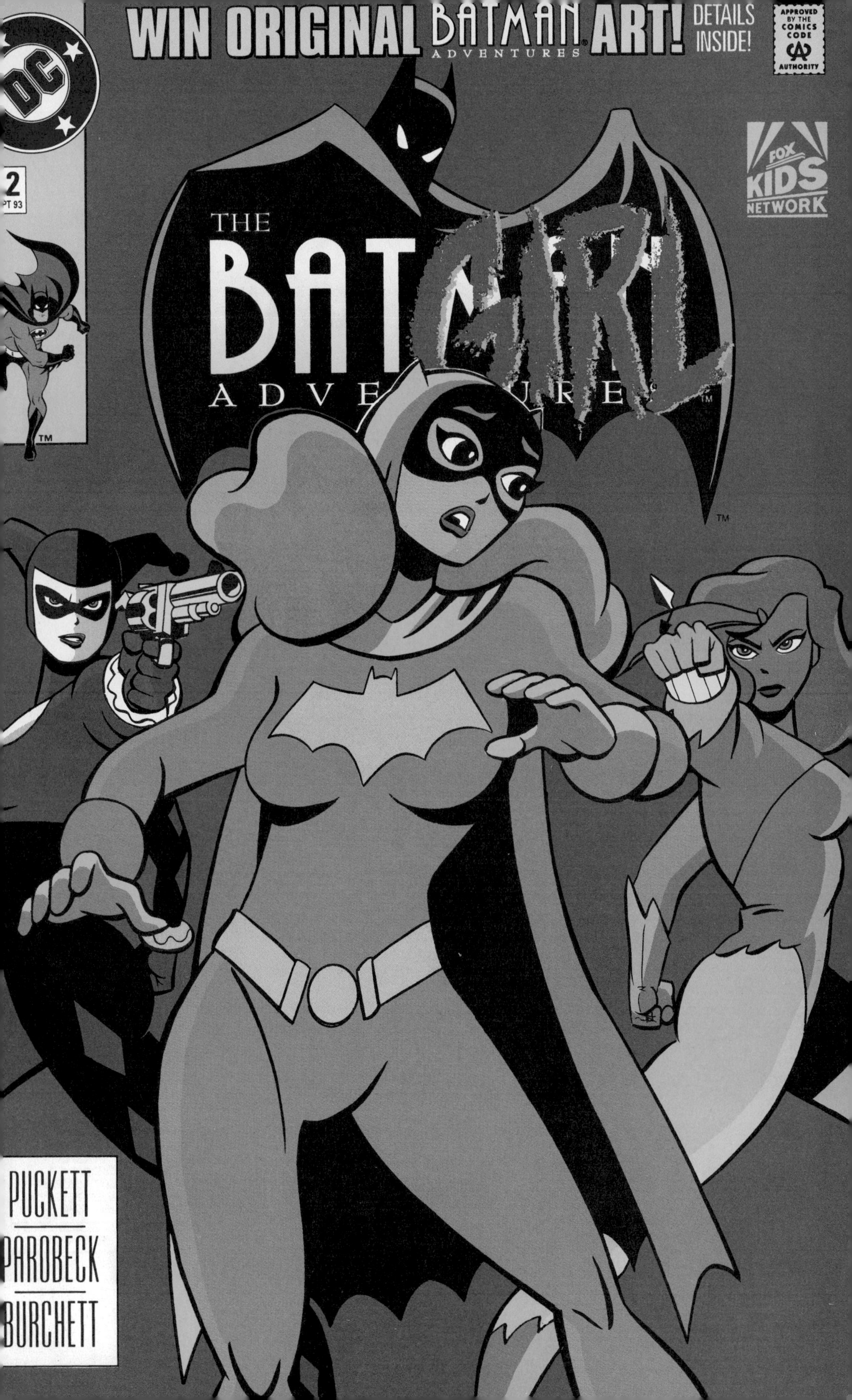

WIN ORIGINAL BATMAN ADVENTURES ART!
DETAILS INSIDE!
APPROVED BY THE COMICS CODE AUTHORITY
DC
2
FOX KIDS NETWORK
THE BATGIRL ADVENTURES
PUCKETT
PAROBECK
BURCHETT

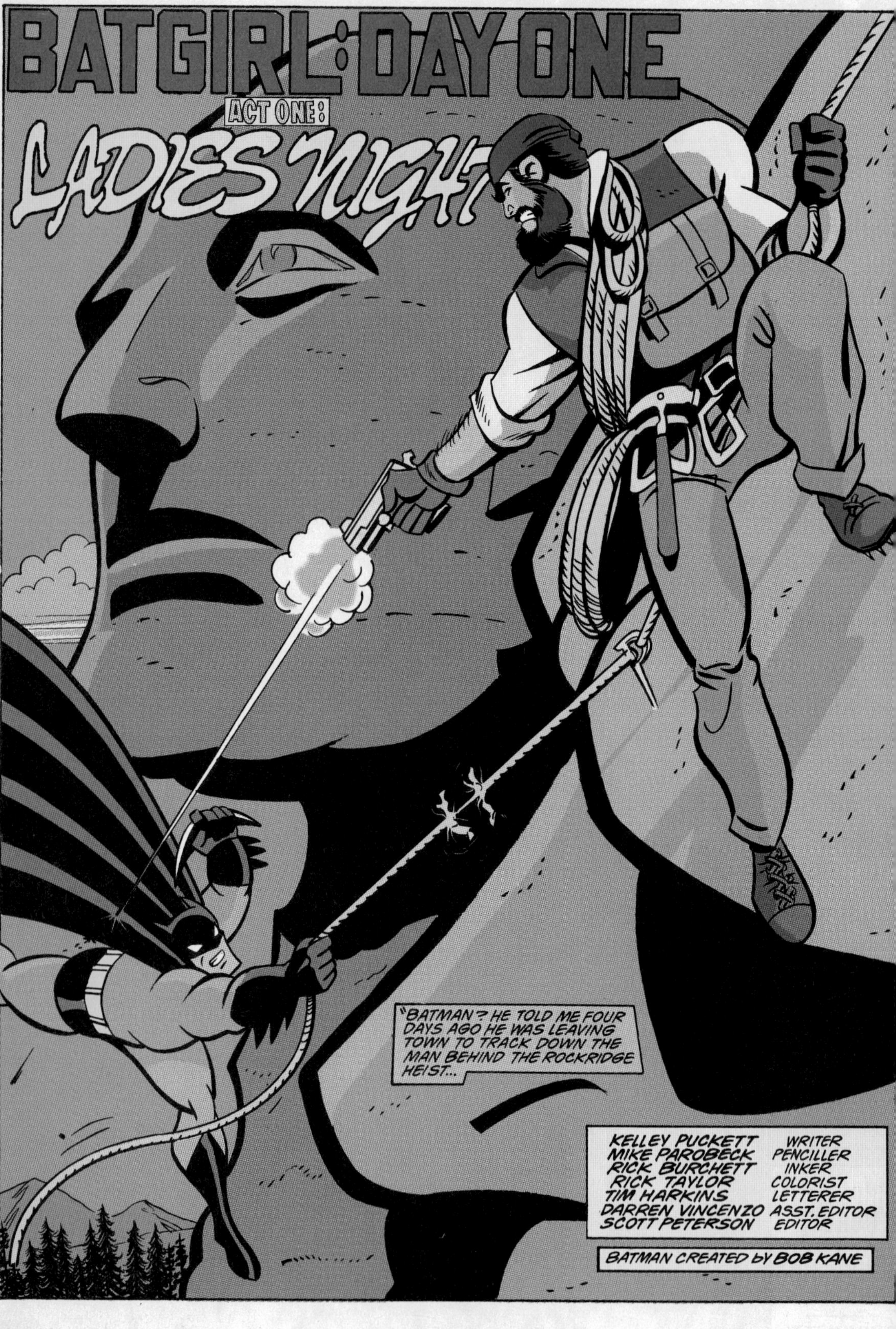
BATGIRL: DAY ONE
ACT ONE:
LADIES NIGHT
"BATMAN? HE TOLD ME FOUR DAYS AGO HE WAS LEAVING TOWN TO TRACK DOWN THE MAN BEHIND THE ROCKRIDGE HEIST...
KELLEY PUCKETT WRITER
MIKE PAROBECK PENCILLER
RICK BURCHETT INKER
RICK TAYLOR COLORIST
TIM HARKINS LETTERER
DARREN VINCENZO ASST. EDITOR
SCOTT PETERSON EDITOR
BATMAN CREATED BY BOB KANE

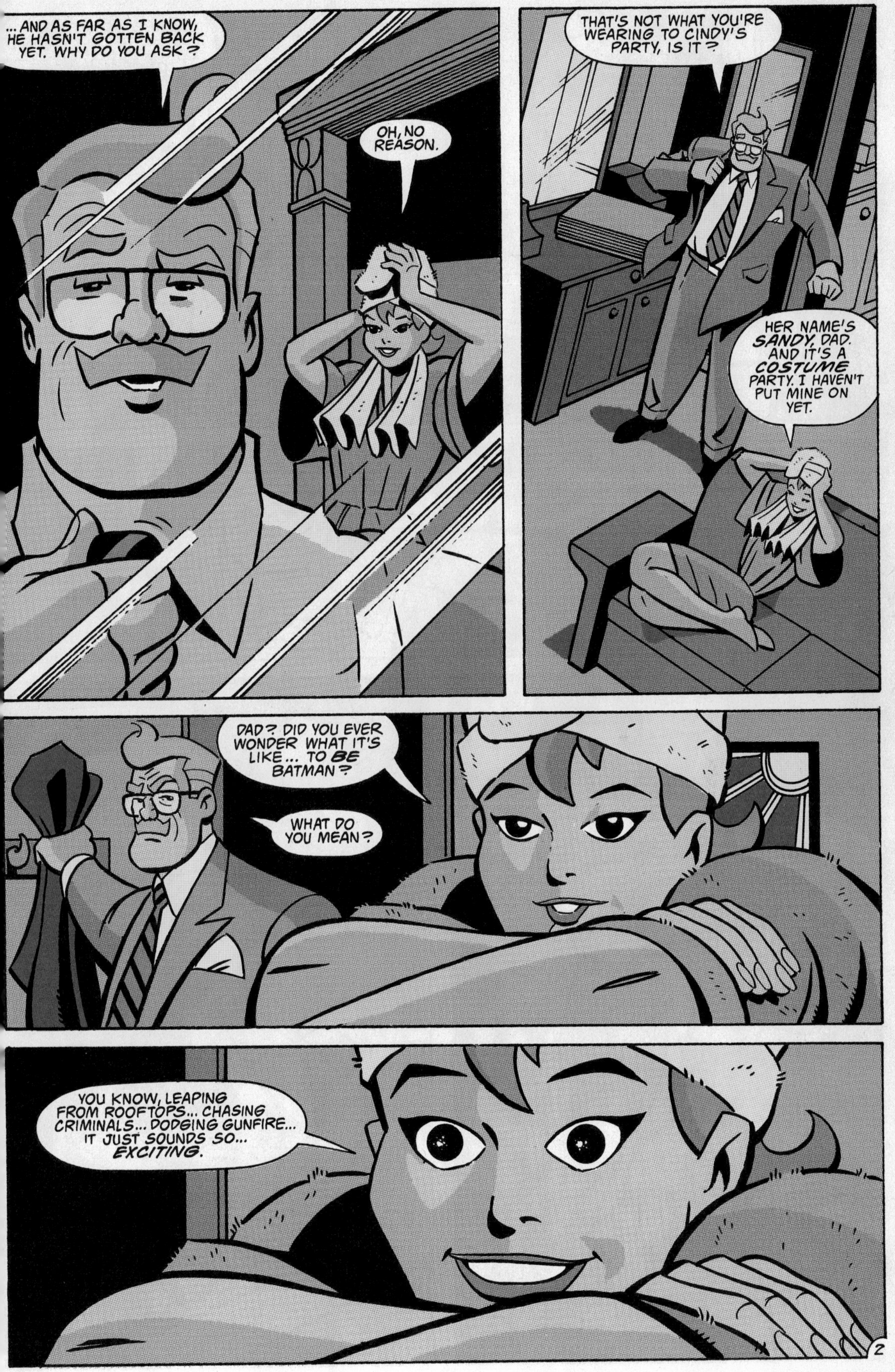
...AND AS FAR AS I KNOW, HE HASN'T GOTTEN BACK YET. WHY DO YOU ASK?
OH, NO REASON.
THAT'S NOT WHAT YOU'RE WEARING TO CINDY'S PARTY, IS IT?
HER NAME'S SANDY, DAD. AND IT'S A COSTUME PARTY. I HAVEN'T PUT MINE ON YET.
DAD? DID YOU EVER WONDER WHAT IT'S LIKE... TO BE BATMAN?
WHAT DO YOU MEAN?
YOU KNOW, LEAPING FROM ROOFTOPS... CHASING CRIMINALS... DODGING GUNFIRE... IT JUST SOUNDS SO... EXCITING.
2

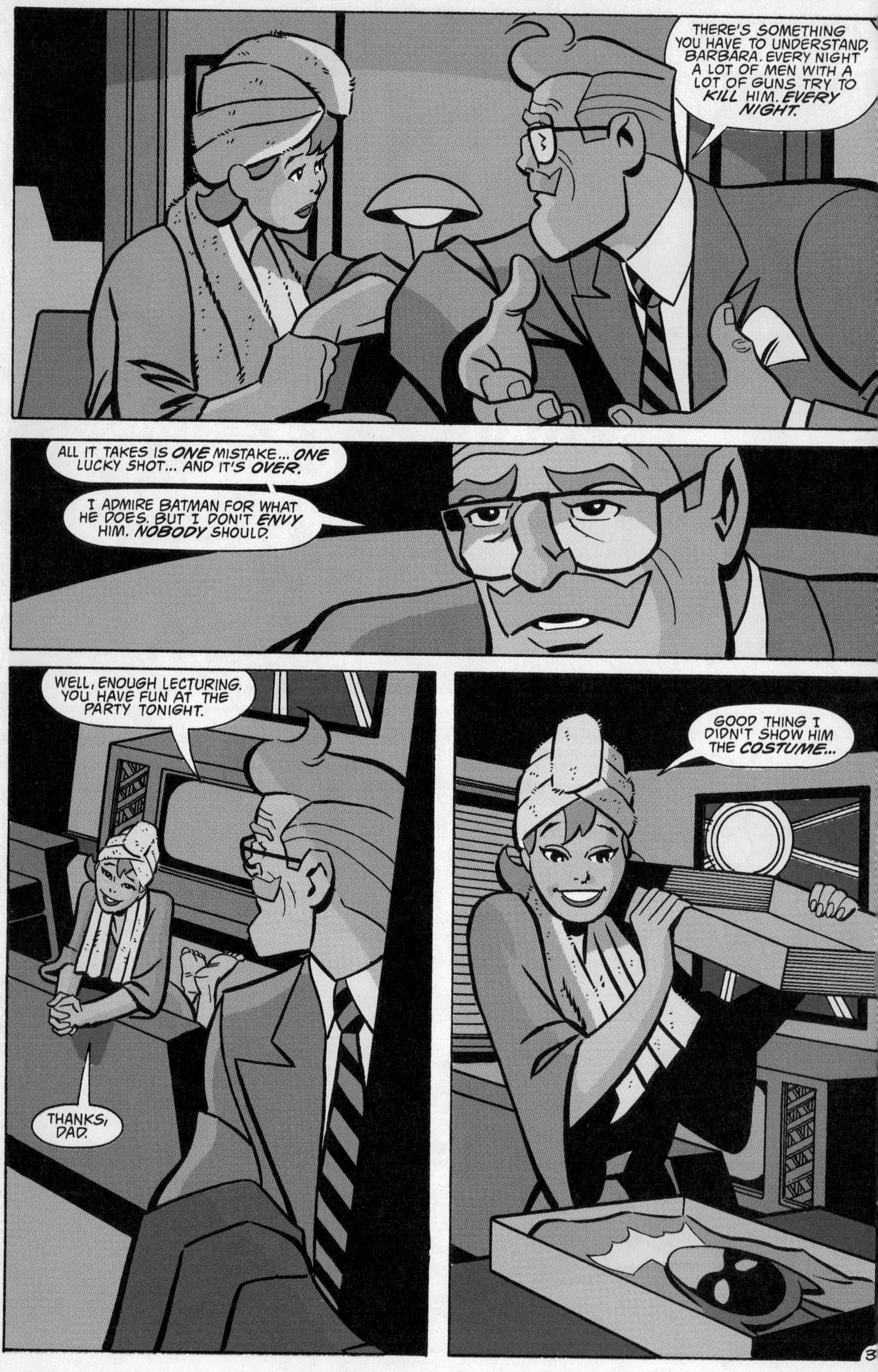
THERE'S SOMETHING YOU HAVE TO UNDERSTAND, BARBARA. EVERY NIGHT A LOT OF MEN WITH A LOT OF GUNS TRY TO KILL HIM. EVERY NIGHT.
ALL IT TAKES IS ONE MISTAKE... ONE LUCKY SHOT... AND IT'S OVER.
I ADMIRE BATMAN FOR WHAT HE DOES. BUT I DON'T ENVY HIM. NOBODY SHOULD.
WELL, ENOUGH LECTURING. YOU HAVE FUN AT THE PARTY TONIGHT.
THANKS, DAD.
GOOD THING I DIDN'T SHOW HIM THE COSTUME...
3

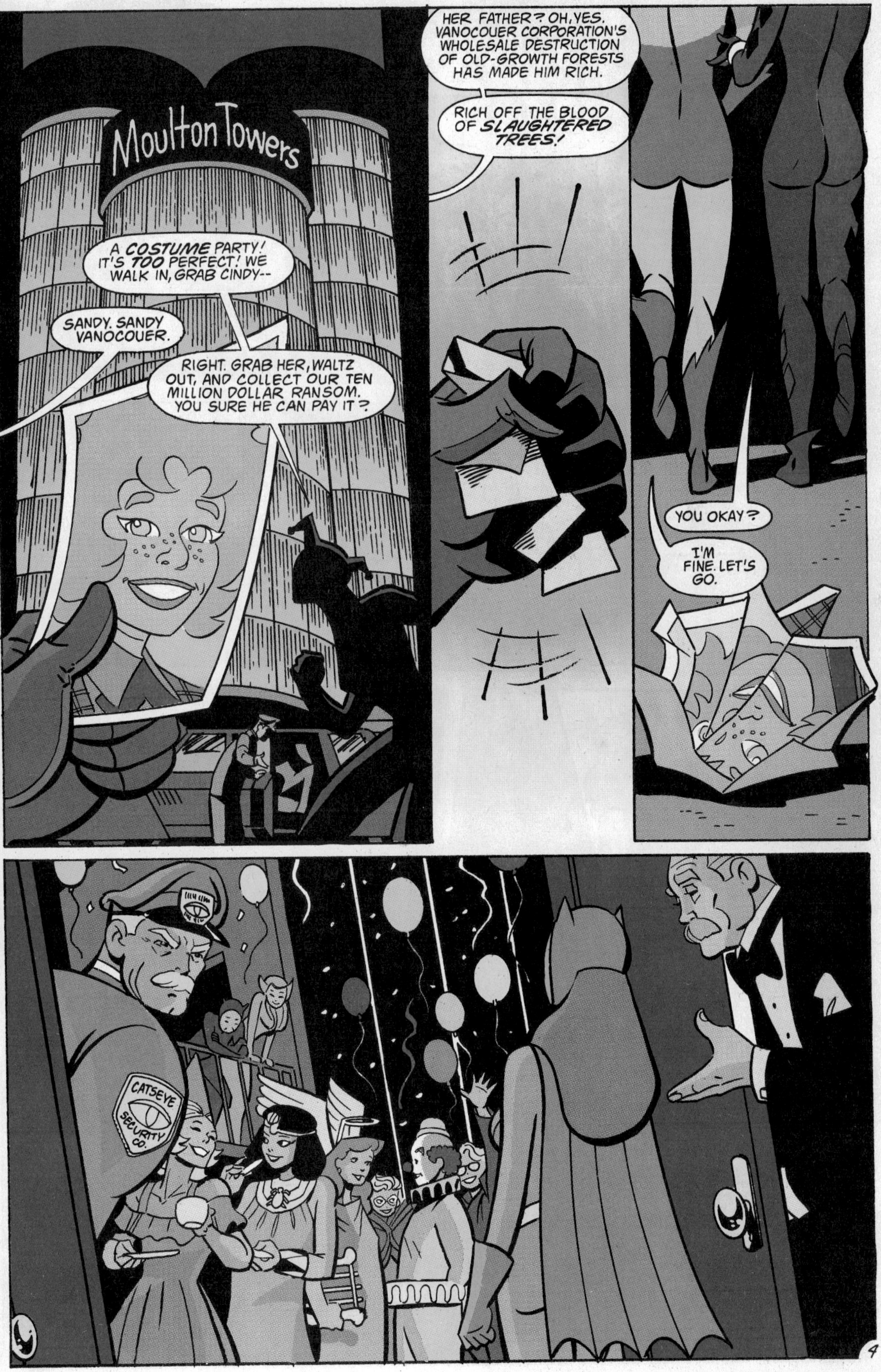
Moulton Towers
A COSTUME PARTY! IT'S TOO PERFECT! WE WALK IN, GRAB CINDY--
SANDY. SANDY VANOCOUER.
RIGHT. GRAB HER, WALTZ OUT, AND COLLECT OUR TEN MILLION DOLLAR RANSOM. YOU SURE HE CAN PAY IT?
HER FATHER? OH, YES. VANOCOUER CORPORATION'S WHOLESALE DESTRUCTION OF OLD-GROWTH FORESTS HAS MADE HIM RICH.
RICH OFF THE BLOOD OF SLAUGHTERED TREES!
YOU OKAY?
I'M FINE. LET'S GO.
CATSEYE SECURITY CO.
4

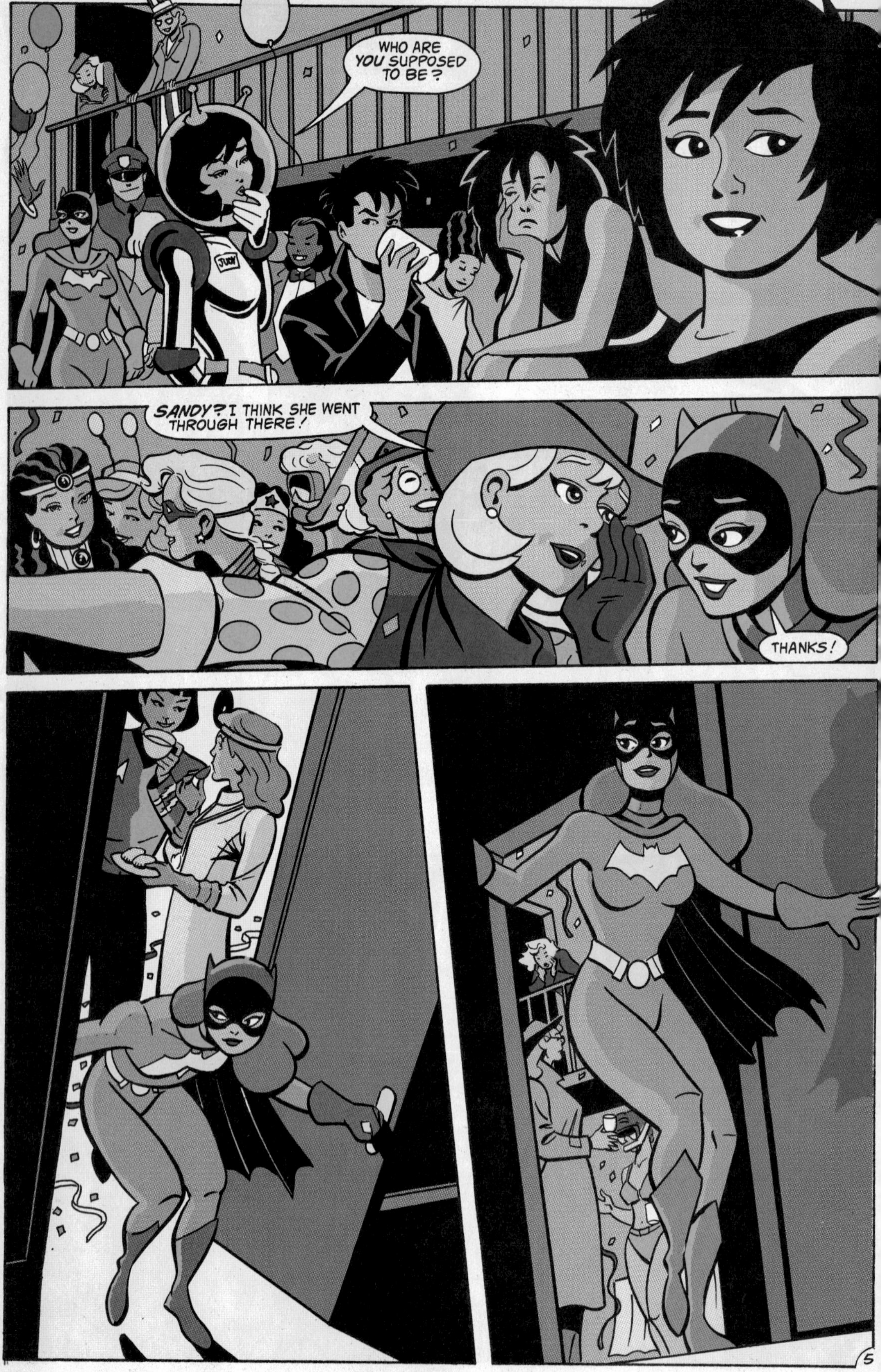
WHO ARE YOU SUPPOSED TO BE?
SANDY? I THINK SHE WENT THROUGH THERE!
THANKS!
5

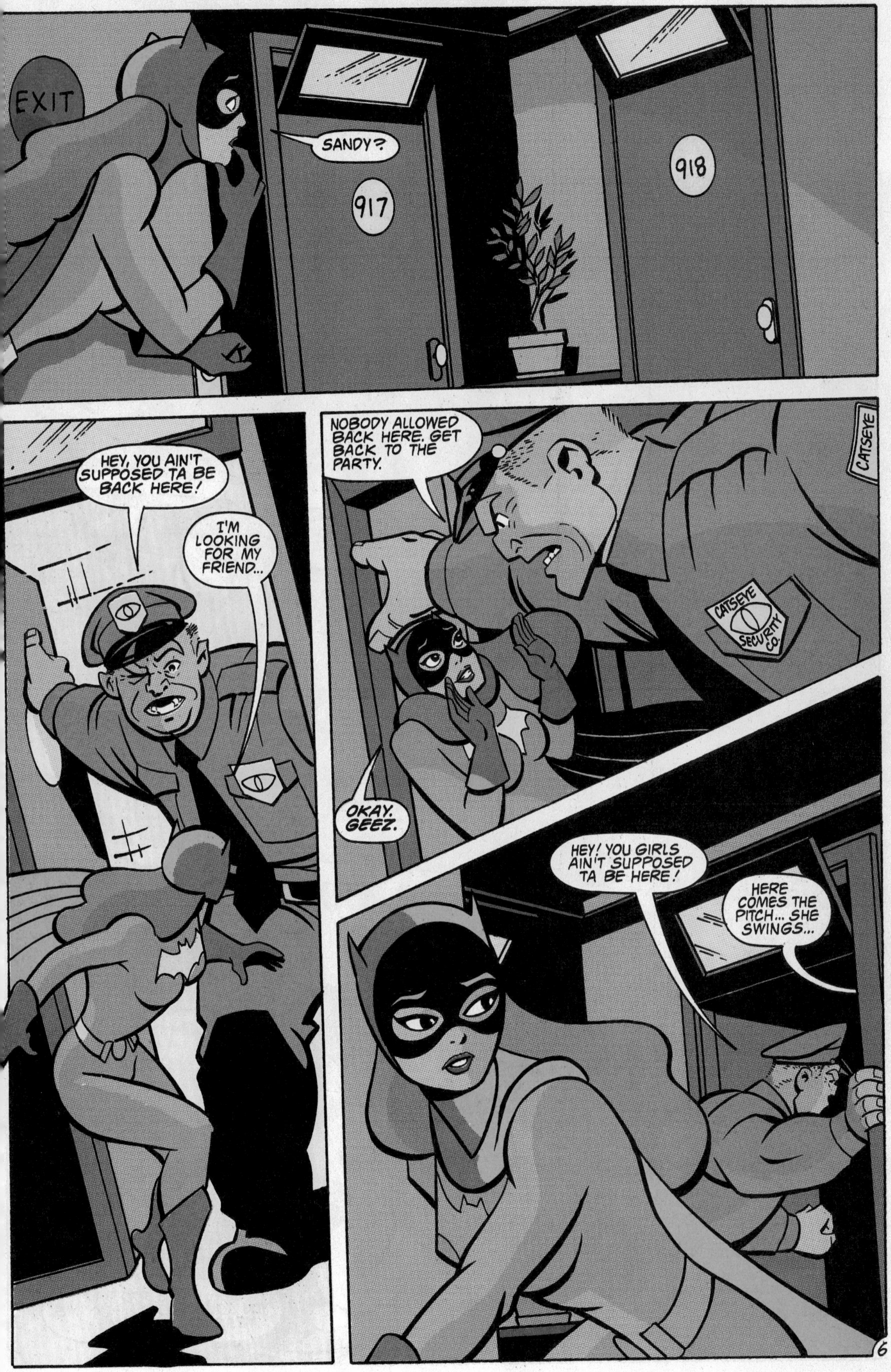
EXIT
SANDY?
917
918
HEY, YOU AIN'T SUPPOSED TA BE BACK HERE!
I'M LOOKING FOR MY FRIEND...
NOBODY ALLOWED BACK HERE. GET BACK TO THE PARTY.
CATSEYE
CATSEYE SECURITY CO.
OKAY. GEEZ.
HEY! YOU GIRLS AIN'T SUPPOSED TA BE HERE!
HERE COMES THE PITCH... SHE SWINGS...
6

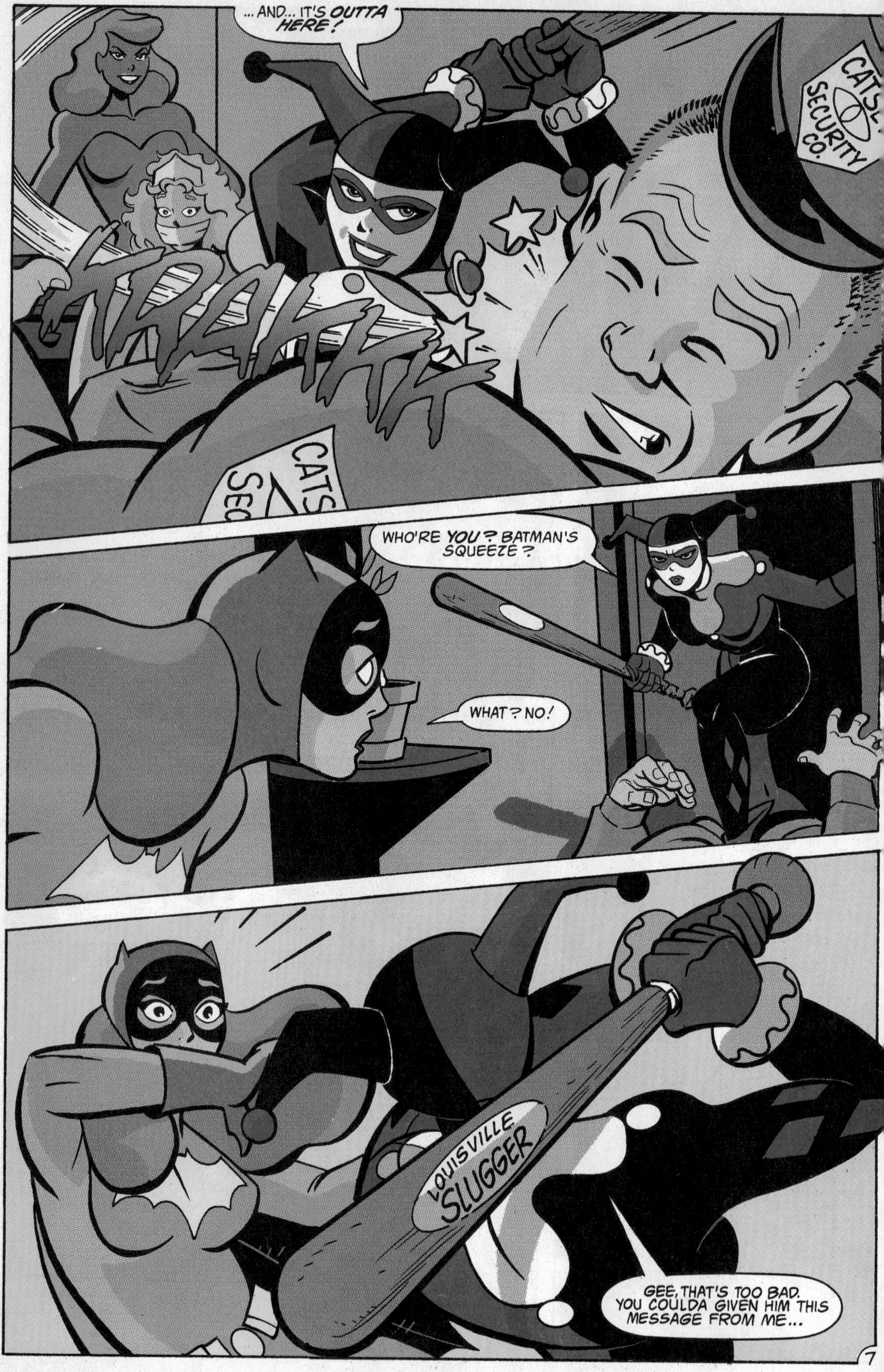

...AND... IT'S OUTTA HERE!
CATS SECURITY CO.
CATS SEC
WHO'RE YOU? BATMAN'S SQUEEZE?
WHAT? NO!
LOUISVILLE SLUGGER
GEE, THAT'S TOO BAD. YOU COULDA GIVEN HIM THIS MESSAGE FROM ME...
7

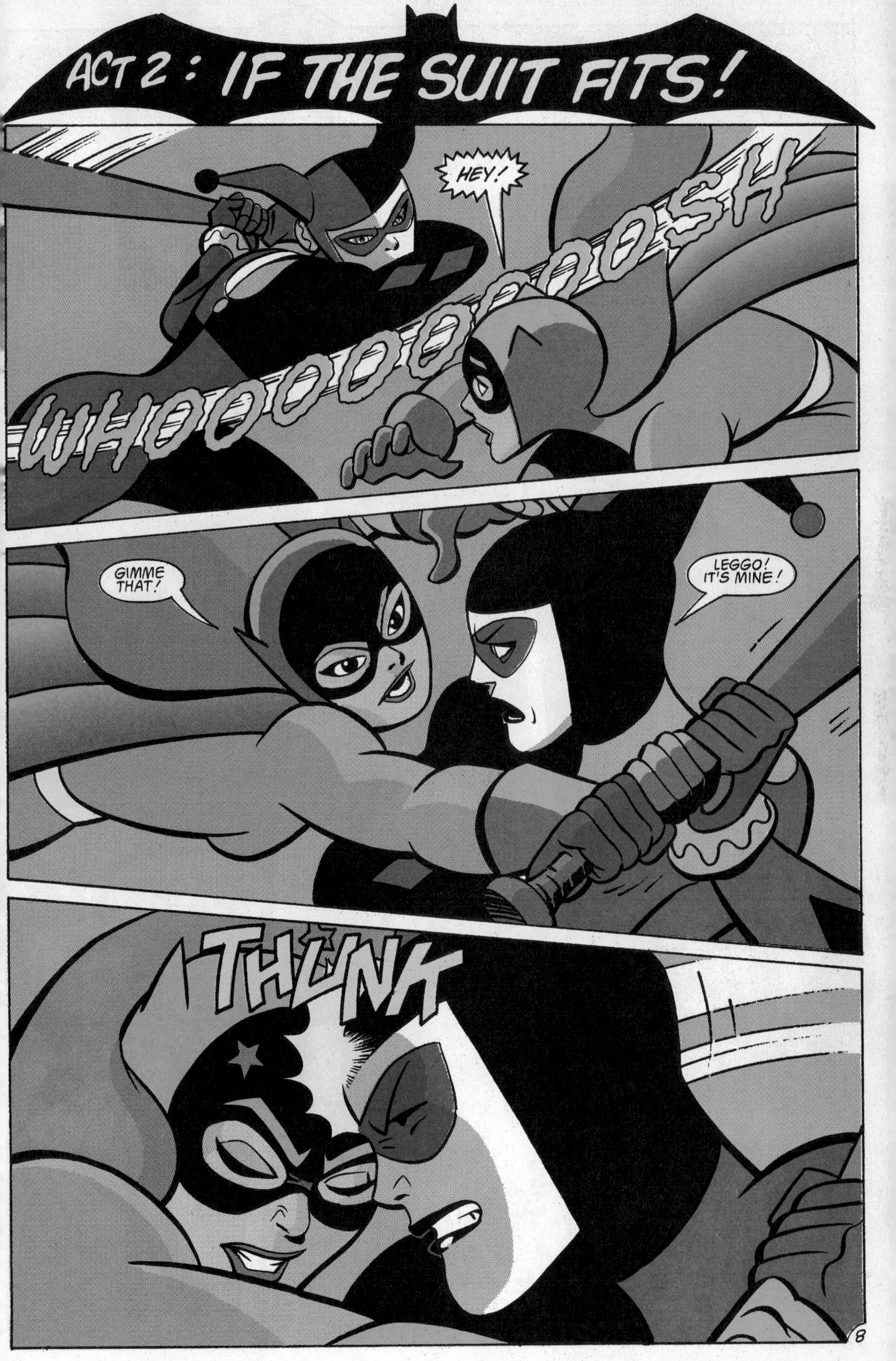
ACT 2: IF THE SUIT FITS!
HEY!
WHOOOOOOOOOOOOSH
GIMME THAT!
LEGGO! IT'S MINE!
THUNK
8

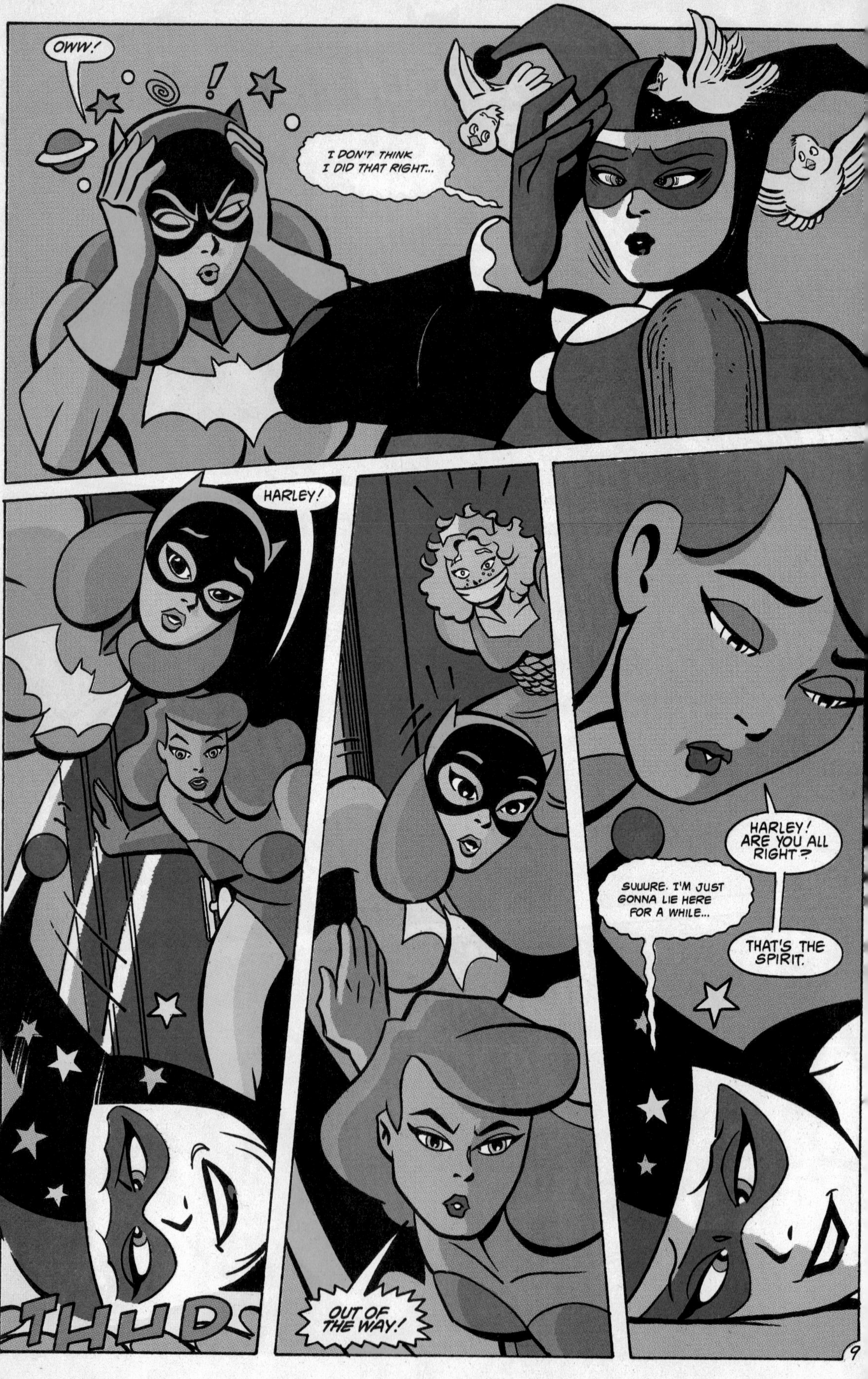
OWW!
I DON'T THINK I DID THAT RIGHT...
HARLEY!
THUD
OUT OF THE WAY!
HARLEY! ARE YOU ALL RIGHT?
SUUURE. I'M JUST GONNA LIE HERE FOR A WHILE...
THAT'S THE SPIRIT.
9

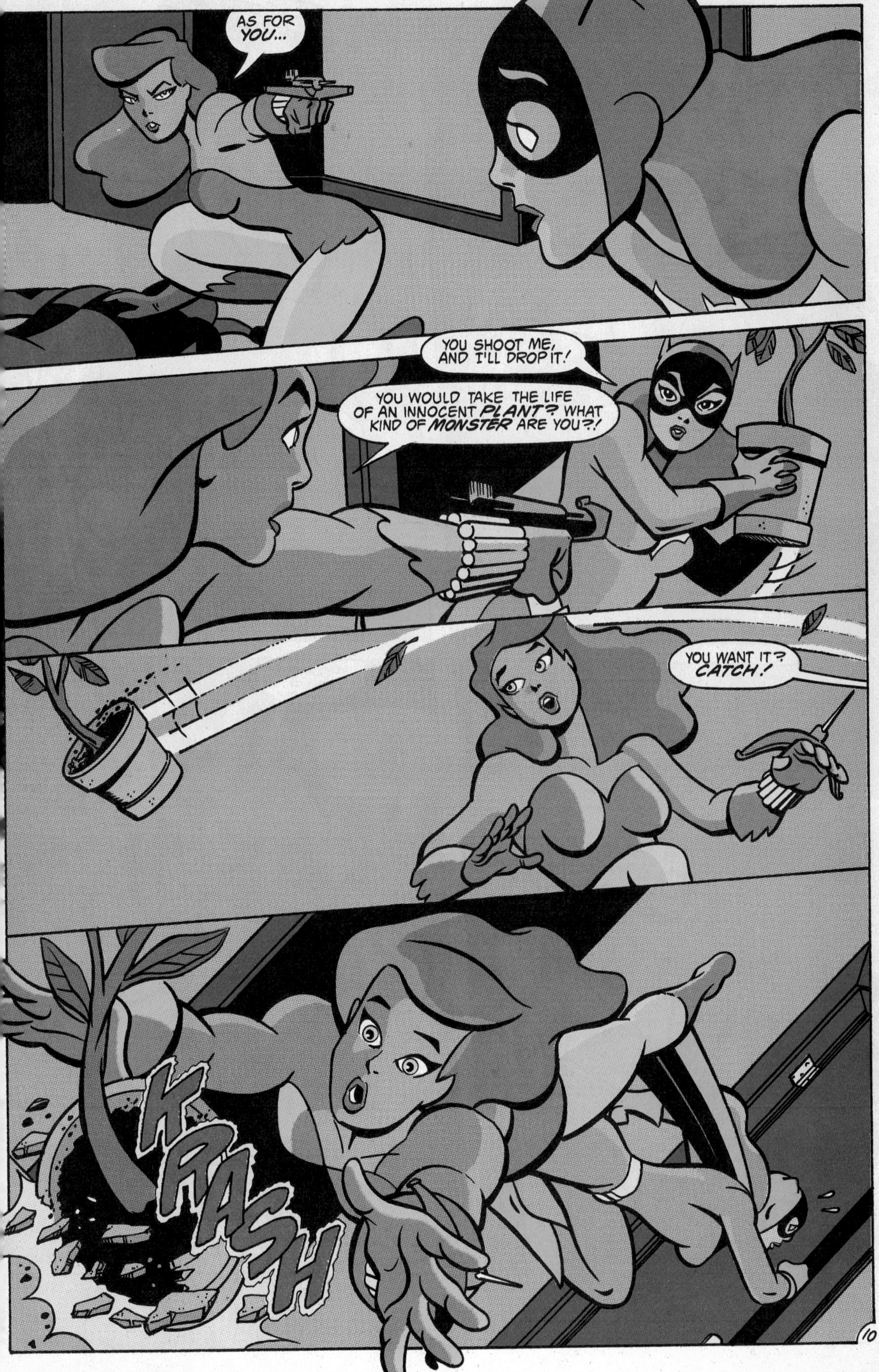
AS FOR YOU...
YOU SHOOT ME, AND I'LL DROP IT!
YOU WOULD TAKE THE LIFE OF AN INNOCENT PLANT? WHAT KIND OF MONSTER ARE YOU?!
YOU WANT IT? CATCH!
KRASH
10

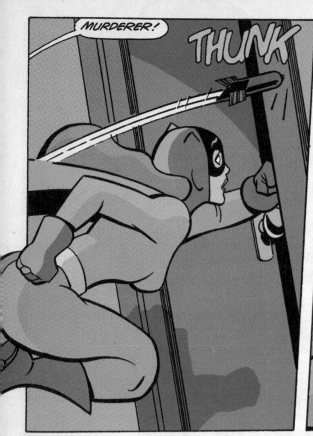

MURDERER!

THUNK

SLAM THUNK

ARE YOU OKAY?

WHO ARE YOU?

I'M... UHH... I'M BATGIRL. BATMAN COULDN'T MAKE IT.

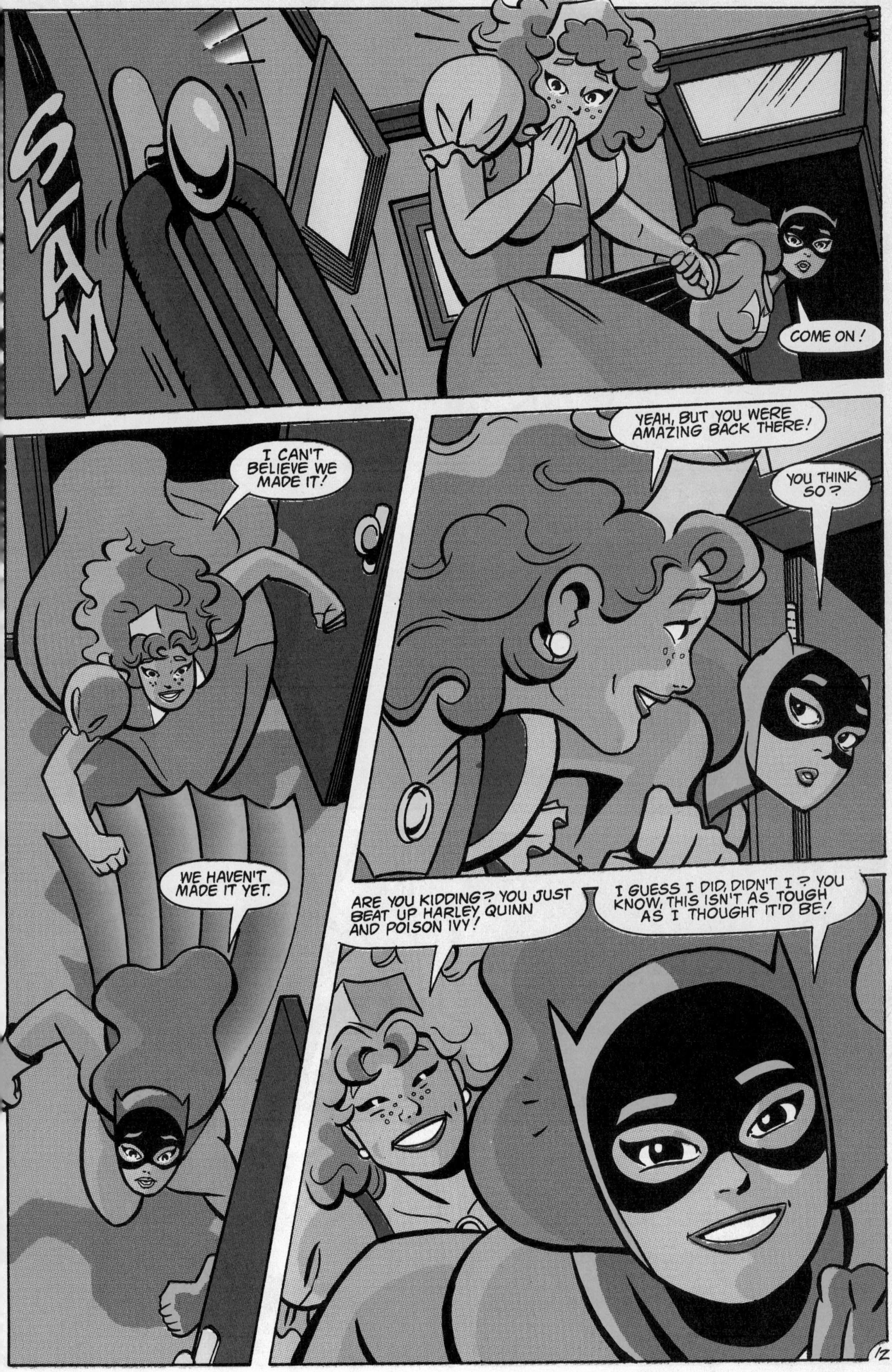
SLAM
COME ON!
I CAN'T BELIEVE WE MADE IT!
WE HAVEN'T MADE IT YET.
YEAH, BUT YOU WERE AMAZING BACK THERE!
YOU THINK SO?
ARE YOU KIDDING? YOU JUST BEAT UP HARLEY QUINN AND POISON IVY!
I GUESS I DID, DIDN'T I? YOU KNOW, THIS ISN'T AS TOUGH AS I THOUGHT IT'D BE!
12

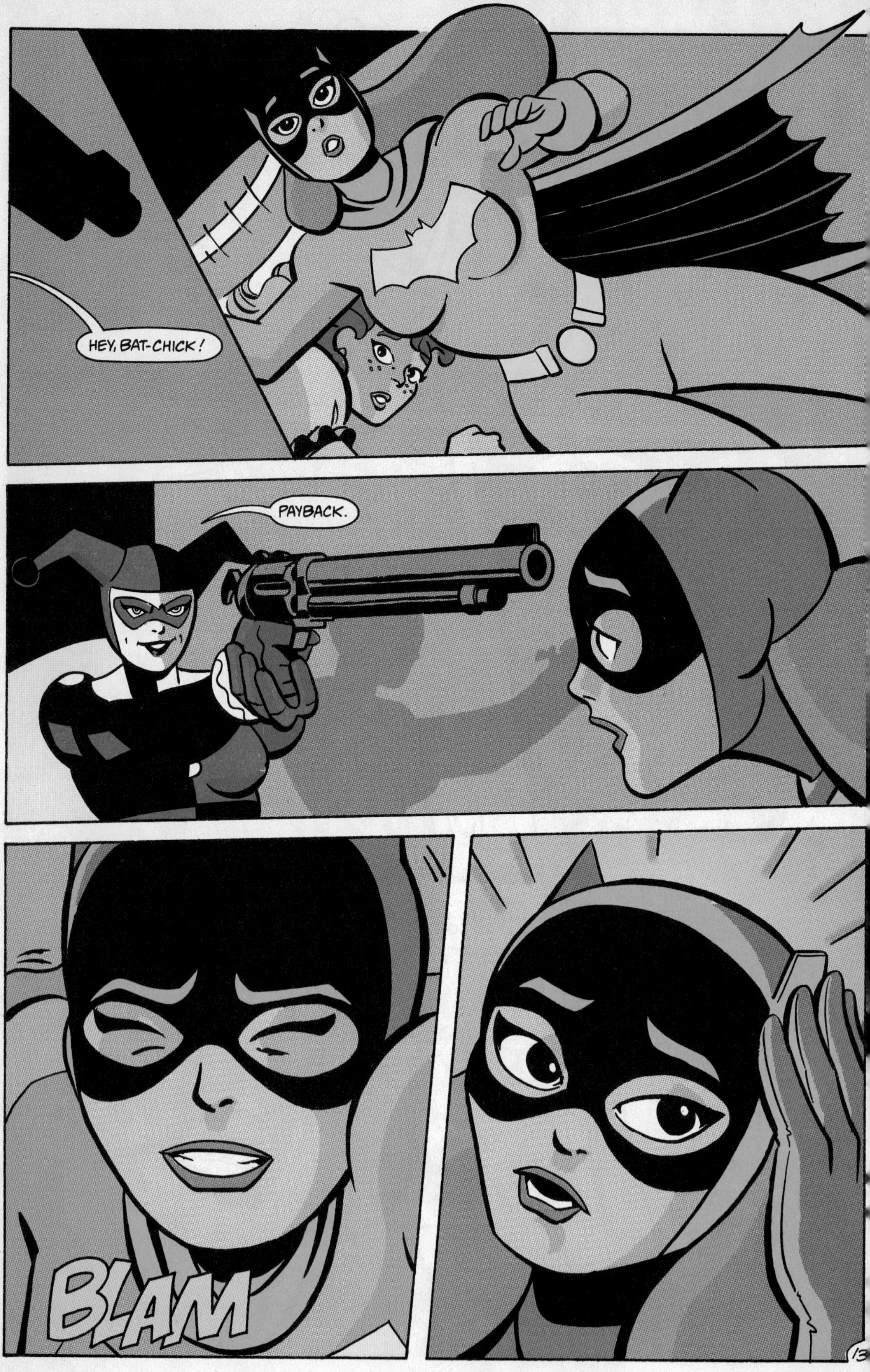
HEY, BAT-CHICK!
PAYBACK.
BLAM
13

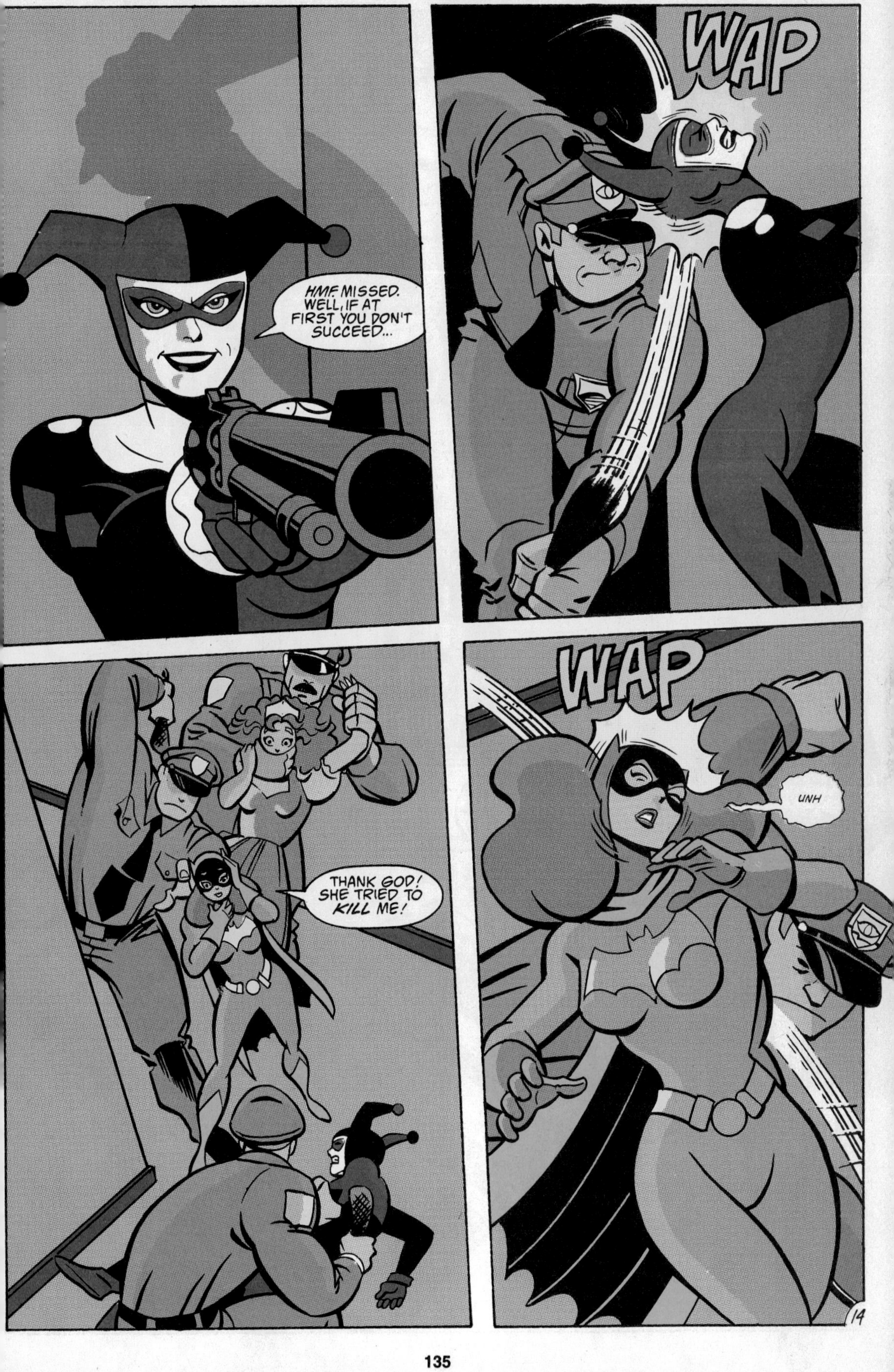
HMF. MISSED. WELL, IF AT FIRST YOU DON'T SUCCEED...
WAP
THANK GOD! SHE TRIED TO KILL ME!
WAP
UNH
14

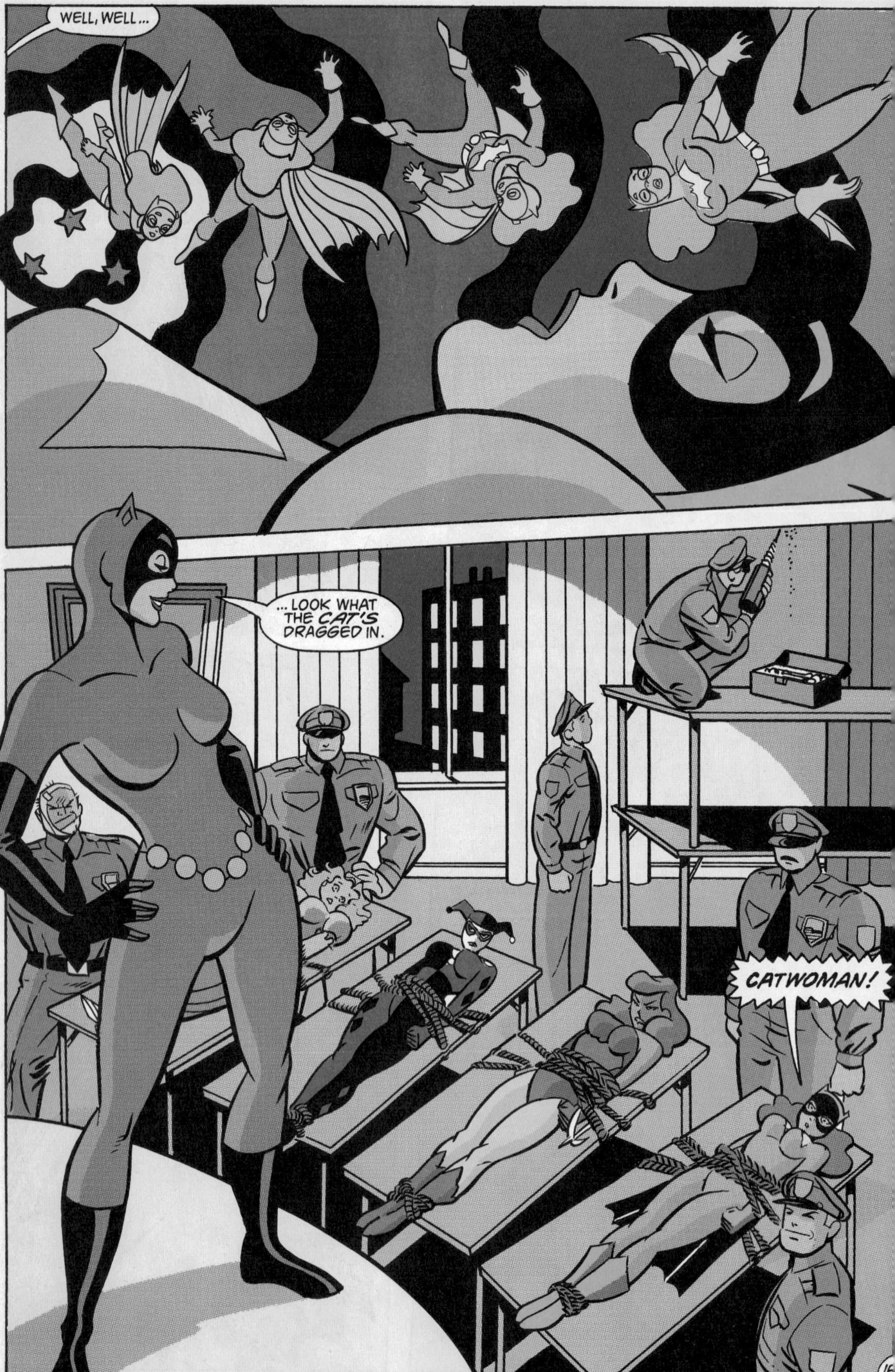
WELL, WELL...
...LOOK WHAT THE CAT'S DRAGGED IN.
CATWOMAN!

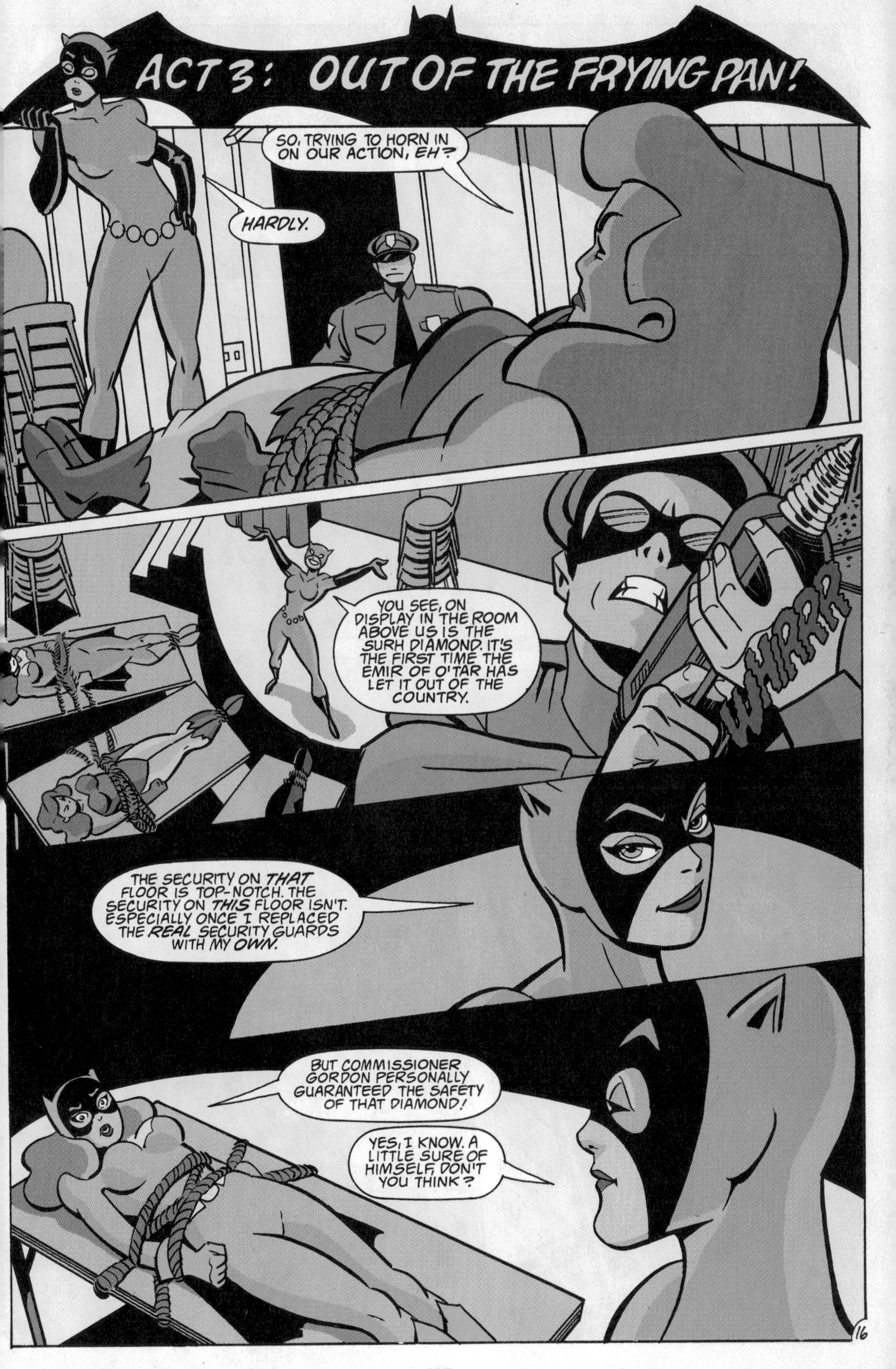
ACT 3: OUT OF THE FRYING PAN!
SO, TRYING TO HORN IN ON OUR ACTION, EH?
HARDLY.
YOU SEE, ON DISPLAY IN THE ROOM ABOVE US IS THE SURH DIAMOND. IT'S THE FIRST TIME THE EMIR OF O'TAR HAS LET IT OUT OF THE COUNTRY.
WHIRRR
THE SECURITY ON THAT FLOOR IS TOP-NOTCH. THE SECURITY ON THIS FLOOR ISN'T. ESPECIALLY ONCE I REPLACED THE REAL SECURITY GUARDS WITH MY OWN.
BUT COMMISSIONER GORDON PERSONALLY GUARANTEED THE SAFETY OF THAT DIAMOND!
YES, I KNOW. A LITTLE SURE OF HIMSELF, DON'T YOU THINK?
16

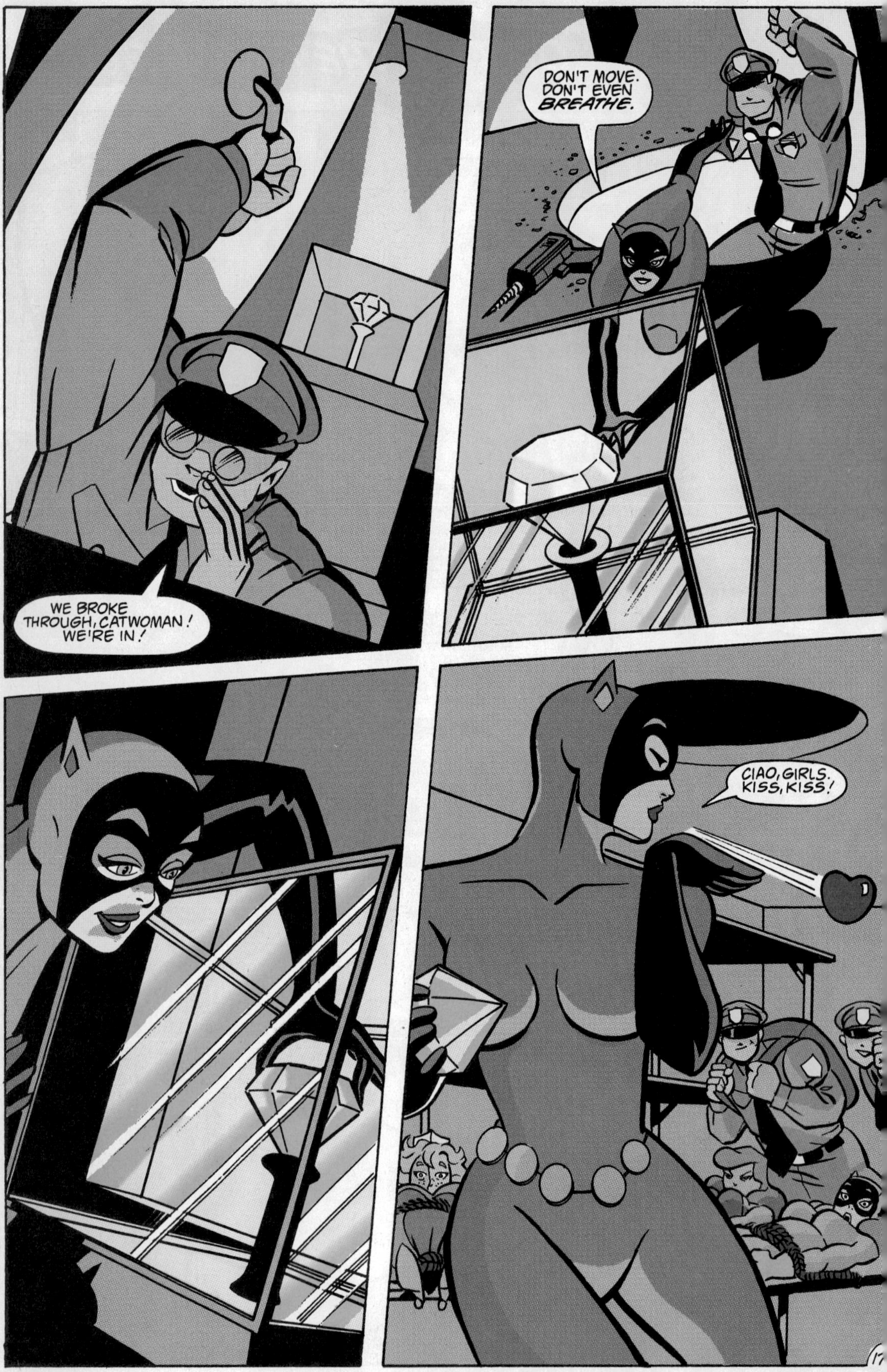
WE BROKE
THROUGH, CATWOMAN!
WE'RE IN!
DON'T MOVE.
DON'T EVEN
BREATHE.
CIAO, GIRLS.
KISS, KISS!
17

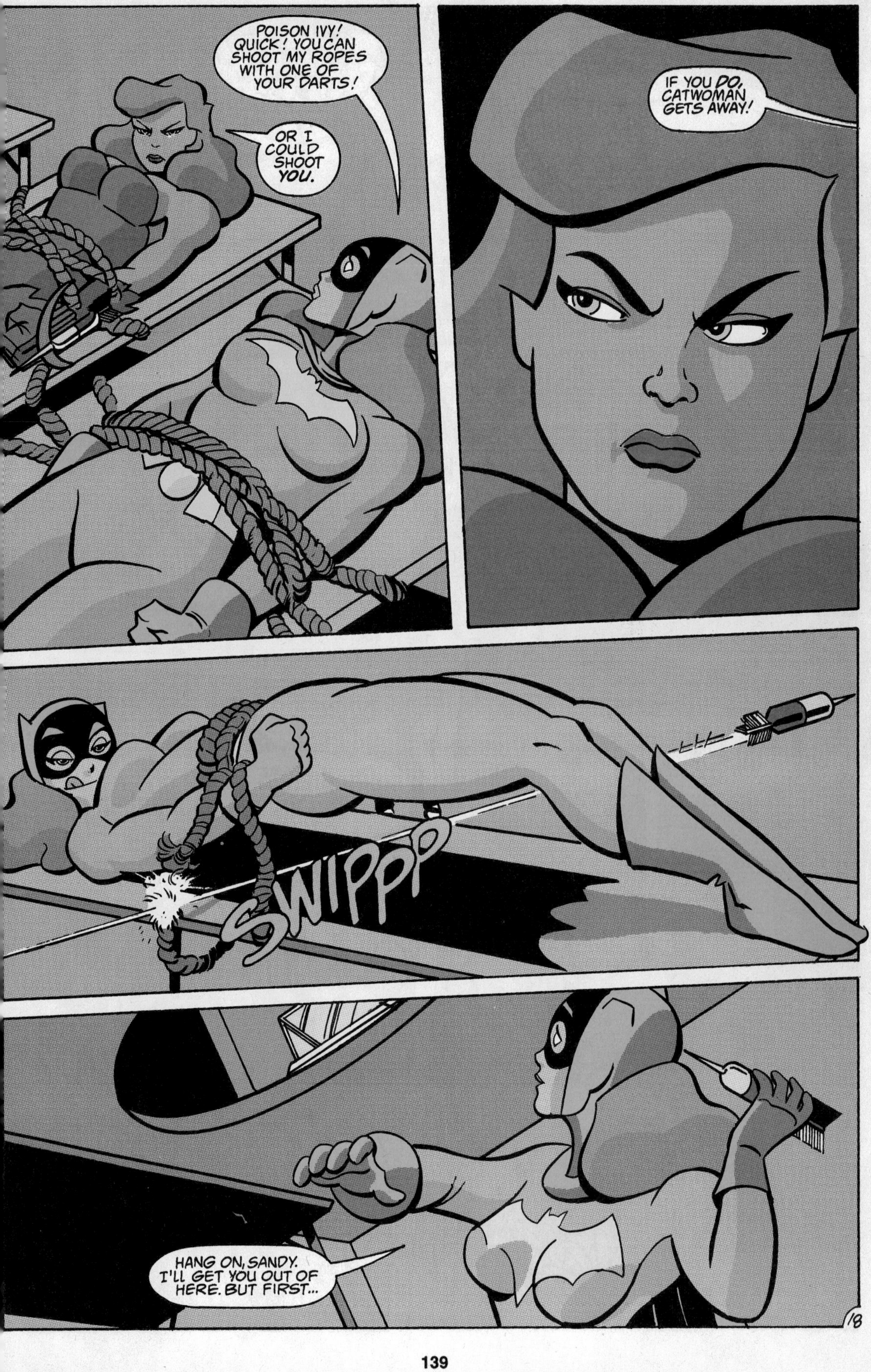
POISON IVY! QUICK! YOU CAN SHOOT MY ROPES WITH ONE OF YOUR DARTS!
OR I COULD SHOOT YOU.
IF YOU DO, CATWOMAN GETS AWAY!
SWIPPP
HANG ON, SANDY. I'LL GET YOU OUT OF HERE. BUT FIRST...
18

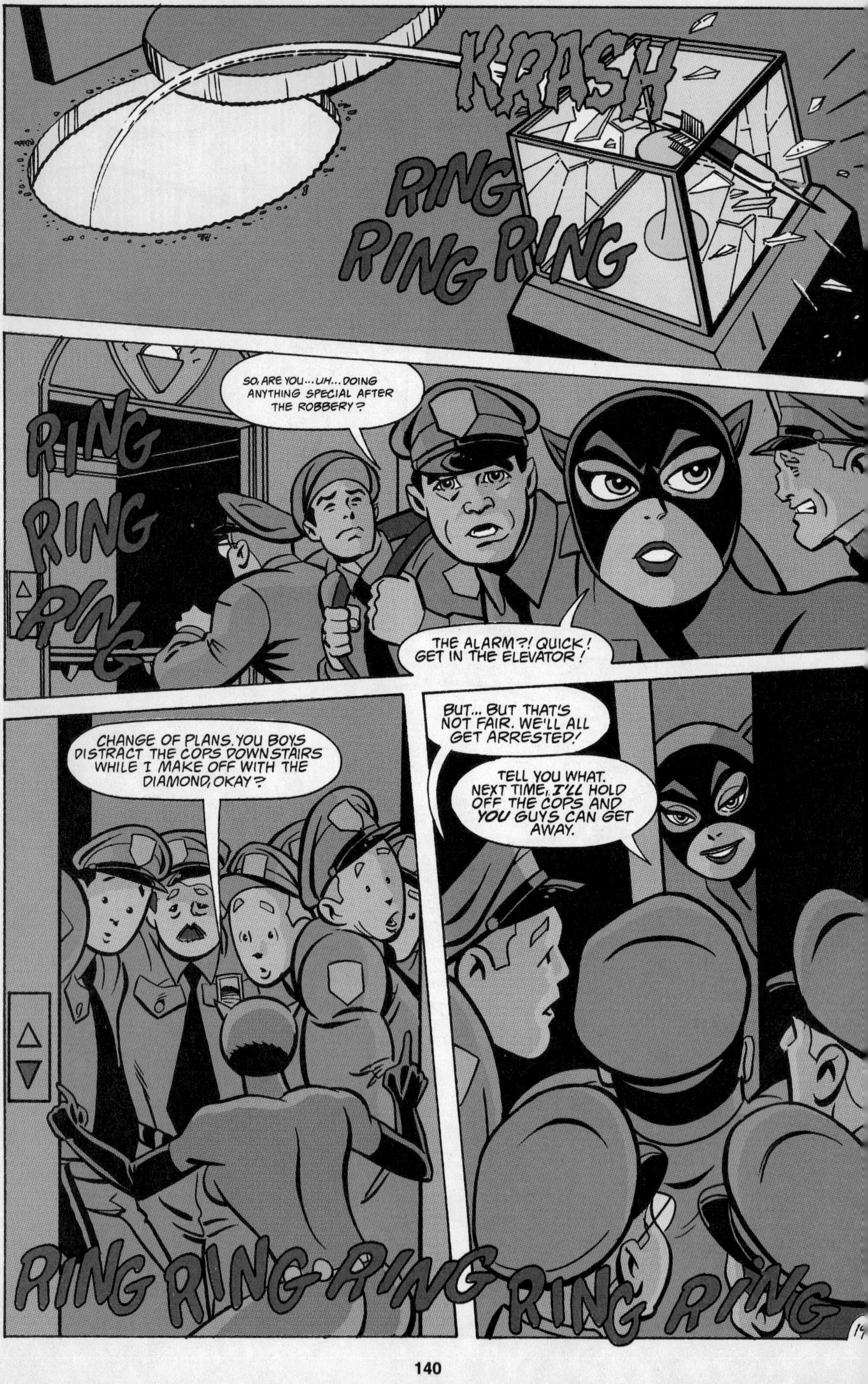
KRASH
RING RING RING
RING RING RING
SO, ARE YOU... UH... DOING ANYTHING SPECIAL AFTER THE ROBBERY?
THE ALARM?! QUICK! GET IN THE ELEVATOR!
CHANGE OF PLANS. YOU BOYS DISTRACT THE COPS DOWNSTAIRS WHILE I MAKE OFF WITH THE DIAMOND, OKAY?
BUT... BUT THAT'S NOT FAIR. WE'LL ALL GET ARRESTED!
TELL YOU WHAT. NEXT TIME, I'LL HOLD OFF THE COPS AND YOU GUYS CAN GET AWAY.
RING RING RING RING RING RING

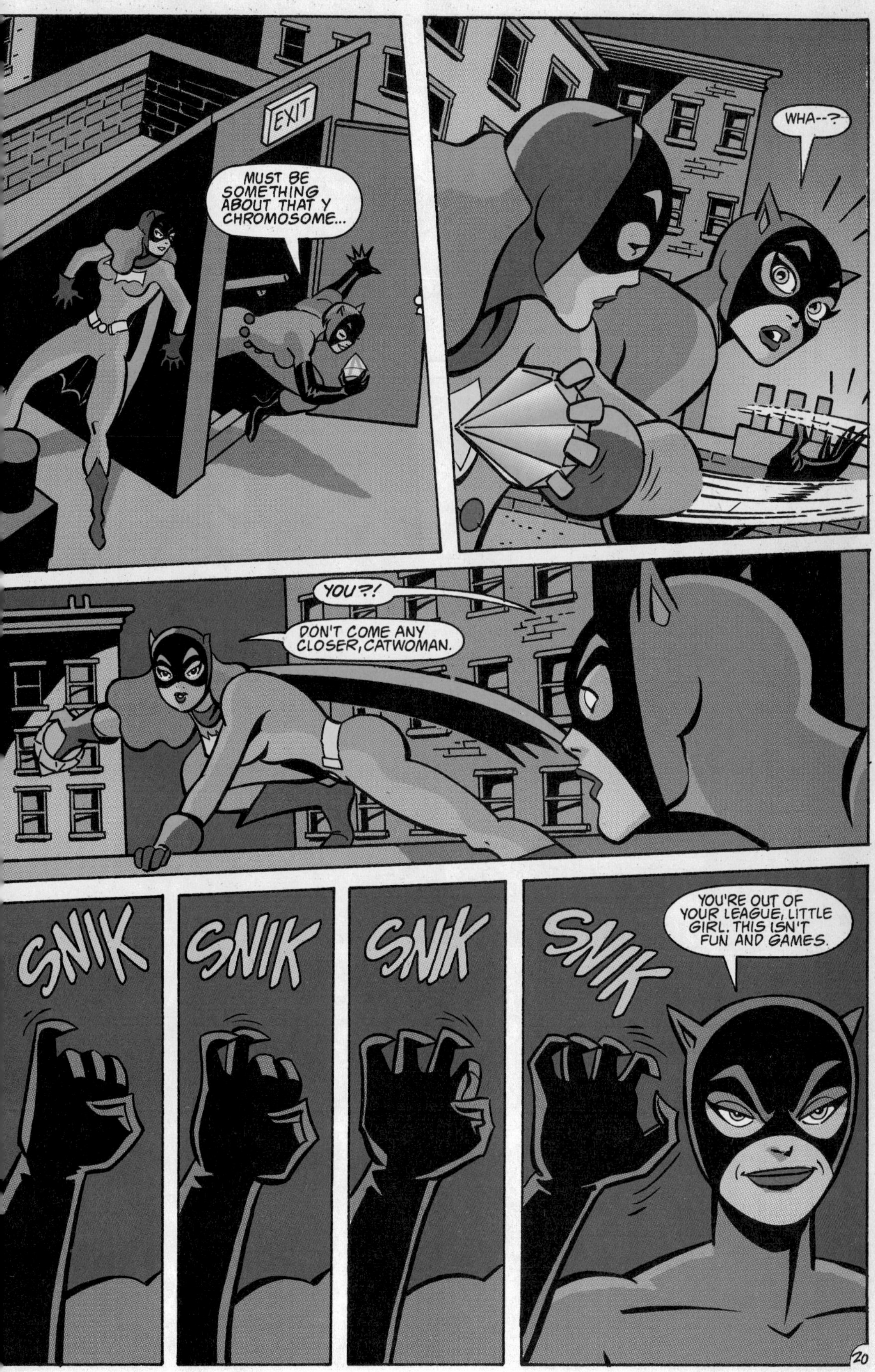
EXIT
MUST BE SOMETHING ABOUT THAT Y CHROMOSOME...
WHA--?
YOU?!
DON'T COME ANY CLOSER, CATWOMAN.
SNIK
SNIK
SNIK
SNIK
YOU'RE OUT OF YOUR LEAGUE, LITTLE GIRL. THIS ISN'T FUN AND GAMES.
20

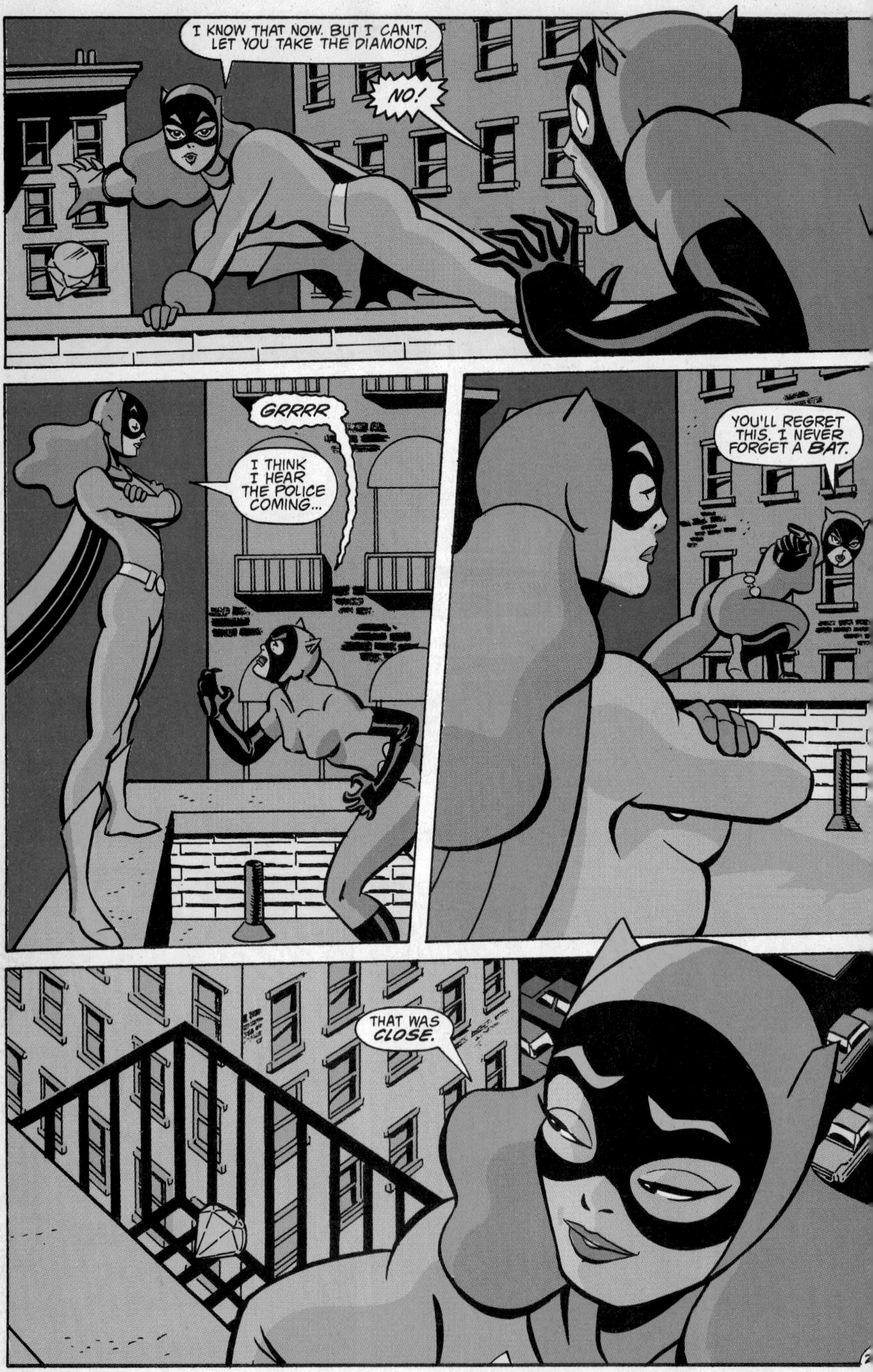
I KNOW THAT NOW. BUT I CAN'T LET YOU TAKE THE DIAMOND.
NO!
GRRRR
I THINK I HEAR THE POLICE COMING...
YOU'LL REGRET THIS. I NEVER FORGET A BAT.
THAT WAS CLOSE.

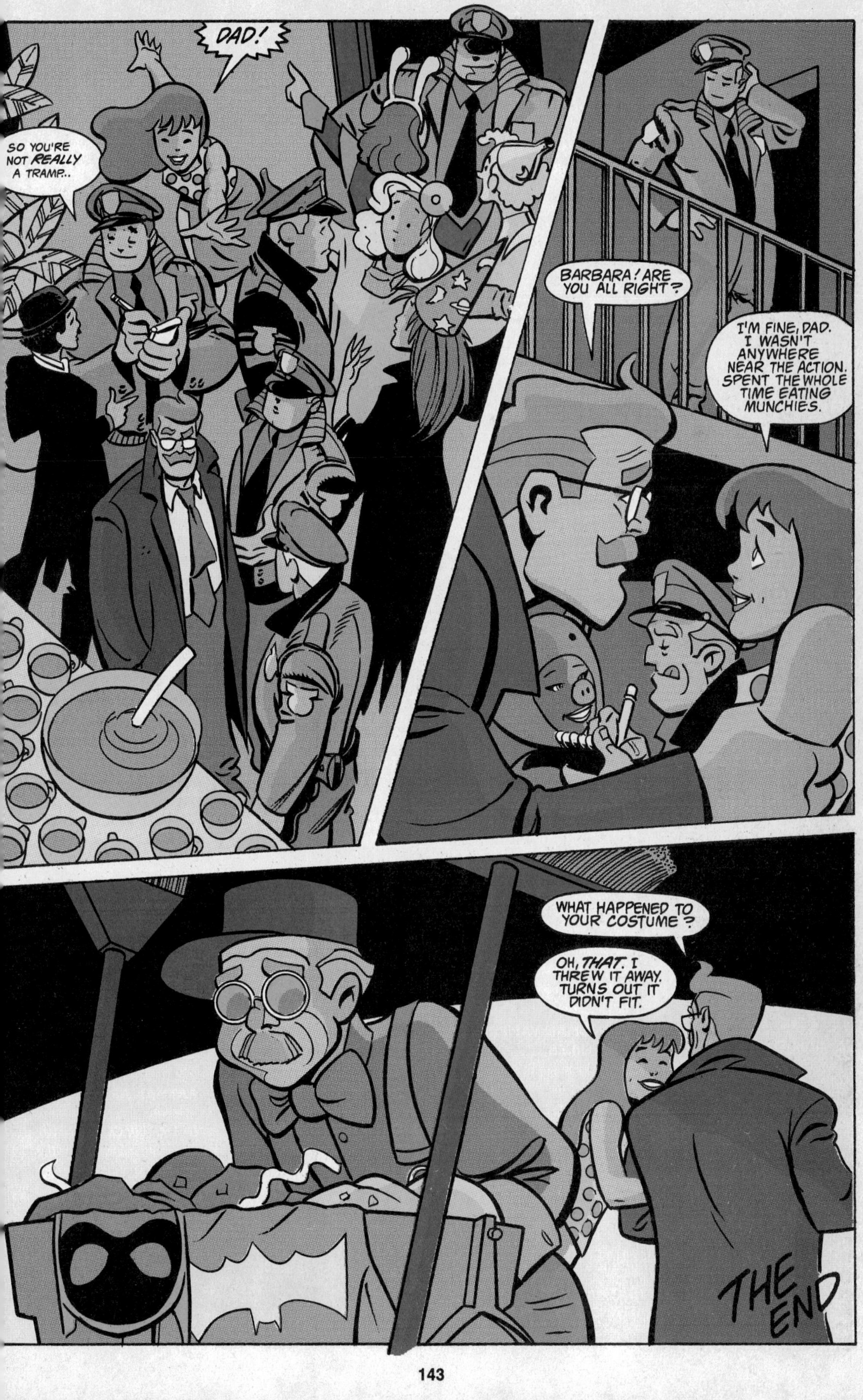
DAD!
SO YOU'RE NOT REALLY A TRAMP..
BARBARA! ARE YOU ALL RIGHT?
I'M FINE, DAD. I WASN'T ANYWHERE NEAR THE ACTION. SPENT THE WHOLE TIME EATING MUNCHIES.
WHAT HAPPENED TO YOUR COSTUME?
OH, THAT. I THREW IT AWAY. TURNS OUT IT DIDN'T FIT.
THE END

The Quest for Justice Continues in These Books from DC:

GRAPHIC NOVELS

AZRAEL/ASH
Dennis O'Neil/Joe Quesada/
Jimmy Palmiotti

**THE BATMAN
ADVENTURES: MAD LOVE**
Paul Dini/Bruce Timm

**BATMAN CHRONICLES:
THE GAUNTLET**
Bruce Canwell/Lee Weeks

**BATMAN & DRACULA:
RED RAIN**
Doug Moench/Kelley
Jones/Malcolm Jones III

**BATMAN & HOUDINI: THE
DEVIL'S WORKSHOP**
Howard Chaykin/John Francis
Moore/Mark Chiarello

BATMAN & SPIDER-MAN
J. M. DeMatteis/Graham
Nolan/Karl Kesel

**BATMAN FOREVER MOVIE
ADAPTATION**
Dennis O'Neil/Michal
Dutkiewicz/Scott Hanna

**BATMAN RETURNS MOVIE
ADAPTATION**
Dennis O'Neil/Steve Erwin/
Jose Luis Garcia-Lopez

BATMAN: ARKHAM ASYLUM
Suggested for mature readers
Grant Morrison/Dave McKean

BATMAN: BANE
Chuck Dixon/Rick Burchett

**BATMAN: BIRTH OF
THE DEMON**
Dennis O'Neil/Norm Breyfogle

BATMAN: BLOODSTORM
Doug Moench/Kelley Jones/
John Beatty

**BATMAN: CASTLE OF
THE BAT**
Jack C. Harris/Bo Hampton

**BATMAN: DARK
ALLEGIANCES**
Howard Chaykin

BATMAN: FULL CIRCLE
Mike W. Barr/Alan Davis/
Mark Farmer

**BATMAN: GOTHAM
BY GASLIGHT**
Brian Augustyn/Mike Mignola/
P. Craig Russell

BATMAN: HOLY TERROR
Alan Brennert/Norm Breyfogle

**BATMAN: THE
KILLING JOKE**
Suggested for mature readers
Alan Moore/Brian Bolland/
John Higgins

BATMAN: MASQUE
Mike Grell

**BATMAN: MASTER OF
THE FUTURE**
Brian Augustyn/Eduardo Barreto

BATMAN: MR. FREEZE
Paul Dini/Mark Buckingham/
Wayne Faucher

BATMAN: NIGHT CRIES
Archie Goodwin/Scott Hampton

**BATMAN: SCAR OF
THE BAT**
Max Allan Collins/Eduardo Barreto

**BATMAN: SON OF
THE DEMON**
Mike W. Barr/Jerry Bingham

**BATMAN/DEADMAN:
DEATH & GLORY**
James Robinson/John Estes

BATMAN/DEMON
Alan Grant/David Roach

**BATMAN/GREEN ARROW:
THE POISON TOMORROW**
Dennis O'Neil/Mike Netzer/
Josef Rubinstein

**BATMAN/JUDGE DREDD:
JUDGMENT ON GOTHAM**
Alan Grant/John Wagner/
Simon Bisley

**BATMAN/JUDGE DREDD:
VENDETTA IN GOTHAM**
Alan Grant/John Wagner/
Cam Kennedy

**BATMAN/JUDGE DREDD:
THE ULTIMATE RIDDLE**
Alan Grant /Carl Critchlow

**BATMAN/RIDDLER:
THE RIDDLE FACTORY**
Matt Wagner/Dave Taylor

**BATMAN/SPAWN:
WAR DEVIL**
Doug Moench/Chuck Dixon/
Alan Grant/Klaus Janson

**BATMAN/TWO-FACE:
CRIME AND PUNISHMENT**
J. M. DeMatteis/Scott McDaniel

**CATWOMAN/VAMPIRELLA:
THE FURIES**
Chuck Dixon/Jim Balent/
Ray McCarthy

**THE JOKER: DEVIL'S
ADVOCATE**
Chuck Dixon/John Ostrander/
Graham Nolan/Scott Hanna

PENGUIN TRIUMPHANT
John Ostrander/Joe Staton/
Bob Smith

COLLECTIONS

**BATMAN VS. PREDATOR:
THE COLLECTED EDITION**
Dave Gibbons/Andy Kubert/
Adam Kubert

**BATMAN VS. PREDATOR II:
BLOODMATCH**
Doug Moench/Paul Gulacy/
Terry Austin

**BATMAN: A DEATH IN
THE FAMILY**
Jim Starlin/Jim Aparo/
Mike DeCarlo

**BATMAN: A LONELY
PLACE OF DYING**
Marv Wolfman/George Pérez/
various

**BATMAN: COLLECTED
LEGENDS OF THE DARK
KNIGHT**
Robinson/Moore/Grant/Sale/
Russell/O'Neil

BATMAN: CONTAGION
Various writers and artists

**BATMAN: THE DARK
KNIGHT RETURNS
10TH ANNIVERSARY
EDITION**
Frank Miller/Lynn Varley/
Klaus Janson

BATMAN: DARK LEGENDS
Various writers and artists

BATMAN: FACES
Matt Wagner

**BATMAN: FEATURING
TWO-FACE AND THE
RIDDLER**
Various writers and artists

**BATMAN: HAUNTED
KNIGHT**
Jeph Loeb/Tim Sale

**BATMAN: KNIGHTFALL Part 1:
BROKEN BAT**
Various writers and artists

**BATMAN: KNIGHTFALL Part 2:
WHO RULES THE NIGHT**
Various writers and artists

BATMAN: KNIGHTSEND
Various writers and artists

**BATMAN: THE
LAST ARKHAM**
Alan Grant/Norm Breyfogle

BATMAN: LEGACY
Various writers and artists

BATMAN: MANBAT
Jamie Delano/John Bolton

BATMAN: PRODIGAL
Various writers and artists

BATMAN: SHAMAN
Dennis O'Neil/Ed Hannigan/
John Beatty

**BATMAN: SWORD
OF AZRAEL**
Dennis O'Neil/Joe Quesada/
Kevin Nowlan

**BATMAN: TALES OF
THE DEMON**
Dennis O'Neil/Neal Adams/variou

BATMAN: THE MOVIES
Dennis O'Neil/various artists

BATMAN: VENOM
Dennis O'Neil/Trevor
Von Eeden/various

BATMAN: YEAR ONE
Frank Miller/David Mazzucchelli

CATWOMAN: THE CATFILE
Chuck Dixon/Jim Balent/
Bob Smith

**CATWOMAN: HER SISTER'S
KEEPER**
Mindy Newell/J. J. Birch/
Michael Bair

**THE GREATEST BATMAN
STORIES EVER TOLD Vol. 1**
Various writers and artists

**THE GREATEST JOKER
STORIES EVER TOLD**
Various writers and artists

**LEGENDS OF THE
WORLD'S FINEST**
Walt Simonson/Dan Brereton

**NIGHTWING: TIES
THAT BIND**
Dennis O'Neil/Alan Grant/
various artists

ROBIN: A HERO REBORN
Chuck Dixon/Tom Lyle/
Bob Smith

**SUPERMAN/BATMAN:
ALTERNATE HISTORIES**
Various writers and artists

WORLD'S FINEST
Dave Gibbons/Steve Rude/
Karl Kesel

ARCHIVE EDITIONS

BATMAN ARCHIVES Vol. 1
(Batman's adventures from
DETECTIVE COMICS 27-50)
Bob Kane/Bill Finger/various

BATMAN ARCHIVES Vol. 2
(Batman's adventures from
DETECTIVE COMICS 51-70)
Bob Kane/Bill Finger/various

BATMAN ARCHIVES Vol. 3
(Batman's adventures from
DETECTIVE COMICS 71-86)
Bob Kane/Bill Finger/various

**BATMAN: THE DARK
KNIGHT ARCHIVES Vol. 2**
(BATMAN 5-8)
Bob Kane/Bill Finger/various

For the nearest comics shop
carrying collected editions and
monthly titles from DC Comics,
call 1-888-COMIC BOOK.

971030